Studies in Ecstatic Kabbalah

SUNY Series in Judaica: Hermeneutics, Mysticism
and Religion
Edited by Michael Fishbane, Robert Goldenberg, and
Arthur Green

Studies in Ecstatic Kabbalah

Moshe Idel

State University of New York Press

Published by
State University of New York Press, Albany

Printed in the United States of America

For information, address State University of New York
Press, State University Plaza, Albany, N.Y., 12246

Library of Congress Cataloging-in-Publication Data

Idel, Moshe, 1947-
Studies in ecstatic kabbalah.

(SUNY series in Judaica)
Bibliography: p.
Includes index.
1. Cabala—History. 2. Ecstasy (Judaism)
3. Abulafia, Abraham ben Samuel, 1240-ca. 1292.
I. Title. II. Series.
BM526.I344 1988 296.8'2 87-6522
ISBN 0-88706-604-6
ISBN 0-88706-605-4 (pbk.)

10 9 8 7 6 5 4

Contents

Preface

The history of the Kabbalah consists of a long series of ideological developments, which trace the peregrinations of Kabbalists and their beliefs from place to place, country to country, and even from one continent to another. The impact of early Kabbalistic writings in Provence at the end of the twelfth century was felt in Catalonia, where large-scale Kabbalistic treatises were composed and disseminated; this phenomenon recurred by the middle of the thirteenth century in Castile. Since the second part of the thirteenth century, Kabbalistic writings become a rather common Spanish phenomenon, with a few insignificant exceptions outside of Spain. One major exception, however, is the development of the ecstatic Kabbalah in Italy and Greece, which was disseminated some time before the arrival of the classical Spanish Kabbalah. Though it was of Spanish extraction, the ecstatic Kabbalah was rejected at the end of the thirteenth century by the Spanish Kabbalists, who felt that its most important representative, R. Abulafia, was a *bête noire* of the classical Kabbalah. This development was inspired by the banishment of Abulafia by R. Shelomo ben Abraham Ibn Adret, the most important Halakhic authority of the Spanish Jewry. However, aside from the anarchic potentialities inherent in Abulafia's claims to be recognized as prophet and Messiah (raising the fears of both Spanish and Italian Jews), his ecstatic Kabbalah was phenomenologically different from the basic mood of the Spanish Kabbalah. In lieu of the theosophical understanding of the divine essence advocated by both the Catalonian and Castilian Kabbalists, Abulafia accepted a philosophically oriented theology congenial to almost all of Maimonides' basic tenets.

In lieu of a theurgical understanding of the commandments, the ecstatic Kabbalah conceived these religious activites as fraught with allegorical meanings, directing the mystic to contemplate the spiritual world rather than influencing it through the intentional performance of the commandments. For Abulafia the *summum bonum* was the attainment of a state of ecstasy—which he designated as prophesy, and which included revelatory experiences understood to reflect the bliss of the world to come—and the messianic state, which was envisioned as an allegory of the spiritual accomplishment.

The combination of the historical fact of Abulafia's banishment and the profound phenomenological differences between the two theologies explains the disappearance of the ecstatic Kabbalah from the spiritual landscape of Jewish mysticism in Spain. Subsequently, Abulafia disseminated his peculiar type of mysticism in countries where the influence of the Spanish Rabbinic authority was not dominant. The results of his propagandist efforts were not, according to his own confession, successful, but his Kabbalah became, nevertheless, a constant component of some of the most important developments in the Italian and Byzantine Kabbalah. The ecstatic Kabbalah reached territories where Abulafia himself did not visit as part of his efforts to spread his views. Already in the nineties of the thirteenth century, conspicuous traces of his mystical techniques and experiences can be located in almost all Kabbalistic writings extant from the Land of Israel. Some novel common denominators in these writings include elements stemming from Sufic mysticism as well as those that reflect the influence of Abulafia's works. This Sufic and Sufi-like transformation of Abulafia's ecstatic Kabbalah in the East is one of the subjects of the present collections of essays. Written after the completion of my thesis on Abulafia himself, most of the essays survey, for the first time in a focused manner, the encounter of Jewish mysticism arriving from Spain with Eastern mysticism as it was cultivated by Muslims and by Jews who were influenced by Sufic mysticism.

This episode in the history of the Kabbalah has been relatively ignored by modern scholars. Centered on the theosophical Spanish Kabbalah, the interest of many scholars has not encompassed the problems posed by ecstatic mysticism nor has it explored implications emerging from the synthesis between Eastern mysticism and the European Kabbalah as it was exposed by Abulafia. In my view, the repercussions from this synthesis for the later development of Jewish mysticism were tremendous: the overemphasis on the importance of *devekut*, or mystical union, of *hitbodedut* (either as seclusion or as mental concentration), or the introduction of the equanimity as having a paramount mystical value, restructured the bosom of Jewish medieval mysticism, and overtly affected the peculiar spiritual physiognomy of some aspects of the Safedian Kabbalah, and later on, led to the formation of Hasidism as a mystical phenomenon. Some of the issues mentioned above will be discussed in the following pages, though some crucial matters concerning the influence of the ecstatic Kabbalah, on Hasidism for example, remain beyond the scope of the present collection of essays.

The topics dealt with here are related either to the ecstatic Kabbalah and its founder, R. Abraham Abulafia, or to the development of the Kabbalah up until the middle of the sixteenth century. I have deliberately ignored the impact of the Abulafian Kabbalah on the Jewish Italian, Byzantine, and Christian Kabbalah; these are issues to be pursued in future studies.

The present essays were written during the last decade, and the occasion of their English translation was an opportunity to update them in accordance with recent findings and studies. Though no substantial changes were introduced in the translation, some issues were elaborated upon, and some of the notes in Chapter 7 were condensed. In addition, to present a more unified discourse, previously published works have been cross-referenced, and the terminology has been adjusted for consistency among the various translations.

Acknowledgments

Chapter 1 is forthcoming in a third volume of studies edited by I. Twersky, which is devoted to Jewish Medieval History and Literature. There Hebrew passages from Abulafia's manuscripts are adduced.

Chapter 2 is a translation, with some additions, of a Hebrew article printed in *Iyuun* vol. 30 no. 2 [1981] pp. 133-140.

Chapter 3 is a translation of a portion of my Ph.D. thesis done by Mrs. Martel Gavarin; it was printed in *Immanuel* vol. 11, Fall 1980 pp. 64-80.

Chapter 4 is a translation of a Hebrew observation printed in *AJS review* vol. 4 [1979] pp. 1-6, Hebrew part.

Chapter 5 is a slightly enlarged version of a Hebrew article published in *Eshel Beer-Sheva, Studies in Jewish Thought* vol. II [1980] pp. 165-176.

Chapter 6 is a translation done by Mr. Naftali Greenwood of an essay published in *Shalem* vol. 3 [1981] pp. 119-126. The English translation, printed in ed. Richard I. Cohen, *Vision and Conflict in the Land of Israel* [Jerusalem-New York, 1985] pp. 102-110, contains some additions to the Hebrew version.

Chapter 7 was published in its fullest form in Hebrew in *Daat* vol. 14 [1985] pp. 35-82 and ibid. vol. 15 [1982] pp. 117-120. A shorter English translation, done by Mr. Jonathan Chipman, was published in ed. Arthur Green, *Jewish Spirituality* vol. 13 of *World Spirituality* [New York, 1986] pp. 405-438. In its present form, this essay is a much longer version of the English translation, though some of the notes of the full Hebrew original were deleted.

Mr. Menahem Kalush has translated chapters 2, 4, 5, and the last section of Chapter 7.

Abbreviations

AJS Review	*Association of Jewish Studies Review*
BN	*Biblioteque Nationale*
HTR	*Harvard Theological Review*
HUCA	*Hebrew Union College Annual*
JAOS	*Journal of American Oriental Society*
JJS	*Journal of Jewish Studies*
JQR	*Jewish Quarterly Review*
JTS	*Jewish Theological Seminary*
MGWJ	*Monatschrift für die Geschichte und Wissenschaft des Judentums*
PAAJR	*Proceedings of the American Academy for Jewish Research*
REJ	*Revue des Études Juives*

Chapter 1

Abraham Abulafia and *Unio Mystica*

I

R. Moses ben Maimon—Maimonides—is the most prominent Jewish author of the Middle Ages. He was a sober lawyer, an important philosopher and physician, an influential spiritual leader, and the subject of fervent devotion as well as bitter attacks. He is unquestionably a central figure in Jewish philosophy. His works have been disseminated, debated, interpreted, and printed again and again.

R. Abraham Abulafia, was a different figure; of poor halakhic education, and a mediocre thinker if judged as a philosopher. Like Maimonides, however, he was the subject of admiration and bitter critiques. Unquestionably, he is a central figure in Jewish mysticism. Abulafia's works were disseminated, debated, and interpreted, but not printed until the second part of the nineteenth century, when less than one percent of his prolific literary output was edited by Adolph Jellinek.

The sober Maimonides and the enthusiastic Abulafia are, *prima facie*, two antipodes of the Jewish medieval intellectual and spiritual arena. Nevertheless, Abulafia is one of the first commentators of Maimonides' *Guide of the Perplexed*, the first scholar who at least temporarily made his living teaching the *Guide* to students, and the only author who has written three commentaries on the secrets alluded to by Maimonides in his book.[1]

Abulafia's deep interest in Maimonides' *chef d'oeuvre* might be explained merely as a biographical incident; he began to study the *Guide* in the early sixties of the thirteenth century,[2] years before he received the first revelation at Barcelona, in 1270.[3] However, this is not sufficient. Abulafia's contemporaries, Kabbalists like R. Isaac Ibn Latif, R. Moses de Leon, and his own student, R. Joseph Gikatilla, began their intellectual careers under the influence of Maimonides, or at least avidly interested in his teachings.[4] A few years later, however, they shifted toward theosophical speculations[5] or neo-Platonic thought[6], becoming critical towards Maimonides and Aristotelianism, or, at least, indifferent to this brand of thought. The single Kabbalist who remained relatively faithful to Maimonides' teachings was Abulafia, despite a tremendous shift in his *Weltanschauung*.

The differing attitudes toward Maimonidean thought among the Kabbalists are the result of two different metaphysical stands. The theosophical Kabbalists, represented by Gikatilla and de Leon, focused their interest upon the nature of ten *sefirot* or divine potencies, which are situated above the ten separate intellects central to Maimonides' metaphysics. According to the theosophical Kabbalists, the Aristotelian philosophy is concerned with a realm inferior to the *sefirot;* to use Louis Gardet's term, this view can be called "un distinction hierarchisée," or, a hierarchical distinction.[7] Abulafia did not accept the importance of the *sefirot* as a special realm beyond the ten separate intellects; roughly speaking, he agreed with Maimonides' metaphysics, but differed by emphasizing the significance of the spiritual possibilities inherent in the Aristotelian scheme. Abulafia was interested in the intensification of the spiritual life, not in the discovery of new realms for contemplation.

The medieval Aristotelianism, according to Maimonides, is primarily a descriptive system: it includes long discussions on the nature of God, the universe, *Torah*, and man, whereas its prescriptive part is rather poor and vague; it recommends Aristotelian works as the main texts of an ideal curriculum which proposes the indirect perception of God's attributes through the medium of contemplation of nature.

Abulafia's doctrine is almost exclusively prescriptive; his acceptance of the Maimonidean scheme continues until his last works; however, he added elaborate techniques for attaining mystical experiences in this life, which, though obviously non-Maimonidean, could be understood in Maimonidean terms.[8]

To illustrate Abulafia's use of philosophical, mostly Maimonidean, terminology, I should like to quote a pertinent passage, from one of Hans Jonas' papers:

> Without an antecedent dogmatism there would be no valid mysticism. And mysticism, let it be noted, wants to be "valid", namely, more than a revel of feeling. The true mystic wants to put himself into possession of absolute reality, which already is and about which doctrine tells him . . . Having an objective theory, the mystic goes beyond theory; he wants experience of and identity with the object; and he wants to be able to claim such identity. Thus, in order that certain experiences may become possible and even conceivable as valid anticipations of an eschatological future, or as actualizations of metaphysical stages of being, speculation must have set the framework, the way, and the goal—long before the subjectivity has learned to walk the way.[9]

Though Jonas was exclusively concerned with ancient texts, Hermetic or patristic, his diagnosis of the relation between philosophy and mysticism is surprisingly adequate also for Jewish authors like Abulafia. Aristotelian thought, (mainly its psychological theories as interpreted by Maimonides, Avicenna, and Averroës), supplied the framework and the goal. The specific techniques, were inherited from other sources, or partly invented by Abulafia himself.[10] I should like to elaborate here upon the goal of Abulafia's mystical activity (i.e. *unio mystica*) and its sources in the philosophical medieval heritage. I suppose that some of Abulafia's mystical experiences were interpreted by him, as unitive states.

II

Before proceeding with the discussion of Abulafia's view of *unio mystica*, some remarks upon Scholem's opinion of *unio mystica* in Judaism are pertinent. According to Scholem,

> it is only in extremely rare cases that ecstasy signifies actual union with God, in which the human individuality abandons itself to the rapture of complete submersion in the divine stream. Even in this ecstatic frame of mind, the Jewish mystic almost invariably retains a sense of the distance between the Creator and His creature . . . he does not regard it as constituting anything so extravagant as identity of Creator and creature.[11]

This view of the most intimate connection of the human soul with God as adhesion or communion—versus *unio mystica*—seems to be an important specific illustration of Scholem's Hegelian[12] theory of the emergence of mysticism.[13] To him, the very existence of mysticism is possible only after two periods of religious development: the mythical epoch, when "the abyss between Man and God has not become a fact of the inner consciousness"; and the period of "classical religion" when there was "a vast and transcendental Being and Man, the finite creature." A third period, when the phenomenon of mysticism became possible, is, in Scholem's view, the romantic period of religion: "Mysticism does not deny or overlook the abyss; on the contrary, it begins by realizing its existence, but from there it proceeds to a quest for the secret that will close it, the hidden path that will span it." Therefore, mysticism can be regarded as the Hegelian synthesis, which includes both the thesis—the first period which denies the divine transcendence—and the antithesis, where the transcendence is central. So also in the case of *unio mystica* according to Scholem: even in its extreme forms, the gap between the Divinity and the human cannot be totally bridged.

Since Scholem's denial of the extreme form of *unio mystica* in 1941, no close examination of this thesis was undertaken by scholars of Jewish mysticism,[14] whereas experts of other religious mysticism unconditionally accepted it and used it in their studies.[15]

I should like to argue three points: (1) that Scholem's view, while correct in general[16] and insofar as it concerns the theosophical Kabbalah (i.e. the main strain of Jewish medieval mysticism which deals with the nature of the *sefirot* and the relations between the commandments and divine harmony) is, wrong with regard to the second important brand of Kabbalah, or the ecstatic or prophetic Kabbalah. (2) that the divergence of the two types of Kabbalah on this issue, stems from their differing conceptions of man, as well as the nature of Divinity. And (3) that the influence of philosophical psychology on the ecstatic Kabbalah is the main reason for the emergence of the extreme type of expressions concerning *unio mystica* in the mysticism of Abulafia and his disciples.[17] I would now like to explore this last assertion and its implications concerning the nature of the various forms of Jewish mysticism.

III

Maimonides' *Guide* is based upon the assumption that *imitatio Dei* can be achieved in the practical domain, with human science being limited to the terrestrial realm.[18] In other words, man *cannot* attain an accurate knowledge of the separate intellects, or of God's nature, *a fortiori* the union of his soul or his intellect with them while alive.

Nevertheless his immediate followers have openly rejected the Maimonidean reticence regarding the possibility of a mystical union. His son, R. Abraham Maimuni, asserts that: "by the union of his (i.e. the righteous) soul and intellect, with the active intellect, he and he become one entity."[19] R. Samuel Ibn Tibbon, the famous translator of the *Guide*, and one of the most important devotees of Maimonides' thought, writes:

> The soul then unites with the Intellect and they become one single thing, for then, the soul becomes divine, of a higher order, immortal as is the Intellect with which it has united, the Intellect [I say] whose being is separate from matter.[20]

Both authors continued philosophical traditions already existing in twelfth-century Spanish thought;[21] but their flagrant contradiction with the doctrine of "the great eagle" indicates that a shift towards a more mystical stand took place already at the beginning of the thirteenth century in the very strongholds of Maimonidean thought.[22]

Their explicit statements about the possibility of a union with the active intellect notwithstanding, evidence about an actual experience of such a union is reported neither in Maimuni's, nor in Ibn Tibbon's works. Moreover, in Ibn Tibbon's passage, the unitive experience is explicitly connected with the eschatological condition of the righteous, whereas Maimuni refers, in the context of his discussion on union, to a Rabbinic *dictum*, implicitly giving his thought an eschatological turn. Therefore, though the union, even total fusion, of the human soul or intellect with the active intellect, was theoretically well-known in Maimonidean circles, it was neither a confession of a personal experience nor a prescription for a type of religious life in this world. Ibn Tibbon's stand on union represents an attempt to infuse in Maimonides' thought an Averroistic direction;[23] Abraham Maimuni may have also been influenced by this brand of thought,[24] though Sufic material may have influenced him as well.[25]

Therefore, the two greatest authorities on the matter of Maimonides' thought, preceding those of Abulafia, explicitly accepted non-Maimonidean Averroistic conceptions of uniting *unio mystica* with the active intellect. Abulafia seems to ignore Maimuni's works, written in Arabic in the relatively remote Egypt; however, he knew at least one of Ibn Tibbon's works,[26] written in Hebrew and in Abulafia's geographical vicinity, Provence, and he could even read, in his intellectual ambience,[27] Ibn Tibbon's Hebrew translation of some of Averroes' most significant texts dealing with the possibility of conjunction with the active Intellect.[28]

In his *Commentary on the Secrets* included in the *Guide*, Abulafia explicitly states that the ultimate transformation of human intellect into the *intellectus agens*, or even God, takes place during the mystical experience. Speaking about the perfect actualization of the intellectual faculty by the active intellect, Abulafia asserts that:

> he prophesies, according to the entity which causes him to pass from

> potentiality into the final and perfect actuality and he and he become one entity, inseparable during this act.[29]

Elsewhere Abulafia elaborates upon the process of prophesying:[30]

> The [place of the] beginning of the real prophecy[31] is the inner intellectual faculty[32] which is created in the heart through the agency of seventy languages, by the 22 sacred letters, all of them being combined in the heart, *in virtu*, by the process of combination of letters done by the intellectual faculty, and *in actu* by *intellectus agens*, which is divine, religious, and prophetic.[33] And from him [the inner intellectual faculty] there will be an emanation on the imaginary faculty and from the imaginary [faculty] [the emanation will pour upon] the appetitive [faculty] and from the appetitive [faculty] on the sensitive [faculty] and from the sensitive on the designative [faculty] which is designed on the book. And it [the prophesying emanation] will also turn to the inverse direction and will reach a high status. It will separate from the designated [status] [and will turn] to the sensitive [faculty] and from the sensitive to the appetitive and from it to the imaginative and from it to the inner rational cogitative [and] designative [faculty] and from it to the prophetic [faculty] and from it to the [*intellectus*] *agens* and will unite with it after many hard, strong and mighty exercises, until the particular and personal prophetic [faculty] will turn universal, permanent, and everlasting like the essence of its cause, and he and he will become one entity.

Abulafia describes what seems to be a complete circle.[34] Beginning with God, and then the *intellectus agens*, the emanation descends upon the human faculties and turns into a written message; thereafter it returns to its origin, causing the ascension of the intellectual faculty and its fusion with the divine *intellectus agens*. A comparison of this passage with other of his writings, enables us to perceive this quotation as dealing with the transformation of spiritual effluence from the *intellectus agens* (elsewhere denoted as "primordial speech")[35] into a written book, through the mediation of the various human inner senses, functioning as an organ of this transformation. However, the particular intellect, while serving as a channel for the divine communication to men, is itself activated and is enabled, by the use of techniques based upon linguistic elements, to unite with the *intellectus agens*. It is obvious that Abulafia's terminology was attentively chosen: the human intellectual faculty is named *dibbur* whereas the universal intellect (*"dibbur qadmon"*) and each of the higher separate intellects are described as *"dibbur"*.

The human prophetic faculty is "particular and personal" vis à vis the universal prophetic faculty. The similarity of these terms conveys the possibility of continuity between human reason and the active intellect:

the particular can turn universal since each is but another aspect of the same intellectual essence. According to Abulafia: "The divine separate intellect and the hylic emanated intellect are two valid witnesses, though they are one."[36] We can hardly miss the Averroistic background of this statement: Though this intellect is only the lowest among the separate intellects—according to the accepted view of medieval Arab or Jewish Aristotelians—it seems that a perfect union with it still deserves the title of *unio mystica,* since it is the total fusion of the human intellect with a comprehensive entity—the divine active intellect. Also, because the spiritual nature of this intellect seems to be, according to Abulafia, similar to God, a clear distinction between the union of the human intellect with the *intellectus agens*, or with God, is rather difficult:

> "image" in this context is a name which designates the natural form, which is [the form of] the species, and it is the soul, which is the human rational intellection, which is similar to the divine [rational intellection] with which it is united and from which its existence [stems] and from It is its being, providence and perpetuity. This is why it is written that [man] was created in God's image and likeness. And the meaning of this secret is that "image", which is the name of the soul which survives after the death, the perpetuity of its survival depends upon its likeness to its Creator, concerning the intellection, the existence and the eternity and the dominion, until this image's name will be like the name of its Master, and it [image] is the special name of the *Intellectus Agens*, an image like his image, as it is written on it and God created man in His Image, in the image of God He created him. The duplication of these words hints to the creator and to the creature, which is called with the name of the creator; this fact hints that they [the Creator and the creature] are one entity, inseparable.[37]

The ambiguity of the identity of the Master, the Artifactor, is crucial: these terms may stand for both God and the *Intellectus Agens*, the latter being denominated, as seen above, as divine. The soul becomes "similar to the divine intellection" and, furthermore, we read about "its likeness to its creator". It is obvious that according to Abulafia, the last term of reference of the soul is the "divine", be it the active intellect, or be it the supreme Deity. The intellectual human faculty is assumed to reach the most similarity to the divine attributes while alive, in order to assure its *post mortem* survival. The two kinds of intellections completely fuse in a supreme act of intellectual love:[38]

> The name [of God] is composed from two parts since there are two parts of love[39] [divided between] two lovers, and the [parts of] love turn one [entity] when love became actuated. The divine intellectual love and the

> human intellectual love are conjuncted being one. Exactly so the name [of God] includes [the words] one one,[40] because of the connection of the human existence with the divine existence during the intellection—which is identical with the intellect in [its] existence—until he and he become one [entity]. This is the [great] power of man: he can link the lower part with the higher one, and the lower [part] will ascend and the higher [part] will descend and will kiss the entity ascending towards it, like a bridegroom actually kisses his bride out of his great and real desire, characteristic of the delight of both, from the power of the name [of God].

The similarity of this passage to the quotations from *Sitrei Torah* is obvious; but in the last description of the conjunction between two kinds of intellections, there is no mention of the active intellect at all, only the "divine existence" being viewed as the entity with which the "human existence" is united. This is also the case in Abulafia's interpretation of Moses' transfiguration:

> His higher soul longed to unite with her root, which is the beginning without end, and the end without beginning . . . and God, may He be exalted, has poured upon him, out of the efflux of His Goodness . . . until He caused his intellect to pass slowly from its human potentiality and caused it to become divine actuality.[41]

Here the actualization of the human intellect is synonymous with its becoming divine. This process of deification by intellection is a natural event, since:[42]

> all the inner forces and the hidden souls in man are differentiated in the bodies. It is however in the nature of all of them that when their knots are untied,[43] they return to their origin, which is one without any duality, and which comprises the multiplicity.

Interestingly enough, Scholem has interpreted this passage as dealing with the connection between the human soul and "the stream of cosmic life—personified for him [Abulafia] in the *intellectus agens* of the philosopher." Nevertheless, Stace, apparently deliberately ignoring Scholem's interpretation of the text, writes:

> The untying of the knots of the souls means their liberation from the fetters of finitude so that they return to their origin, which is the Infinite One.[44]

It seems that Stace's intuition on the real significance of Abulafia's passage, can be corroborated by other discussions found in the writings of the

Kabbalist. On the same page, Abulafia indeed describes man in these terms:[45]

> the ultimate composite,[46] which is man, who comprises all the *sefirot*, and whose intellect is the active intellect; and when you will untie its knots, you will be united with it [the active intellect] in a unique union.

The affinity between Abulafia's description of Divinity as comprising the multiplicity and his perception of man as comprising both the ten *sefirot* and the active intellect, is obvious. This perception of Abulafia's intention to compare man and his intellect with Deity, is corroborated by his own statement in one of his untitled works:[47]

> . . . and since God wanted us, He announced to us . . . the mysteries of this world, which is sealed with His name,[48] in order to untie all the knots, by whom they [the knots] were knotted according to Him [the name] and with it [the name] we were composited, so that we are able to become simple[49] [spiritual], loose from all remaining compositions, and he will remain uncomposite, neither the composition of his natural disposition, nor material composition, and we shall become innovated entities, possessing simple [spiritual] ideas, separated of any matter and composited of all forms; we shall become the caused [entities], of all the divine causes, the simplest of them being composited out of all the others and the most composite of them being the simplest one [the most spiritual].

According to Abulafia, the untying of knots results in a total spiritualization of human intellect, which leaves the material knots and becomes bound to spiritual bonds, passing from the most composited being in the material realm, to the most composited entity in the spiritual world (i.e. formed out of the forms—the ideas—separated from matter). This total transformation renders the stripped human intellect similar to God, who is presented as the most composite out of the simplest [i.e. spiritual] entities. It seems that God is the first composite entity, whereas man is the last (i.e. ultimate composite one).

Man therefore undergoes a spiritual transition from his natural condition as a composite entity in the material realm, to his *status* as a composite entity in the spiritual realm, thus making him similar to God and, according to the passages out of Abulafia's letter, making him capable of forming a perfect union with the active intellect and, afterwards, with God.

This gradation is evident from Abulafia's statement in his *Ḥayyei Ha'Olam HaBa'*:

> the benefit of the knowledge of the name [of God] is its being the cause

> of man's attainment of the actual intellection of the active intellect and the benefit of the intellection of the active intellect is the ultimate aim of the life of the intellectual soul and it is the reason of the life of the next world; this aim is the union of the soul, by this intellection, with God forever.[50]

Here, the Kabbalist unequivocally states that the soul can unite not only with the active intellect but with God Himself, evidently asserting the possibility of the supreme *unio mystica.* According to another text of Abulafia, if the mystic:[51]

> has felt the divine touch and perceived its nature it seems right and proper to me and to every perfected man that he should be called "master" because his name is like the Name of his Master be it only in one, or in many, or in all of His Names.[52] For now he is no longer separated from his Master, and behold he is his Master and his Master is he; for he is so intimately united[53] with Him, that he cannot by any means be separated from Him, for he is He . . . and there is no difference between them, except that his Master has his supreme rank by his own right and not derived from other creatures, while he is elevated to this rank by the intermediary of creatures.

This passage is of utmost importance for the understanding of Abulafia's view of *unio mystica* as well as Scholem's view of Abulafia. The Kabbalist directly asserts that after the identification of the mystic with his Master, both of them are on the same rank: it is the supreme rank; the difference between them is merely "historical": the human intellect becomes universal *post rem*, whereas the Master is universal *ante rem.* Furthermore, the connection between the mystic and the Master is so close that "he cannot by any means be separated from Him, for he is Him." Therefore, Scholem's translation of the word "dibbuk" as "adhering" seems to miss the point. Since, according to Abulafia, there is no more separation, why not regard the conjunction as an outright union? Scholem has attempted to attentuate the unitive overtone of the formula "He is he" or "huwa huwa", by interpreting it as a "famous formula of advanced Moslem pantheism." However, the context where the formula occurs does not support this opinion; as a pantheistic affirmation, without unitive insinuation, this formula may appear only as a confession which is not connected to a transformation of the mystic's personality. However, when such a transformation is explicitly asserted, the formula "hu' hu'" indicates a recognition of the nature of the *new* state the mystic has reached. It is not the "unity of being" "waḥdat al wuġud" that is affirmed by Abulafia, but the union of being with God.

To suppose that this passage deals with *unio mystica* is confirmed also by the transfer of the Divine Name or Names to the mystic. This transfer is already known in Jewish mysticism, in connection with Enoch's translation into an angel—Metatron. In the ancient Jewish mysticism, a metamorphosis of the patriarch into a high angel is accompanied by his receiving one or seventy divine names, although the concept of union is unknown to the ancient texts.[54]

The similarity of Abulafia's assertion about the mystic who receives a divine name, to the ancient Jewish view of Enoch's translation, is obvious. Like the case of Enoch, Abulafia suggests a deep transformation of the mystic's personality, which takes place during the unitive experience.

IV

Before leaving our discussion of *unio mystica*, let me present an intriguing passage found in a treatise which was written either by Abulafia, or more probably, by one of his disciples:[55]

> He told me: Thou art my son, this day I have begotten you [Psalm 2,7], and also: See now that I, even I, am he [Deut. 32,39], and the secret [of these verses] is the union of the power—i.e. the supernal divine power[56] called the sphere of prophecy[57]—with the human power; and it is also said: I I [Jes. 43,11].

Therefore, beside the formulae "He is He", and "I am He and He is I" we get the formula "I - I": its Biblical sources notwithstanding, the signification of this phrase is given by the Kabbalist as union of the human and the divine. We may then ask the intention of the author who has chosen to use the formula "I - I" in lieu of "I am He", since in both cases, the basic meaning is the mystical union. In other words, who is the real speaker, God, as in the Biblical sources, or the mystic, who may pronounce this formula as the assertion of his identity with God (perceived as the I-ness)? I am inclined to accept the second solution for two reasons: (1) Preceding the above-mentioned passage, the author quotes a midrashic interpretation on the meaning of the name "Eheyeh asher Eheyeh":[58]

> And it is written: I am with you in trouble etc. [Psalms, 91,15] and this is in entirety when you will be with Him. But if you are not with Him, He also will not be with you; however, if you are with Him [then] from your flesh;[59] and I shall tell you: "But my dwelling," [signifies] "But I am with you" [and signifies] I shall be a dwelling. This is the way our [ancient] sages interpreted this secret in connection with the name I shall be

> whatever I shall be, and the Holy, may He be blessed, said to Moses: Moses, be with me and I shall be with you. And the adduced proof [for this interpretation] is from the verse: The Lord is thy shade upon thy right hand [Psalms, 121,5] as it is exposed in Midrash Hashkem.[60]

Here the Divinity is completely passive, and His activity is described as purely reactive to the human initiative. The meaning of the appelation "I shall be whatever I shall be" is, in this Kabbalist's view, "I shall be wherever you will be". In other words, the activation or actuation of the human intellect is tantamount to the dwelling of the Divine within the human.

Furthermore, the duplication of the divine name: "I shall be whatever I shall be" is clearly related to the "I - I" in the passage immediately following our quotation. The divine existence, then, seems to be tantamount to its I-ness; both are closely correlated to human intellectual activity.

Because of this correlation, it seems that the phrase: "I - I" is an exclamation by a mystic, indicating his awareness of becoming divine. (2) An interesting parallel to our analysis of the passages of *Sefer HaMalmad*, can be adduced from a discussion of the Spanish philosopher and theosophist, Ibn Sabin. Professor Shlomo Pines has kindly drawn my attention to an interesting interpretation of Al-Hallaj's dictum "'Ana al-Ḥaqq", found in Ibn Sabin's, *Yemenite Answers to Sicilian Questions*;[61] according to the Spanish author: "I" is related to the term "anniyah", which can be conceived both as "existence"—including divine existence—as in the regular philosophical usage of this term,[62] and as "I-ness". Therefore, Al-Hallaj's exclamation expresses, according to this view, not only the identification, or identity, of a particular mystic with God, but also the possibility of applying the I-ness to the Godhead by the mystical union of human with divinity, or as a result of such an event.

V

It is worth remarking that Abulafia's mysticism includes not only the transformational unitive component, but also a limited pantheistic facet; according to this Kabbalist, the various intellectual parts of the existence are part of one *continuum*:[63]

> Intellect is a term [applied] to the entity which rules over everything, i.e. the first cause of all; and it is[64] called the form of the intellect. The [term] intellect is also [applied] to the entity separated from matter,[65] which is emanated[66] from the first cause; by the means of this emanation the first entity rules over the moving heavens.[67] However[68] He, may He

> be exalted, is the simple[69] intellect. The [term] intellect is the name of the first cause which is close and acts upon whatever exists beneath the heavens,[70] and this is the active intellect which causes [the emergence of] the intellect in the human soul. Therefore there are three stages, all three being but one essence; God, His emanation which is separated [from matter], and the emanation of this emanation which is attached to the soul and the soul is attached to it in a very tenacious way, though the two [i.e. the soul and the emanation of God's emanation] are but one essence.

Essentially, all the intellectual phenomena are one; therefore, the actualization of the human soul is tantamount to her divinization, or to put it in Abulafia's own words:

> the grasping [of the soul] the human intellect which is emanated from the separated active intellect, causes the union of the soul to her God; this union is the cause of the soul's eternal life, similar to the life of her God.[71]

The acquisition of the intellect renders man similar to the supernal man (i.e. the spiritual world):[72]

> the supernal man has four [elements] which are: soul,[73] emanated intellect,[74] separated intellect,[75] and the first cause of all; so also the terrestrial man has four [elements] which are: soul, emanated intellect, separated intellect and the first cause of all.

The integration of intellectual forces into the human *aggregatum* joins them to the spiritual *continuum* whose first part is God.[75] The human intellect is a humanized God; therefore, the total union of human soul to God, and even her fusion with Him can be easily deducted from the common denominator of God as intellect, intelligibilia and intellection, and separate intellects—all of which are various aspects of the spiritual.[76] This view may be defined as a "limited pantheism", and is described by Abulafia as the presence of the separate (i.e. the spiritual) everywhere.[77] A visual representation of Abulafia's intellectual pantheism is found in the collectanea which include excerpts from *'Or HaSekhel;* there a flame is painted, with God at its top, while its lowest point is human intellect.[78]

The immediate source of Abulafia's view is obvious; it is Aristotelianism which presented God as the intellect, intelligible, and intellection.[79] This conception was introduced in Jewish thought by R. Abraham Ibn Ezra[80] and endorsed by Maimonides in the *Guide*.[81] Jewish philosophers, however, never intended to integrate their perception of Divinity into a mystical approach that uses the intellectualization of God as a means to bridge the gap between the human and divine intellect. Moreover, Maimonides stressed a distinction between the human mode of intellection and the divine one.[82] We see again the emergence of one of Abulafia's mystical views (i.e. the intellectual pantheism) as an elaboration of already existing philosophical conceptions.

VI

The texts discussed above, convincingly indicate that Abulafia maintained that the human intellect can fuse with the active intellect and even with God Himself. This view, explicitly based upon philosophical epistemology, places Abulafia among the "mystical theorists", to use Dodds' terminology.[83] The question must be asked if these theoretical statements could be connected with the details of Abulafia's biography; an affinity, or affinities between his texts and his life would indicate that general assertions, relevant for all "prophets" (i.e. mystics) are meaningful also for Abulafia's own spiritual activity. It seems to me that there are reasons to believe that Abulafia's mystical theory regarding the possibility of *unio mystica* corresponds to other pertinent biographical events, such as the following:

a) Abulafia inherited, or developed, highly complicated techniques, whose final purpose was to attain "prophecy" (i.e. a mystical experience). These techniques are exclusively based upon linguistic elements, such as those mentioned in the analysis above wherein the combinations of letters and the divine names were mentioned. Though there is no explicit statement on the practical arrival of *unio mystica* through the use of these techniques in Abulafia's extant writings, we cannot ignore the possibility that such an experience indeed occurred. Mystical experiences of other types—revelatory or demonic experiences—were related in Abulafia's autobiographical remarks.

b) The first and most elaborated discussions on the nature of the union of human intellect with higher entities, occur in *Sitrei Torah* and in the commentary to *Sepher HaYashar*. Both were written in 1280 when Abulafia was forty years old. This age was considered by philosophers and Kabbalists —including Abulafia himself—as the acme of human intellectual development. Abulafia expressed this view in two books written in 1280.[84] Therefore, it would seem reasonable to link the emergence of discussions about *unio mystica* with those about the perfection of the intellect to the same year. This would indicate that Abulafia reached a union with the "divine existence" in 1280. This year was of utmost importance for Abulafia's spiritual life; it was the date when he was supposed to meet

the Pope. The encounter never took place, however, because of the sudden death of the Pope.[85] It may be pertinent to this discussion to remark that the preceding years were a period of intensive revelations, which inspired Abulafia to meet with the Pope.[86]
c) In 1279 Abulafia began the writing of a series of prophetic books. The last of them, and the single extant one, was composed in 1288.[87] Abulafia's commentary to the *Book of the Testimony*, written in 1280 in Rome,[88] includes intercalations of phrases stemming from the original book, and beside them, Abulafia's interpretations.[89]

> He[90] said that he was then at Rome and [God] revealed him what he shall do and what he shall say in His Name, and he will announce to everyone that: The Lord reigneth, let the people tremble [Psalms, 99,1] . . . And he said: and I have called his name Shaddai like My name[91] and its secret[92] is the corporeal Shaddai and you shall understand its meaning. And he also said: He is I and I am He; and it is forbidden[93] to disclose this issue in a more explicit fashion than was already done. But the secret of the corporeal name[94] is the Messiah of God and Moses will rejoice etc.

The intent of this cryptic passage is to convey the Messianic installation of Abulafia as the spiritual King of Israel. As part of the process, his name is changed to Shaddai. Abulafia probably hints that he, namely, "the corporeal Shaddai" is the Messiah of God. In this context, the occurrence of the formula "He is I and I am He" is highly significant: its affinity to the other formula, "He is he" is obvious, and its connection to Abulafia is almost explicit. It seems, therefore, that the prophetic and messianic tension, which characterizes this period of Abulafia's life, is fraught with an additional dimension: the experience of a mystical union. A decisive piece of evidence marking 1280 as the year when Abulafia experienced mystical union is found in *Ḥayyei Ha'Olam HaBa'*, the most important handbook of ecstatic techniques, written in Rome in 1280:[95]

> in this manner he should transpose all its letters [of the Divine Name] frontwards and backwards, using many tunes . . . [96] and he must master very well the secrets of the law and their science in order to recognize [the meaning of the combinations of letters resulting from] the transposition of the combinations and his heart will become aware of the intellectual, divine and prophetic mental concept. And the first thing which will come out of the combination [of letters] during his concentration[97] upon it, is the emergence of fear and trembling upon him, the hairs of his head will stand up whereas his limbs will convulse. Afterwards, if he is worthy [of this experience] the Spirit of the living God will dwell upon him . . . and he will feel as if his whole body, from tip to toe, were annointed with the unction oil, and he will be the Messiah[98] of God and His messenger

> and he will be called the angel[99] of God, and his name is like the name of his Master[100] which is Shaddai which was named as Metatron,[101] the Angel of Presence.

Here, Abulafia is not only theoretically examining the union with Metatron (i.e. the active intellect), but also the corporeal and spiritual phenomena accompanying this experience. A passage asserting the "apotheosis" of the mystic occurs in the commentary to *Sefer HaMeliẓ* written in 1282 at Messina:[102]

> By his intellect he [the mystic] became superior to their species[103] and he became different from them and became [part of] another species, divine,[104] after he was human.

According to Abulafia, the mystic's duty is to remain in the spiritual state known as the unitive experience. The only reason "to return from God"[105] or to escape this state, is when there is an urgent need to instruct the people, in order to bring them "under the wing of the Divine Presence."

It seems therefore that Abulafia's "objective" treatment of the problem of the union between the human and the divine intellects reflects not only his acceptance of philosophical epistemology, but also his personal experiences which occurred exactly the same year. In other words, Abulafia read Maimonides in Avicennian and Averroistic keys, decoded his own spiritual adventures according to Maimonides' teaching in the *Guide*, and added philosophical conceptions out of Arabic philosophy.

At this stage in our discussion, we must seriously question Abulafia's use of Maimonides' teachings and his *Guide* as a point of departure for his non-Maimonidean view of *unio mystica* (which probably points to a real mystical experience). It is obvious that philosophy supplied him with concepts and terms, but why did he stick to the *Guide*, interpreting its secrets which hint at the possibility of mystic union, instead of commenting upon the *Song of Songs*?

It seems that one answer can be found in Abulafia's peculiar method of interpreting the *Guide*. In contrast to all the other commentaries on the *Guide*, which follow the sequence of chapters as they are written by the author, Abulafia's three commentaries exclusively treat the thirty-six secrets which, in his view, are hidden in the *Guide*.[106] He comments upon each of the secrets, bringing together other pertinent discussions in the *Guide*, and attempting to uncover Maimonides' remarks on the way the book is to be decoded.[107] Why was Abulafia so eager to reveal Maimonides' secrets? It is because of his feeling that he is the Messiah and his period is worthy of such a disclosure.[108] What is the nature of these secrets?

According to Abulafia, Maimonides' *Guide* (I, 71), has reconstructed the lost secrets of the Law, the "Sitrei Torah". Since biblical stories are viewed as allegories of spiritual progression of the human soul,[109] the Law, according to Abulafia, is aimed at directing man to attain the prophetic experience. By decoding Maimonides, then, Abulafia has revealed the true Jewish path of the ultimate felicity[110]—a path relevant to everyone, everywhere.

According to Maimonides and Abulafia, the *Guide* is a crucial stage where biblical secrets were recrystallized, after their loss during the exile period. Abulafia seems to have perceived his commentaries as furthering the disclosure of the secrets, which were germane to his own mystical experiences. He has found in Maimonides not only a reliable source of philosophical terminology, but also a respectable and authoritative intermediary between biblical spirituality, as he has conceived it, and his own spiritual experiences. Moreover, the philosophical terminology served as keys to self-understanding, and as a way of communication; in Abulafia's period, the Aristotelian epistemological concepts were already spread among the Jewish *intelligentsia*. Abulafia uses the terminology to convey the significance of his mystical experiences as he understood them, though they are almost totally absent in the short descriptions of his visions. We may add to Hans Jonas' view, that speculation was one of the main sources for the language used in speaking about intellectual mysticism, by observing that philosophical jargon molded the raw material of the inner experience into messages that became intelligible to the educated audience. The occurrence of philosophical terminology in Abulafia's work also seems to be a deliberate attempt to allure or attract philosophically biased Jewish scholars to his Kabbalah, in that it served to bridge philosophical scholarship and the more advanced stages of Kabbalistic training.[111]

It is worthwhile to compare Abulafia's transformation of Maimonides' philosophical system with a parallel phenomenon in Christian mysticism. Meister Eckhart similarly transforms and uses philosophical material, including Maimonides' *Guide*, as starting points for his own theosophy. In both cases, Aristotelian elements serve as important instruments for the formulation of intellectual mysticism. According to Eckhart, "God and I, we are one in pure knowledge."[112]

The phenomenological affinity between Abulafia and Eckhart's mystical use of Aristotelian concepts is remarkable. Though they were of different mental and spiritual constitutions, they casually used and misused philosophical views in order to express their *intuiti mystici*. Like other prominent mystics, such as Pseudo-Dionysios, Shankara or Ibn Arabi, they express their experimental knowledge of God in philosophical idioms; the respective philosophical systems served to explain idiosyncratic experiences in universal terms, thereby transforming the perceptions of their unitive lives into intellectual formulations.

VII

The mystical achievement according to Abulafia, consists of the fusion of the human intellect and the active and/or the divine intellect. This is made possible by the reduction of ideal human being to its intellectual faculty. This reduction, or simplification is the *sine qua non* for an individual's attainment of the universal or the divine. The prophetic Kabbalah can properly be described as the way of disintegrating the human *aggregatum*, and uniting its highest component with its source; other facets of the personality, the material or the emotional, are suppressed. This type of intellectual mysticism needs, theoretically speaking, neither the halakhic way of life, nor the Jewish community as a means for its consummation; the techniques of Abulafia are non-halakhic ways of cleaving to God, and they can be perfectly exercised only in complete solitude.[113] These two features sharply distinguish the ecstatic Kabbalah from the main trends of Kabbalah in general; almost all other types of Kabbalah are chiefly interested in the halakhic *dromenon*, which, when performed according to the Kabbalistic intention, are directed to restoring the primordial dynamic unity in the bosom of the revealed divinity: the ten *sefirot*. This type of activity requires highly educated and spiritually powerful personalities, who are able to perform the Kabbalistic ritual.

This performance employs all of the main facets of the human being and integrates the Kabbalist in the communal rituals. The theurgical Kabbalah, as opposed to the ecstatic one, was theosophically oriented and only secondarily interested in the mystical accomplishment of every Kabbalist. This theurgical trend is a continuation of ancient Jewish conceptions concerning the ultimate role of the performance of the commandments.

Abulafia's Kabbalah, based on the Aristotelian view of God as the intellect, the intelligible, and the intellection, was unable to influence processes in the divine realm, nor was it interested in seriously discussing the meaning of the actual performance of Jewish commandments; it was concerned only with the ultimate intellectual rationale of some commandments. This type of Kabbalah therefore represents a major departure from the development of the medieval Kabbalah. The most important symptom of this departure is its urge to immerse into the ocean of Divinity instead of the effort to contribute to the divine harmony. Though deeply interested in the perfection of the individual, the ecstatic Kabbalah ends with his complete disintegration; this is obviously the continuation of the philosophical tendency to suppress the non-intellectual parts of the human personality, reducing him to a purely intellectual being.

The theurgical Kabbalah, notwithstanding its theosophic tendency, aimed at the amplification of the Kabbalist's capacities; or, to use Jungian terminology, the theurgian Kabbalist underwent a process of individuation,[114] vis à vis the "regression" of the intellect into the bosom of divinity according to the prophetic Kabbalah. In other words, Jewish mysticism may be described as a realm whose border with philosophy is a region of passive contemplation and where the inhabitants tend towards solitude and intellectual inwardness. Governing this parcel is the active intellect, whereas its Lord is Aristotle's self-intellecting first cause.

In the opposite direction, Jewish mysticism is a greater domain, deeply penetrated by halakhic activity, where energized contemplation is attained in communal worship. This realm is directly governed by divine potencies or powers—the *sefirot*—whose lord is either the Neoplatonic-biased concept of *Ein Sof*, or, more rarely, the concept of the anthropomorphic supernal essences forming the hidden primeval Adam.[115] The ecstatic Kabbalah presents the mystic as a receptacle of divine emanation and energy; a quasi-female intellect impregnated by the active intellect which is treated as a male.[116] In the theurgical Kabbalah, the mystic is viewed as a source of energy which is projected into the realm of *sefirot;* the last of them, *Malkhut*, is sometimes conceived as the supernal wife of the righteous.[117] The basic divergence between the two types of Jewish mysticism may be illustrated by a comparison of two dicta: the theosophical Kabbalah would prefer as its slogan the biblical verse, "And thou, Solomon my son, know thou the God of thy father, and serve him" (I Chronicle, 28,9). Here, knowledge of God is presented, but only in anticipation of the proper religious service, the latter being the ultimate purpose of man.[118] Abulafia and his disciples, however, would choose the well-known maxim "He who knows himself knows his Lord," whose metamorphoses were traced by A. Altmann. Knowledge of God is treated as the highest perfection of man, and it is explicitly connected, according to several medieval philosophers, with man's union with the active intellect.[119]

The typology above notwithstanding, I should like to point out what seems to be a striking discrepancy between our description of the prophetic Kabbalah, and the personality of its most important exponent, Abraham Abulafia. He was indeed a very active figure, roaming from city to city and acquiring devotees and disciples through his teaching, prolific writings, and intensive preaching to Jews and Christians. Nevertheless, this activity, fraught with messianic overtones, was considered, by Abulafia, to be a necessary evil, obviously inferior to the experience of being with God.

Thus, his public activity was considered an escapist interruption to the unitive experience.[119]

VIII

Most of the above-mentioned texts remained in long-forgotten manuscripts, and, prima facie, exert little influence on the development of Jewish and European thought. Nevertheless, it seems that some themes of Abulafia's thought found their way to a larger intellectual audience than one might expect. The *Sitrei Torah* is extant in at least twenty-five manuscripts,[120] and small portions of it were printed anonymously.[121] Furthermore, it was translated, together with other works of Abulafia, into Latin, and it became one of the cornerstones of Pico della Mirandola's Kabbalah, as the late Ḥaim Wirszubski has convincingly proved.[122] I should like to suggest that Pico's view on man's union with God might be influenced by Abulafian views.[123]

On the other hand, Abulafia's passage from *'Or HaSekhel*, dealing with human intellectual love and "divine intellectual love", was copied by a late fifteenth-century author and printed one hundred years later. For the time being, the last phrase is closest to the wording of Spinoza's famous expression, "*amor dei intellectualis.*"[124]

Notes to Chapter 1

The writing of this study was made possible by a grant from Memorial Foundation for Jewish Culture.

1. See Moritz Steinschneider, "Die Hebräischen Commentare zum 'Führer' des Maimonides", *Festschrift A. Berliner* (Frankfort, 1903): 345-363; Altmann, "Maimonides' Attitude" pp. 200-219; Idel, *Abraham Abulafia* pp. 8-12, Wirszubski (note 18 below).

2. Cf. Adolf Jellinek, *Bet Ha-Midrash*, vol. III (Jerusalem, 1938) p. XLI (German section).

3. See Idel, "Abulafia and the Pope", p. 1-2 n.3.

4. Isadore Twersky, "Religion and Law" in *Religion in a Religious Age* (ed. S. D. Goitein, Cambridge, Mass., 1974) p. 74.

5. See Scholem, *Major Trends* pp. 194-195.

6. See S. O. Heller-Willensky, "Isaac Ibn Latif—Philosopher or Kabbalist." In *Jewish Medieval and Renaissance Studies*, ed. A. Altmann (Cambridge, Mass.

1967) pp. 185-237.

7. Louis Gardet, *Études de philosophie et de mystique comparées* (Paris, 1972) pp. 268-270; see also Scholem, *Major Trends*, pp. 23-4.

8. Idel, *The Mystical Experience* pp. 13-71. Abulafia was deeply influenced by Maimonides' theory of prophecy: see idem, *Abraham Abulafia* pp. 86-128 and compare to Altmann "Maimonides' Attitude" p. 206.

9. Hans Jonas, "Myth and Mysticism: A Study of Objectification and Interiorization in Religious Thought" *Journal of Religion* 49 (1969) pp. 328-329.

10. Idel, *The Mystical Experience* pp. 22-24.

11. Scholem, *Major Trends* pp. 122-123: compare also pp. 55-56; idem, *Kabbalah* pp. 174-176; idem, *The Messianic Idea* pp. 203-204. A more cautious formulation can be detected in Scholem's relatively late paper "Mysticism and Society" *Diogenes*, vol. 58 (1967) p. 16: "The Jewish mystics used the term *devequth* to denote this ultimate aim. The term, meaning literally "cleaving" or "adhering" to God . . . The necessity to compromise with medieval Jewish theology dictated this terminology, not the act itself, which *may* or may not include a state of mystical union."

Scholem's assumption that the use of the rather ambiguous term *devequth* was dictated by the need to compromise with Jewish theology, i.e. the philosophically biased thought, is not supported by the following discussion; not only has Abulafia been influenced by philosophical unitive terminology; we can find philosophical texts which openly speak about the possibility of total union with God: see, e.g. the statement of one of Abulafia's contemporaries, R. Isaac ben Yeda'yah who wrote about the Nazirite that by the disattachment of his soul from matter and the purification of his intellect, he will find a direct presence of God "and his soul will cleave to Him in a complete and unseparable union, which lasts forever." *Commentary on Avot* (Jerusalem, 1973) p. 65. cp. also to p. 62 and for another discussion of the same author, adduced in Marc Saperstein "R. Isaac b. Yeda'ya: A Forgotten Commentator on the 'Aggada" *REJ*, vol. 138 (1979) p. 31. Saperstein has the merit to have established the real author of this commentary.

On Abulafia's influence on R. Abraham Shalom, a fifteenth-century Jewish theologian, see Chapter IV where I have evinced the influence of Abulafia's description of *unio mystica* in *'Or Ha-Sekhel.*

12. The unfolding of the Hegelian mold of Scholem's view was briefly described by Natan Rotenstreich, *Judaism and Jewish Rights* (HaKibbutz Hameuchad Publishing House, 1959) pp. 119-120 (Hebrew).

13. Scholem, *Major Trends* pp. 7-8.

14. Minor exceptions are the statements of Tishby, *The Wisdom of the Zohar*, vol. II p. 289 n. 69; Gottlieb, *Studies* pp. 237-238; Altmann, *Faces* pp. 78-79, 89-90, and note 38 below. See also, Idel, *Kabbalah: New Perspectives* ch. III-IV.

15. See Robert C. Zaehner, *Hindu and Muslim Mysticism* (University of

London, 1960) p. 2; and *At Sundry Times—An Essay in the Comparison of Religions* (London, 1958) p. 171.

16. See Idel, *Kabbalah: New Perspectives* ch. III-IV.

17. We are concerned here only with Abulafia's own view of *unio mystica;* the views of his followers can be the subject of another study; see Idel, *Kabbalah: New Perspectives* ch. IV and essay VII below.

18. See Shlomo Pines, "The Limitations of Human Knowledge According to Al-Farabi, Ibn Bajja, and Maimonides" In *Studies in Medieval Jewish History and Literature*, ed. I. Twersky (Cambridge, Mass: Harvard U. Press, 1979) pp. 82-109; also Pines, "Les limites de la metaphysique selon Al-Farabi, ibn Bajja et Maimonides . . . ," in *Miscellanea Mediaevalia*, Vol. 13/1 (Berlin, New York, 1981) pp. 211-225. This agnostic position notwithstanding, Maimonides was considered by some Jewish and Christian Kabbalists as a genuine mystic: see Gershom Scholem, "Maimonide dans l'oeuvre des Kabbalistes" *Cahiers juifs* 3, (1935) pp. 103-112; Chayyim Wirszubski, "*Liber Redemptionis*—the Early Version of R. Abraham Abulafia's Kabbalistic Commentary on the *Guide of the Perplexed* in the Latin Translation of Flavius Mithridates," in *Divrei Ha-Akademia Ha-Le'umit Ha-Yisraelit Le-Mada'im*, vol. III (Israeli Academy of Science, Jerusalem, 1970) pp. 139-149. This "Kabbalization" of Maimonides is generally connected with conceptions belonging to Abulafia's Kabbalistic school. I subscribe to Pines' assertion that ". . . Maimonides is no mystic. His intention is not to recommend progressive detachment from the knowledge of all things that are not God, but to further that kind of knowledge by teaching people to avoid misplaced references to God's essence": in the "Translator's Introduction" to *The Guide of the Perplexed*, tr. S. Pines, (Chicago, 1963) p. xcvi. For a mystical interpretation of Maimonides' thought see David Blumenthal "Maimonides' Intellectualist Mysticism and the Superiority of the Prophecy of Moses" *Studies in Medieval Culture* vol. X (1981) pp. 51-67.

19. *Milḥamot HaShem* (Hanovre, 1840) p. 22. See Vajda, *Recherches*, p. 27 n. 2.

20. Samuel Ibn Tibbon, *Ma'amar Yikkawu Ha-Mayyim* (Presbourg, 1837) p. 91. See Georges Vajda "An Analysis of the Ma'amar Yiqqawu ha-Mayim by Samuel b. Judah Ibn Tibbon" *JJS*, X (1959) p. 147 n. 28; idem *Recherches*, p. 26 n. 3.

21. Compare R. Yehudah ha-Levi's presentation of the philosophic view in *Kuzari* I, 1; IV, 13 cf. Vajda, *Recherches* p. 23 n; idem, "An Analysis", p. 147 n. 28.

22. Vajda, *Recherches* p. 27 n. 2.

23. As pointed out by Vajda, *Recherches*, pp. 27-28 n. 3.

24. Maimuni highly appreciated Ibn Tibbon, and could be influenced by his Averroistic view.

25. See the bibliography referred to by Gerson D. Cohen, "The Soteriology

of R. Abraham Maimuni" *PAAJR*, 35 (1967) p. 25 n. 2.

26. See Idel, "On the History" p. 16. Abulafia uses Ibn Tibbon's translation of *The Guide.*

27. Abulafia's teacher, R. Hillel ben Samuel of Verona, introduced him to the *Guide* and also copied at length, parts of Averroes' treatise on the conjunction with the active intellect (see n. 28 below) in his work *Tagmulei HaNefesh.* Though this book was written only years after the meeting of Abulafia with R. Hillel, it seems reasonable to suppose that R. Hillel could be one of the sources of Abulafia's knowledge of Averroes; on Hillel's usage of Ibn Tibbon's translation, see Joseph B. Sermoneta, *Hillel ben Samuel ben Eleazer of Verona and His Philosophy* (Ph.D. thesis, University of Jerusalem, 1961) pp. 355-401 (Hebrew).

28. See J. Hercz, *Drei Abhandlungen über die Conjunction des separaten Intellects mit dem Menschen von Averroes (Vater und Sohn), aus den Arabischen übersetzt von Samuel Ibn Tibbon*, (Berlin, 1869); see also the anonymous undated Hebrew translation of Averroes' *Über die Möglichkeit der Conjunction oder Über den Materiellen Intellect*, ed. Ludwig Hannes (Halle, 1892). On the problem of union in Averroes see Alfred Ivry "Averroes on Intellection and Conjunction" *JAOS* 86 (1966) pp. 76-85 and Philip Merlan, *Monopsychism, Mysticism, Metaconsciousness* (The Hague, 1963).

29. *Sitrei Torah*, Ms. Paris, BN 774, fol. 140a.

30. Ibid., fol. 155a. Compare this text to the quotation which R. Isaac of Acre quotes in the name of R. Nathan, in his book *Me'irat 'Einayim*, cf. essay VII n. 50. R. Nathan, which in my opinion, was a student of Abulafia, describes the descent of the divine intellect, through the intellectus agens until the level of human soul which is lower than the passive intellect, and then the human soul's return to, and union with, the divine intellect. On the affinity of R. Nathan's text to an Averroistic view see Hercz (n. 28 above) p. 22 (Hebrew part). R. Nathan seems to have been one of Abulafia's disciples: see chapter V.

31. "Amitat Ḥ aNevuah"

32. "Dibbur Penimi"

33. This expression occurs again in Abulafia's other work, *Ḥayyei Ha'Olam HaBa'*, Ms. Oxford, 1580, fol. 11a; which was composed in the same year as *Sitrei Torah*, namely, 1280.

34. Compare to the circle which occurs in Ibn al-Sid Al-Batalyawsi's (1052-1127) *Book of the Circles:* see David Kaufmann, *Die Spuren Al-Batlajusis in der jüdischen Religionsphilosophie* (Leipzig, 1880) p. 25 (Hebrew part). Though the elements of these two circles are not identical, they share a common feature: the *intellectus agens* is considered both the origin and the end of man's psychological activity. Furthermore, in the quotation from Abulafia's *Sitrei Torah*, he uses the concept of "prophetic faculty" in this seems to be the unique passage in all of Abulafia's numerous works where it occurs. This concept may stem from

Al-Batalyawsi's view of "the prophetic soul"; see Kaufmann, ibid. pp. 15-16 (Hebrew part). Moreover, according to both Al-Batalyawsi and Abulafia, the prophetic faculty unites with the *intellectus agens:* see Kaufmann, pp. 15-16. Finally, Abulafia uses in his *Sitrei Torah* the term "ma'agalei ha-meẓiut," (the circles of existence) which, though missing in Al-Batalyawsi's work, conveys a concept central to its outlook (see Ms. Paris, BN 774, fol. 118a). Al-Batalyawsi's book might have been already translated by 1280, when Abulafia had written his *Sitrei Torah* by Moses Ibn Tibbon (according to Colette Sirat, *REJ* 138 (1979) p. 505, Ibn Tibbon's last dated traduction was done in 1274). It is also possible that another Hebrew translation of this work, done by R. Salomon Ibn Daud (See Benjamin Richler, *Kiryat Sefer*, vol. 53 (1978) p. 577) may be dated in the middle of the thirteenth century, if R. Makir, for whom the translation was dedicated, is the son of R. Sheshet Nasi, who flourished in the first third of the thirteenth century in Provence.

35. "Dibbur Kadmon" cf. Abulafia's epistle called *Ve-Zot Li-Yihudah*, ed. by Adolf Jellinek, *Auswahl Kabbalistischer Mystik*, (Leipzig, 1853) vol. I p. 16 (Hebrew Part); there Abulafia describes the union of the inner intellectual faculty with the supernal logos. On the *intellectus agens* as "speech" (i.e. reason), see Idel, *Abraham Abulafia* pp. 92-93. The ascension of the intellectual faculty beyond the "primordial speech" (i.e. the *intellectus agens*), and its readiness to receive the "divine speech" probably points to the possibility of contact between the human and the divine. Compare to the quotation adduced in note 50 from *Ḥayye Ha'Olam HaBa'.*

36. *Sitrei Torah*, Ms. Paris, BN 774, fol. 131b.

37. *Sitrei Torah*, Ms. Paris, BN 774, fol. 120a.

38. *'Or HaSekhel*, Ms. Vatican, 233, fol. 115a. Compare also to another passage from the same work printed and discussed by Francesco M. Tocci, "Una Tecnica recitativa e respiratoria di tipo sufico nel libro *La Luce dell'Intelletto* di Abraham Abulafia," in *Annali della Facolta di Lingue e Letterature Straniere di Ca' Foscari*, vol. XIV, 3 [1975] p. 227. On page 236, n. 36, Tocci asserts that "*devekut*", which occurs in the Abulafian text is "analogo ma no identico a quello di unio mystica."!

39. "Love" (in Hebrew, "Ahavah") is formed of letters whose numerical value is 13: two loves 13+13=26: see note 40 below. Abulafia's theory on the nature of love is mainly Maimonidean, though the sexual imagery is more pronounced: see Idel, *The Mystical Experience*, ch. IV. Georges Vajda, *L'Amour de Dieu dans la theologie juive du Moyen Age* (Paris, 1957) pp. 203-204, 299.

40. The divine name is composed of four letters whose numerical value is 26. In Hebrew, "one"—'Eḥad—is formed from letters whose numerical value is 13; twice "one" is therefore the numerical value of the divine name. See note 39 above.

41. Ms. Paris, BN 774, fol. 118a.

42. *VeZot LiYihudah*, (see note 35 above) p. 20. I accepted Scholem's

translation, almost entirely, see *Major Trends*, p. 131; on the forces and souls distributed in bodies, compare the second text adduced in note 38 above.

43. On the meaning of this phrase see Scholem, *Major Trends*, p. 131; Idel, *The Mystical Experience* pp. 134-137. On binding and loosing see also Mircea Eliade, "The "Gods who Binds" and the Symbolism of Knots" *Images and Symbols* (New York, 1969) pp. 92-124; J. Duncan M. Derrett, "Binding and Loosing (Matt. 16:19; 18:8; John, 29:23)" *JBL* 102 (1983) pp. 112ff.

44. W. T. Stace, *Mysticism and Philosophy* (London and Basingstoke, 1972) p. 116.

45. Jellinek, *Auswahl* (n. 35 above) p. 20.

46. This term stemming from the *Guide*, II, 40 occurs several times in the Abulafian literature: see Ms. Sassoon, 290, p. 234 and the anonymous works *Ner 'Elohim*, Ms. Munchen, 10, fol. 143a; the anonymous work *Sha'arei Ẓedek*, Ms. Jerusalem, 8° 148, fol. 55b-56a. However, it seems that Maimonides' description of man indicates the result of the process of creation, whereas Abulafia's use of the phrase points to the ontological *status* of humanity. Cf. also the material referred to by note 72 below.

47. Ms. Sassoon 290, pp. 234-235. "Notarot" is obviously a pun: it may mean both "remaining" and "untied".

48. According to Jewish ancient texts, the world was created by and was sealed with the name of God at the time of creation: see Nicholas Sed, *La Mystique cosmologique juive* (Paris, Berlin, New York, 1981) pp. 79-131. Abulafia presents his teaching as a technique of untying the knots which emerge with the creation of the world or of man.

49. This verb means "to strip oneself" and figuratively points to the separation from materiality. See also n. 69 below.

50. Ms. Oxford 1580, fol. 41b. See also n. 35 above and 71 below.

51. Abulafia's commentary to his *Sefer HaYashar*, written in 1279, Ms. Rome, Angelica, 38, fol. 31b-32a; Ms. München, 285, fol. 26b. I have generally accepted Scholem's rendering of this passage.

52. See Joseph Dan, "The Seventy Names of Metatron" *Proceedings of the Eighth World Congress of Jewish Studies*, Division C (Jerusalem, 1982) (English Section) pp. 19-23.

53. Scholem translated "adhering".

54. The apparently earliest known text which uses the phrase "hu' hu'" in the context of Enoch's translation into Metatron, was written by a thirteenth-century anonymous Kabbalist, whose discussion remained in Ms. Oxford, 1947, fol. 10a-10b. It is pertinent to our discussion that Enoch's translation is due to his intellectual activity, the ancient mystic conception of corporeal ascension and

metamorphoses being interpreted here figuratively. Compare also to R. Baḥiya ben Asher on Genesis V, 24, who asserts that Enoch cleaved to the supernal light through his endeavour to understand the nature of Metatron. See also n. 98, 123, below.

55. Ms. Oxford 1649 fol. 206a.

56. The comparison of these phrases to two passages above (notes 37-38) convincingly evinces that here we have an elliptic expression, which points to the divine intellectual power and the human intellectual power.

57. "Galgal ha-Nevu'ah": "the sphere [or circle] of prophecy" may stand for the union of the two powers into one sphere during the prophetic experience; Compare to the view of the anonymous Kabbalist, a disciple of Abulafia, who wrote in his work *Sha'arei Ẓedek*, Ms. Jerusalem, 8° 148, fol. 55a:

> because Yod, whose form is a semisphere will move whenever its sphere will be fulfilled . . . and this is the matter of the terrestrial man who will ascend and become supernal [man], i.e. the man who is [sitting] upon the chair.

Here, the perfect sphere or circle stands for the perfect man, who is, in Abulafia's view, the prophet. Compare also to *Sha'arei Ẓedek*, fol. 56 ab. In another anonymous treatise of Abulafian mold, *Ner 'Elohim*, Ms. München, 10, fol. 139a, we learn about the prophetic vision which is connected with "the sphere of law." See also Idel, *Kabbalah: New Perspectives*, ch. IV.

58. *Sefer ha-Malmad*, Ms. Oxford 1649, fol. 205b. For an interesting parallel to this usage of the formula "I am what I am" see Eckhart's assertion that "were I wholly that I am, I should be God", cf. C. F. Kelley, *Meister Eckhart on Divine Knowledge* (New Haven and London, 1977) p. 210 and p. 273, n. 85. For the influence of Maimonides on Eckhart and the parallelism between the latter's and Abulafia's relation to Maimonides see Scholem, *Major Trends* p. 126, and note 112 below.

59. The author obviously hints to the verse "From my flesh I behold God" (Job, 19:26). For the mystical interpretations of this verse, see Altmann, "The Delphic Maxim" pp. 208-213 and Chapter VII below, n. 132, where references to interpretations from the works of another ecstatic Kabbalist, R. Isaac of Acre, are quoted.

60. On this Midrash see H. G. Enelow "Midrash Hashkem quotations in Alnaqua's Menorat ha-Maor" *HUCA* 4 (1927) pp. 311-343, especially p. 319. Compare also to the quotation discussed in my paper "The Magical and Theurgic Interpretation of Music in Jewish Sources from the Renaissance to Hassidism" *Yuval*, vol. 4 (1982) p. 47 (Hebrew Section), and Idel, *Kabbalah: New Perspectives*, ch. VIII, par. I.

61. Louis Massignon, *Receuils des textes inedits concertant l'histoire de mystique en pays d'Islam* (Paris, 1929) p. 127. See also R. C. Zaehner, *Hindu and*

Muslim Mysticism (London, 1960) pp. 113-114.

62. Franz Rosenthal "Al-Sayh al-Yunani and the Arabic Plotinus Source" *Orientalia*, vol. 21 (1952) pp. 478-480, Shlomo Pines, "Ecrits 'Plotiniens' Arabes et Tradition 'Porphyrienne'" in *Le Neoplatonisme* (Paris, 1971) pp. 303-313.

63. The text translated above is the summary of Abulafia's discussion in his *'Or HaSekhel*, Ms. Vatican, 233, fol. 117b-118b, as it is found in two *collectanaea* of Kabbalistic materials: Ms. Oxford, 1949, Ms. Paris BN, 776, fol. 192b. The slight differences between Abulafia's version and that in the *collectanaea* will be pointed out in the following footnotes.

64. "and . . . of the intellect" missing in *'Or HaSekhel.*

65. In Abulafia's work: "from all matter" ("Mikol ḥomer").

66. "an emanation emanated" in Abulafia: "sekhel nishpa'".

67. Here a lengthy discussion on the nature of the intellect and *intelligibilia* occurs in Abulafia's work.

68. "However . . . . intellect" missing in *'Or HaSekhel.*

69. I.e., the most spiritual intellect; see also note 49 above.

70. Some statements on the various religious terms referring to the active intellect, occurs in *'Or HaSekhel.*

71. *'Or HaSekhel*, Ms. Vatican 233, fol. 119b. Compare to the text referred to in note 50 above.

72. Ibid., fol. 119a. cf. the material referred to in note 45 above.

73. I.e., *anima mundi*, which is referred to as "the soul of heaven": "nefesh ha-shamayim" *'Or HaSekhel*, fol. 118a.

74. I.e., the human intellect; compare to the prior quotation and to note 36 above.

75. I.e., the ten intellects separated from matter or only the active intellect: see *Guide* I, 68 (Pines' translation, p. 164).

76. The supernal world is referred to as supernal man also in the *collectanaea* mentioned above (note 63): "The Supernal Man points to the Supernal World, the Spiritual [One] that is the world of the Separate Intellects." Ms. Paris, BN 766, fol. 193a.

77. *'Or HaSekhel*, Ms. Vatican, 233, fol. 118a. Compare to the *Guide* II.6 (Pines' translation, p. 264) on the forces which pervade reality; this discussion of Maimonides is quoted in one of Abulafia's commentaries on the secrets of the *Guide*, *Sefer Ḥayyei HaNefesh*, Ms. Münich, 408, fol. 90b.

78. Ms. Paris, BN 766, fol. 192b. Compare to Maimonides' statement that it is impossible to divide the spiritual realm in the *Guide* II,4. See also Idel, "Between

the Concept of Sefirot as Essence or Instruments in Renaissance Kabbalah" *Italia*, vol. III, no. 1-2 pp. 99-100, n. 70 (Hebrew).

79. *Metaphysics* 1072b, 18-27. See Richard McKeon, *The Basic Works of Aristotle* (Random House, New York, 1941) p. 880.

80. See his commentary on *Exodus*, XXXIV, 6. Ibn Ezra asserts in his treatise *Yesod Mora*, ch. X, that the soul can cleave to God. Ibn Ezra influenced Abulafia's thought and he is quoted by him several times.

81. *Guide*, I, 68 (Pines' translation, p. 163); *Hilkhot Yesodei Torah*, II 6, 10.

82. Ibid. I, 55.

83. See E. R. Dodds, *Pagan and Christian in an Age of Anxiety*, (Cambridge, 1969) p. 70.

84. See Idel, "On the History," p. 8.

85. Idel, "Abulafia and the Pope," pp. 8-9.

86. Ibid. pp. 2-6.

87. Idel, *Abraham Abulafia*, pp. 13-15.

88. Ibid. p. 14.

89. Ms. Rome-Angelica, 38, fol. 14b-15a, Ms. München, 285, fol. 39b.

90. I.e., the author, namely Abulafia.

91. See above the texts from *Sefer ha-Yashar* and the quotation from *Ḥayyei Ha'Olam HaBa'*, cited immediately below.

92. "Sod" its meaning is *gematria:* see n. 94 below.

93. literally "impossible".

94. The Hebrew phrases: "corporeal name"—"HaShem HaGashmi," the Messiah of God, "Mashiaḥ HaShem" and Moses will rejoice "Ysmaḥ Moshe" have the numerical value of 703.

95. Ms. Paris, BN 777, fol. 109a.

96. On this issue see Idel, *The Mystical Experience* ch. II.

97. "*Behitbodeduto*": for this significance of the term see Chapter 7.

98. A clear pun upon the double meaning of the root m-sh ḥ: "to annoint" and "Messiah". It is worth remarking that Enoch's transformation into a high angel, one of the "Glorious Ones", is described as annointment with oil: see II Enoch, *Le livre des Secrets d'Henoch*, ed. A. Vaillant (Paris, 1952) 26; 18-27; 2. Abulafia regarded the mystic union in terms very close to Enoch's translation: see notes 52, 54 above.

99. In Hebrew "mal'akh" signifies also messenger.

100. Cf. *BT, Sanhedrin*, fol. 38b.

101. The Hebrew letters of Shaddai and Metatron have the same numerical values, i.e. 314. Cf. also the aforecited passage out of *Sefer Ha'Edut.*

102. Ms. Rome-Angelica, 38, fol. 9b; Ms. München, 285, fol. 12b.

103. I.e., the human species, which is described beforehand as including figuratively beasts and animals, in comparison to the nature of the mystic.

104. In the Rome manuscript, the version is "'Eloah" i.e. God, and I prefer the reading of the München Ms: "'Elohi" "divine".

105. *Ḥayyei Ha'Olam HaBa'*, Ms. Oxford, 1582, fol. 79b. See also Idel, *Abraham Abulafia* pp. 404-405. Compare also to the sequel of the passage quoted above from the commentary of *Sefer HaMeliẓ*.

106. For the list of those secrets, see Idel, *Abraham Abulafia*, p. 9.

107. Cf. Maimonides' *Introduction* to the *Guide* (Pines' translation, pp. 6-7).

108. See Idel, "Abulafia and the Pope", p. 3.

109. Cf. Idel, *Abraham Abulafia* pp. 185-192, 239-240.

110. The titles of Abulafia's three commentaries on the secrets included in the *Guide* are highly significant: a) *Sefer HaGeulah*—the Book of Redemption; b) *Sefer Ḥayyei HaNefesh*—the Book on the [Spiritual] life of the Soul; c) *Sefer Sitrei Torah*—the Book on the Secrets of the Law. Since these commentaries are but three versions of a single list of secrets, it seems that their titles are, at least partially, synonyms: the real redemption is the true life of the soul which can be attained through knowledge of the secrets of the law. See especially Abulafia's statement in his introduction to *Sitrei Torah:* "All the secrets [of the *Guide*] are thirty-six, and whoever will meditate upon them in order to understand them by the means of speculation and to comprehend their real meaning, he will be redeemed (*Levit.* XXV, 31)". Ms. Paris, BN 774, fol. 117a. Here, Abulafia hints to the redemptive role of the 36 secrets, skillfully using the pun upon "Ge'ulah tiḥieh lo": lo = 36; He regards the two purposes of the *Guide* as the explanation of the homonimies in the Bible and of the parables found in the prophecies, whereas the two aims of his commentary are the explanation of the cause of the life of the intellectual soul and of the worship of God out of love; cf. Ms. Paris, BN 774, fol. 115b.

Therefore, in the introduction to *Sitrei Torah* Abulafia overtly hints to both the redemption and the spiritual life of the soul, as emerging out of Maimonides' *Guide.* In his introduction to *Ḥayyei HaNefesh*, we read:

> I will open my mouth (to speak) without parables or allegories in order to save the intellectual soul from the elements . . . and I shall tell her secrets.

Ms. München, 408, fol. 1b. Again, the three main motifs occur together: the salvation of intellectual soul by disclosure of secrets.

111. See R. Shelomo ben Abraham Ibn Adret, *Responsa* (Vienna, 1812) fol. 71c-72a no. 548 where he characterizes Abulafia's books as a mixture of philosophical discussions and "gematriaot" both of them used in Abulafia's exegesis of the Jewish texts. Compare also the description of one of Abulafia's students to a dialogue with his master: "why then do you, Sir, compose books in which the methods of the natural scientists are coupled with instruction in the Holy Names?" He answered: "For you and the likes of you among the followers of philosophy, to allure your human intellect through natural means, so that perhaps this attraction may cause you to arrive at the knowledge of the Holy Name." Adduced by Scholem, *Major Trends*, p. 149.

112. Meister Eckhart, *Die deutschen Werke*, vol. I, ed. J. Quint (Stuttgart, 1938) p. 90. Cf. Kelley, *Meister Eckhart* (n. 58 above) p. 26. Eckhart, like Maimonides and Abulafia, designates God as Intellect; he asserts, like Abulafia, that the human intellect can be assimilated to the unconditional Intellect (see Kelley, p. 204, 235). Moreover, according to Kelley (p. 205) "when contemplation is pure . . " the term I or Selfhood refers to the Light of Intellect-as-such" and compare this view to our discussion in part IV above, especially n. 87.

113. Abulafia seems to be the first Kabbalist who stresses the importance of solitude as a condition for Kabbalistic spiritual activity; see Idel, *The Mystical Experience*, pp. 37-39.

114. According to the *Zohar*, the highest spiritual *status:* the *neshamah*, is acquired by the means of Kabbalistic performance of commandments. Salomon Munk's remark that the Zoharic psychology is influenced by the philosophical view of conjunction, is to be taken *cum grano salis;* see his *Melanges de philosophie juive et arabe* (New York, 1980) pp. 279-280.

115. See Moshe Idel "The Image of Man above the Sefirot". *Daat*, vol. 4 (1980) pp. 41-55 (Heb.).

116. Idel, *The Mystical Experience*, pp. 184-194, and see above, note 38.

117. See Chapter 7 n. 66.

118. See R. Meir ben Salomon Ibn Avi Sahulah's definition of Kabbalah as the science of the ten *sefirot* and mystical significance of the commandments. Cf. Scholem, *Les origines de la Kabbale* p. 48.

119. Altmann, "Delphic Maxim" p. 228; see also Altmann "Ibn Bajja on Man's Ultimate Felicity" *Studies in Religious Philosophy and Mysticism* (Ithaca, New York, 1969) pp. 73-107.

120. See Idel, *Abraham Abulafia*, pp. 42-43 n. 43; on the influence of this book see p. 12.

121. See *Liqqutei Shikheḥah ufeah* (Ferrara, 1556) fol. 23r-35v.

122. Ḥaim Wirszubski *A Christian Kabbalist Reads the Law*, (Jerusalem,

1977) pp. 23, 30-31, 38 (Hebrew); Compare also his article referred to in note 18 above.

123. See *Oratio on the Dignity of Man*, trans. by A. Robert Caponigri, (Chicago, 1967) pp. 8-9, 14, especially pp. 9-10 where the transformation of Enoch into "the angel of divinity" i.e. "malakh HaShekhinah", is referred to. Compare note 54, 98 above. On the influence of Maimonides' concept of death by kiss on Pico's view of *mors osculi* see Ḥaim Wirszubski, *Three Studies in Christian Kabbala* (Jerusalem, 1975) pp. 11-22 (Hebrew); cf. Edgar Wind, *Pagan Mysteries in the Renaissance* (Penguin Books, 1967) pp. 154-157.

124. See Chapter 4 below.

Chapter 2

Was Abraham Abulafia Influenced by the Cathars?

The exposure of relationship between Kabbalistic ideas and ideas found outside of Judaism is a valuable means of understanding the development of the Kabbalah. Gnostic and neo-Platonic influences were noted by scholars as having been instrumental in forming the character of the Kabbalah, yet much work remains in explicating these relationships.[1]

Recent attempts have been made to prove the influence of two additional streams of thought from the Medieval period upon the Kabbalah. Y. Baer wrote that the religious movement originated by Joachim de Fiori influenced the author of the *Sefer Ra'ya Meheimna* and the *Tikkunei HaZohar*,[2] whereas Shulamit Shaḥar posits a close relationship between the ideas of the Cathars and those of the *Sefer HaBahir*.[3] She also claims that there is a close relationship between the Cathars and one of the works by R. Abraham Abulafia.[4] This paper will examine these claims of similarity as well as the possible influence of the Cathars upon Abulafia, as proposed by S. Shaḥar.

Shaḥar wavers between two designations regarding the ideas found among both the Cathars and Abulafia. The title of her article speaks of "shared images and ideas." Elsewhere in the article she assumes that the ideas found in Abulafia's work "are analogous to classic conceptions and images found in both the theology and the popular belief of the Cathars" (p. 351). By the end of her article, these "analogous" and "shared images and ideas" become definite influences: "It seems to me that these shared images and ideas are not merely isolated developments in the personal Kabbalistic doctrine of Abulafia, rather, they are a result of Cathars' influence on Abulafia's spiritual atmosphere and conceptual framework during a particular period of his life" (p. 360). We thus find a clear designation of "similarity."

I will not be concerned here with the possibility of a shared "spiritual atmosphere," between the Cathars and Abulafia, since I doubt whether such concerns can bear much fruit. However, indications of direct Catharic influence on Abulafia's ideas and images, if they do indeed exist (as Shaḥar claims), would constitute an important discovery in the historical research of the Kabbalah. Therefore, a thorough investigation of these claims is important.

Shaḥar analyzes brief quotes from Abulafia's commentary on the *Sefer Yeẓirah.* Based on the ambiguous meanings of these quotes, she draws a weighty conclusion: Abulafia's ideas regarding the place of Satan in the world, and the function he performs therein, come very close to what the "moderate Cathars" believed. In the course of her article, Shaḥar explains that, according to these "moderate" Cathars, although Satan did not indeed create the world, he assisted God in the work of creation and became the "mover of the world,"[5] and the one who laid down the laws of nature. She continues: "This is the case, in like degree, according to Abulafia. For although the world was created by God, . . . Satan is the mover of bodies. Therefore, the embodiment of motion is Satan. This is to say that he has a part in the creation of the world. For Abulafia says that he (Satan) rules in this world." (pp. 353-354) Before we go into an analysis of the abstruse quotation upon which the author bases her statement, we will examine Abulafia's opinions regarding the nature of Satan from those sources where his meaning is not obscure or open to varying interpretation.

In *Sefer Mafteaḥ HaSefirot* (Abulafia's commentary to the biblical book of Numbers), we read: "And the philosophers brought proof to refute all of these thoughts and illusions, and said that demons do not exist. Yet, whatever receives a form, that is generated and corrupted, is the demon, and the imagination is Satan, the king of all demons."[6] Two designations are associated here with Satan: he is the material realm that changes form, and he is the power of the imagination. The first designation, which is most relevant to our discussion, recurs in other texts by Abulafia. In *Sefer 'Oẓar 'Eden Ganuz* he writes: "And so, this intermediary between us and God is called Satan, and he is also called Job. He is called Satan because he is the evil body[7] and has no durability or [real] substance. But he roams the earth and wanders about in it,[8] for he is the realm of the generated and corrupted matter, i.e. the matter of the four elements."[9]

This conception of Satan is not new. For example, a contemporary of Abulafia, R. Zeraḥiah ben She'alti'el Ḥen, in his commentary to the book of Job, explains the concept of Satan as follows: "The meaning of Satan is the material world, i.e. these natural individua composed of both matter and form . . . for the level of the material, beneath the level of the form is called Satan . . . and matter denotes that which undergoes generation and corruption and is constantly changing; whereas the forms of the species do not deteriorate."[10]

According to these writings, Satan is a designation for the nature of matter which is constantly changing form (i.e. Satan is the characteristic of matter that comes into existence and passes away). This is a philosophical concept whose source is in the writings of Aristotle, and is given the name "Satan" in the writings of Abulafia and Zeraḥiah ben She'alti'el Ḥen. Given this background, we can now explain Abulafia's statement in *Perush Sefer Yeẓirah* that was examined by Shaḥar:

> Adam and Eve, who are my father and mother, are blood and ink and include the seventy nations. And from them you will know that all grass is seed just as all seed is grass, with the form of semen whose secret is Metatron, Angel of the Countenance, who is the Angel of Hosts, the motion of the heavenly spheres within which nature imparted the motions of the belly. And from them you will understand that Satan causes motion in bodies, for the body of motion was Satan, and this world was created by means of (the letter) He (of the Tetragrammaton), as we have already indicated in (our explanation of) the secret of the letter Yod (of the Tetragrammaton). We shall therefore indicate now the secret of the He, for by Yod He, God is the everlasting fortress. Place a Vav upon the fortress "ẓur," together with Yod He so that by Yod He Vav Tetragrammaton is the everlasting fortress, (of both) this and the coming world. From this you would know that the coming world was created with the Yod, and this world was created with the He. And when you combine them you will find within them both, glory (Hod) and vaporous mist (Ed), which correspond to joy and sighing. Now the He and the He and five (Ḥamishah) taken together are the secret (i.e. the numerical value) of the Satan. And indeed he rules in this world and has no part in the coming world."[11]

The pairs "Adam and Eve," "my father and mother," and "blood and ink," all have the numerical value of seventy. What is implied is that "Adam," "my father" and "ink" represent the formative aspect of existence, whereas "mother," "blood," and "Eve" represent the material aspect of existence. This interpretation is borne out, beyond a doubt, by Abulafia's commentary to the secrets of Maimonides' *Guide of the Perplexed* which he called *Sitrei Torah.* There, in the course of explaining form and matter, he writes the following: "But I will tell you something new, and will curtly explain it. Know that "Adam and Eve" have the same numerical value as "my father and mother" and their secret is "blood and ink."[12]

Moreover, in the course of Abulafia's commentary on *Sefer Yeẓirah* we find other examples of pairs of opposites.[13] These pairs, in my opinion, contrast the spiritual aspects of existence, as they are symbolized by Metatron (Angel of the Countenance, or Angel of Hosts) who is the Active Intellect, with the material aspects of existence as they are symbolized by Satan, semen, and so forth. Such a contrast continues in the commentary: According to Talmudic tradition, the coming world was created by the letter Yod. This letter, according to Abulafia's Kabbalah, symbolizes the Active Intellect, and one who cleaves to it acquires the world to come. At times, the Yod also symbolizes the ten separate intelligences. The world (i.e. the material world), was created with the letter He. The words of R. Joseph Gikatilla, who in his *Sefer Ginnat Egoz* characterizes the material world as follows: "Know that the aspect of the world composed of complex adulterated forms was said to have been created with the letter He, i.e. the five structures built from ten parts. Indeed, regarding what the sages have said, that the world to come was created with the letter Yod, how goodly and how pleasant when ten parts are formed that are pure without intercombination, adulteration; for the world to come is the world of the intellect, of simplicity without adulteration."[14]

We return to the words of Abulafia who, in his commentary to *Sefer Yeẓirah*,[15] indicates that Satan rules over the adulterated world (i.e. the world composed of form and matter). Coming into existence and passing out of existence occurs only in this world and not in the world to come—in the world of the intellect there is no adulteration. Satan, who moves the bodies, is merely a symbol for the continuous movement of the forms that modify matter. He is not "the fallen angel" (the opinion of the "moderate" Cathars), and not the partner of God in the creation of the world. He is merely a designation, both in the writings of R. Abraham Abulafia and R. Zeraḥiah ben She'alti'el Ḥen, which is used to describe an aspect of matter, or matter itself, but he has no independent existence.

We can draw a parallel between Abulafia and the Cathars only if we fail to analyze the words of Abulafia. Upon analysis of Abulafia's *Perush Sefer Yeẓirah*, however, all similarity ceases to exist. This is also true with regard to the section of *Perush Sefer Yeẓirah* quoted by Shaḥar:

> It is worth taking note, that the warp and woof (the Cross) which is undoubtedly the covenant of Esau, the Angel of Abomination, rules according to the Torah, at the gate of chaos. They are twelve tens of failure, which are 120. He is the secret of the gate, and the house within collects

the fruit of the bodies. He is the head of the corners, he is the Angel of the Elements, and being flesh, he teaches us the secrets of illicit forms of sexuality. His aspect is the element of the flesh, front and back, and includes the visions of fire . . . including two angels, right and left.[16]

Relying on part of this quote, Shaḥar writes that Abulafia is repulsed by sexuality and reproduction, and she posits a relationship between Satan and reproduction (p. 356). In fact, a close reading of the text does not reveal an allusion to Satan, nor is sexual reproduction explicitly mentioned. What is mentioned are "the secrets of forbidden sexual conduct," and the meaning of these "secrets" is indicated in Abulafia's work, *Ḥayyei Ha'Olam HaBa'*, where he writes:

> The secrets of illicit forms of sexuality, the secrets regarding the creation and the secrets of the Chariot, all of them Divine sciences, are highly exalted topics. Indeed, the secrets of the creation involve the natural sciences, the secrets of the Chariot involve the wisdom regarding the Godhead, and both are Divine Sciences, and no form of human science can comprehend them [. . .] Indeed, the secrets of illicit forms of sexuality are matters of Torah, whose true meaning the philosophers did not comprehend. They also did not call it by that name. However, the true Torah that makes whole all that is deficient, informs us of this. And although these secrets also include the secrets of the creation and the Chariot, we know this particular secret from Adam and Eve, who represent everyone in the likeness of form and matter. For they are the onset and the beginning of the entire work of creation, and so, the first Adam is likened to form and Eve, his spouse, created from his rib, is likened to matter.[17]

We have just read the authoritative definition of "the secrets of illicit forms of sexuality." They refer to, in symbolic form, the relations between matter and form. We find here no proscription of sexual activity, nor do we find a definite connection between sex and Satan.[18]

In this setting, we can understand the words of Abulafia in his commentary to *Sefer Yeẓirah* "And when you attach the serpent to Adam and Eve, you find that man is a satan just as satan is a man."[19] In other words, when we add the power of the (illusory) imagination to matter and form, or to matter and intelligence, then man becomes transformed into a satan, since the power of illusion is found within man.[20] Regarding the implications of the relationship among Adam, Eve, the serpent, and Satan, Abulafia writes in *Ḥayyei Ha'Olam HaBa'*:

> It is written in the Midrash[21]: "as soon as woman was created Satan was created with her" and it is written[22] "Samael is the Satan who rides on the

> serpent, and he beguiles the woman," His measure is inanimate matter (Golem) for he is the camel (Gamal)[23] who carries a heavy load. He entices the potential human intellect before it becomes actualized[24] and prevents it from grasping the truth . . . Indeed the truly intelligent person, who is the true human being, will not be enticed into following the knowledge of the woman who is enticed by the Serpent.[25]

We turn now to the last topic associated with Satan. Abulafia writes: "And within the blood is Satan and within Satan is blood."[26] Shaḥar finds further indication of Catharic influence in this sentence (p. 356). However, it seems to me that the sentence was borne by an idea found in Maimonides' *Guide of the Perplexed* where he says that the power of imagination is found only among living organisms who possess a heart.[27] Abulafia relates this idea to the blood and the imagination. For example, he says, "Beware of the blood that is held [!] for it is the cause of error, and from it the imagination is created and heated up i.e. from the blood circulation. Rather, cleave to intelligence and it will cleave to you."[28]

As we saw earlier, "Satan" is a term denoting the illusory imagination. Here too we find a relation between the power of the illusory imagination that causes error[29] and the traditional portrayal of Satan as the one who causes error. However, we must emphasize that we are not dealing with the popular conception of Satan, but of the Maimonidean conception as it was portrayed by Abulafia. Accordingly, Satan is the Angel of Death, the evil inclination, the illusory imagination.[30]

Continuing from the last quote from the commentary of *Sefer Yeẓirah*, Abulafia goes on to say, "You will understand by (observing) those who have Satan in their bellies, who are satisfied by the fat wheat berry, the wheat made fat in smoke (!); all are grasses, which include all grass. Thus fat wheat is called 'seventy' and is the grain of the He."[31] According to Shaḥar, this text is influenced by a Catharic text which reads, *"fumus positus in terra faciebat pulchra blada."* Shaḥar translates "fumus" as smoke, despite the fact that as of the twelfth century "fumus" also carried the definition of "fertilizer" (as Shaḥar points out in note 27). Yet, in order to make the Catharic passage coincide with Abulafia, she chose the denotation "smoke" for "fumus", although it is contextually strained. Even if we were to accept this translation, the meaning of the sentence in the Catharic text, which conceptually associates wheat grain with "fumus", is far from the meaning in Abulafia's text, where the association is determined by a numerological device. In addition, the relation between the words of Abulafia, "You are man, you are angel, and you are Satan,"[32] and the very general Catharic conception indicated by the author (p. 357) is untenable. Abulafia himself explains, unequivocally, the meaning of this sentence. In *Perush Sefer HaMeliẓ* he writes, "Man is obliged to become angel, due to his intelligence, Satan on account of his illusory imagination, and human on account of his feelings."[33] We find here three ways to attain knowledge, and man is tested by his preference.

I will now examine another one of Shaḥar's conclusions regarding Abulafia's writing. Again, I will quote the section in its entirety, more fully than did Shaḥar:

> And the revolution (gilgul) from generation to generation, and its dominion with "generation to generation," this is my remembrance from generation to generation. A generation goes and a generation comes. Thy name is eternal and thy remembrance is from generation to generation. . . . This having been said, we may state that the moon is the measure for all heavenly bodies.[34]

According to the author, one ought to understand this section as a discussion of the transmigration of the soul—in her words, its "metamorphosis." She adduces this from a quotation from Ecclesiastes, "a generation goes and a generation comes," which, as far back as *Sefer HaBahir*, was interpreted as referring to metempsychosis. Also, the word "gilgul" (which can be taken to mean transmigration of the soul) indicates to the author that Abulafia, like the Cathars, believed in the transmigration of the soul (p. 358). Even if such an analysis were true, we need not assume Catharic influence, since both the *Sefer HaBahir* and the Gerona School of Kabbalists believe in metempsychosis. Therefore, this belief, if found in Abulafia's writings, is not a novel one. Indeed, there is no doubt that Abulafia did not intend the word "gilgul", in this context, to mean metempsychosis. A few lines later we read, "And to us it is common knowledge from the revolutions. . . . which revolve from 216 to 216 revolutions, etc."[35] Here, as in the section quoted by Shaḥar, the meaning of "gilgul" is "revolution" or "cycle," and it is clearly associated with the movement of the heavenly bodies—in this instance, the moon. Such was the topic under discussion in this manuscript (ff. 11-12), wherein we find no reference to the soul. This again, instructs us that the removal of a quote from its context will likely cause a distortion of its sense.

Finally, I will address certain notions of time and place mentioned in Shaḥar's article. The time of the writing of Abulafia's *Perush Sefer Yeẓirah*, from which we quoted, is not known. However, the author believes that is was written between 1270-1275, in Spain. For the sake of strengthening this assumption, she quotes Abulafia's autobiographical work, *'Oẓar 'Eden Ganuz*. The quote adduced by Shaḥar speaks in general, of the writings of Abulafia. Although I have no clear proof, it seems to me that the time of writing of the *Perush Sefer Yeẓirah* was approximately 1289, not 1270-75, and its place of composition was Italy, not Spain. I make this claim because seven of the ten manuscripts from this work appear in their respective editions after the work *Vezot LiYihudah*—an epistle sent from Sicily to Barcelona at the end of the 1280s.[37] If I am correct, this work was not written in a Catharic-influenced region at all, and we need not assume that Abulafia hedged away from this work at a later date, as Shaḥar suggests (p. 359).

To summarize, when the meaning of Abulafia's text appears obscure (which is quite frequently the case in his writings), one must search thoroughly through his other writings to find a text that clarifies the obscurity. In most instances such a search will result in a clear, or at least partially clear, interpretation.[38] Generally, the solution is to be associated with widespread philosophical beliefs of the medieval period, such as the relationship between matter and form, or intellect and imagination.

Parallels between Abulafia's writings and concepts outside the Jewish sphere, interesting though they may be, cannot be adduced before making a thorough analysis of Abulafia's works and achieving clear understanding of them. Nonetheless, it is most reasonable to assume that Abulafia's sources for the topics dealt with in this paper are more likely to be found among the philosophies of his contemporaries rather than among the writings of the Cathars.

Notes to Chapter 2

1. See in particular Scholem, *Les Origines de la Kabbale.*

2. Y. Baer, "Hareka' Hahistori shel haRaya Mehemna" in *Ẓion* 5 (1940) pp. 1-44.

3. S. Shaḥar, "Hakatarism VeReshit HaKabbalah BeLanguedoc" *Tarbiẓ* 40 (1971) pp. 483-508.

4. S. Shaḥar, "Ecrits Cathares et Commentaire d'Abraham Abulafia sur 'Le Livre de la Creation,' Images et Idées Communes" *Cahiers de Fanjeaux* 12 (1977) (Juifs et Judaisme de Languedoc) pp. 345-361. [All parenthetical page citations refer to the last article mentioned here.]

5. In the author's words: "le moteur de ce monde." She however does not bring any parallel for this expression from any Catharic sources.

6. MS. Milano-Ambrosiana 53 fol. 180a.

7. In Hebrew, "guf ra'" = 359 = "Satan" (numerically). This numerological equation recurs in Abulafia's *Sefer Ḥayyei Ha'Olam HaBa'*, and its source is, as Scholem pointed out, from R. Barukh Togarmi, commentary on *Sefer Yeẓirah.*

This Rabbi was Abulafia's teacher (see Scholem *MS.* p. 28.) These are Togarmi's words: "The secret meaning of Satan is "guf ra'" (evil body), the "gush 'afar" the clod of dust. Thus one may say dust (the element of earth) is Satan." (Scholem, *Abraham Abulafia*, p. 233.

8. Job 1:7 "Earth" in this verse is interpreted as "matter" and Satan who "wanders" is seen as the "illusory imagination" associated with matter.

9. MS. Oxford, 1580, fol. 134a.

10. *Tiqvat Enosh—Commentaries on Job*, ed. Y. Schwartz (Berlin, 1868) p. 182. See also R. Ya'akov Anatoli, another author who lived in Italy before Abulafia and Zeraḥiah: "And the name Satan refers but to nature that tends towards matter" (*Sefer Malmad HaTalmidim* [Lyck, 1866] f. 184a). See also Naḥmanides' *Kitvei Haramban*, ed. Chavel (Jerusalem, 1963) vol. I, p. 24: "The sages of Israel associated all of those names (the angel of death, the evil inclination) to him (Satan) for they believed that he is indeed an angel, not a natural phenomenon or one of the powers." Naḥmanides attacks here the ideas of the Maimonideans regarding Satan, and takes for himself a different approach.

11. MS. Paris, BN. 768 fol. 11a.

12. MS. Paris, BN. 774 fol. 166a.

13. "Shekol 'esev zera'" (all grass is seed) = "shekol zera' 'esev" (all seed is grass) = "shikhvat zera'" (semen) = "Bitenu'at Hagalgal" (in the motion of the heavenly sphere) = "Tenu'at habeten" (the motions of the belly) = "hasatan yaniya' hagufot" (Satan will set bodies in motion) = 999. By contrast, "Metatron sar hapanim" (Metatron, Angel of the Countenance) = "sar ẓeva'ot" (Angel of the Hosts) = 999.

14. Published in Hanau 1615 fol. 56b.

15. "He" + "He" + "ḥamishah" i.e., 6 + 6 + *353* = 365, whereas "hasatan" = 364. However, according to the exegetical principles of numerology one digit makes no difference.

16. MS. Paris BN. 768 fol. 10a: "Sheti va'erev" (warp and woof) = "Berit 'Esau" (covenant of Esau) = "Sar hato'evah" (angel of abomination) = "Besha'ar hatohu" (at the gate of chaos) = "Yod-bet 'asarot" (twelve tens) = "sha'ar uvayit" (gate and house) = "kibbuẓ peri hagufot" (collection of the fruit of the bodies) = "rosh pe'ot" (head of the corners) = "sar hayesodot" (Angel of the Elements) = "shebe'arayot" (within illicit sexual relations) = "yesod habasar, panim veaḥor" (the element of the flesh, front and back) = "mar'ot ha'esh" (the images of fire = "shnei mala'khim, yamin usemol" (two angels, right and left) = 988. Expressions like "two angels" or "front and back" refer to polarities existing in human nature deriving from the polarity of matter and form.

17. MS. Oxford 1582 fol. 5b-6a. More on Abulafia's view on the concept of 'Arayot and its Maimonidean background see M. Idel "Sitrei 'Arayot in Maimonides'

Thought" in eds. S. Pines-Y. Yovel *Maimonides and Philosophy* (Dordrecht, Boston, Lancaster 1986) pp. 79-91.

18. Indeed, elsewhere in *Sefer Ḥayyei Ha'Olam HaBa'* we read: "And the secrets of illicit forms of sexuality refer to the seduction of Eve by the serpent. For he is the adulterer and it was he who placed the contamination within her" (MS. Oxford 1582 fol. 6b). However, as we read in what follows we see that Abulafia is not referring to sexual relations but to the relation of imagination and matter (i.e., potential intelligence to form (i.e. activated intelligence).

19. MS. Paris BN. 768 fol. 11a. Shaḥar translates: "Quand tu changeras [sic] serpent avec Adam" (pp. 352, 354). No doubt the true meaning is otherwise: when you add ("tishtatef" attach) "serpent" ('naḥash') to "'Adam Ḥava" [i.e., numerologically—"naḥash" = 358 + "'Adam Ḥava" [= 64] = 422] they equal [the numerical value of] the expressions "ha' Adam Satan 'eḥad" (man is a Satan) as well as 'hasatan 'Adam 'eḥad' [Satan is a man] [= 422]

20. For the "Catharic" interpretation of this passage, see Shaḥar p. 354.

21. *Genesis Rabba* 17, Theodor-Albeck edition (Jerusalem 1965) p. 157.

22. *Pirkei de R. Eliezer* chapter 13, also Maimonides' *Guide of the Perplexed* II, 30.

23. In both the Midrash and Maimonides' *Guide*, the text reads "kesh'iur gamal" (like the measure of a camel). Abulafia engages in a play on words—"gamal" (camel) = "gelem" or "golem" (inanimate matter), both words being composed of the same letters. This, in order to indicate that Satan who rides on the serpent is the power of imagination that rides on (the ass—'hamor' i.e. matter). This is based on the philosophical notion that the illusory imagination is contained in the power of matter (also, 'ḥamor'—ass, contains the same letters as 'ḥomer'—matter). See Maimonides' *Guide* II, 36. Regarding the word-play "gamal"—"gelem" or "golem" see Abulafia *Sefer 'Oẓar 'Eden Ganuz* MS. Oxford 1580 fol. 128b and also M. Idel, "Types of Redemptive Activities in the Middle-Ages" in ed. Z. Baras, *Messianism and Eschatology—A Collection of Essays* (Heb.) (Jerusalem 1983) pp. 255, 260 and the notes there.

24. This refers to Eve who symbolizes matter as well as the potential intellect that was defined in the *Guide* as a faculty inherent in the human body and inseparable from it; see I, 72. By contrast, Adam symbolizes form, or intellect *in actu*, upon which the illusory imagination holds no sway.

25. MS. Oxford 1582 fol. 6b-7a, correlated and corrected by MS. Paris BN. 777 fol. 107a-107b. It is reasonable to assume that Abulafia, unlike other commentators on Maimonides' *Guide*, II, 30, does not clearly distinguish between Satan and the serpent.

26. MS. Paris BN. 768 fol. 11a "Ve-hadam bo hasatan" (within the blood is Satan) = "ve-hasatan bo hadam" (and Satan, within him is the blood) = 422.

27. Maimonides' *Guide*, I, 73, introductory note.

28. MS. New York, JTS 1801 fol. 10a. The text of this unique MS. is faulty. We may assume a relationship between the word 'dam' (blood) and the word 'dimayon' (imagination, illusion) even before Abulafia's posited association between them. Numerologically, 'hadimiyon' (the illusory imagination) = 'galgal hadam' (circulation of the blood) = 115.

29. *Sefer Ḥayyei Ha'Olam HaBa'* MS. Oxford 1582 fol. 4a. There we read: " . . . the imagination which causes the human intellect to err."

30. Maimonides' *Guide* II, 12; Abulafia, *Sitrei Torah*, MS. Paris BN. 744 fol. 171b. In his *Sefer Ḥayyei Ha'Olam HaBa'* regarding Satan, we read: "Do not remove your thought from God for any reason in the world, and even if a dog or a cat or a mouse jumps in front of you, or something else that wasn't with you in the house, they are all acts of Satan. For he roams the mind and gives birth to things that have no existence at all, and he is appointed on all." [Published by Scholem *MSS* p. 29]. The description of Satan as one who roams the mind is in my opinion associated with the blood, and the characterization of Satan as appointed on all things that have no real existence corresponds to the nature of the illusory imagination as depicted in Maimonides' writings. Regarding this, see Z. Harvey, 'HaRamban ve-Spinoza al Yedi'at Tov Vera'' in *Iyyun* 28 (1978) p. 178 note 76. We ought to emphasize that the "acts of Satan" i.e., the appearance of the various animals are nothing but figments of the imagination that occasionally embody frightening forms. In the circle of Abulafia's students the demonic element of the illusory imagination becomes more emphasized. However, this emphasis is a result of Sufi influence. See below ch. 5.

31. MS. Paris BN. 768 fol. 11a. This entire section is based on the numerological equations mentioned in note 19: "Satan babeten" (Satan in the belly) = "masbia'" (satisfies) = "ḥitah shemenah" (fat wheat) = "be'ashan" (in smoke) = "'asavim" (grasses) = "kol 'esev" = "shiv'im" (seventy) = "gargir heh" (the grain of the letter He) = 422. Despite my search in the writings of R. Abraham Abulafia, I have yet to find a reasonable explanation for the term "ḥitah shemenah" (fat wheat); however it is reasonable to assume that it is an allegorical designation for matter.

32. MS. Paris BN. 768 fol. 16a.

33. MS. Rome-Angelica 38 fol. 11b; compare with *'Oẓar 'Eden Ganuz* "The partnership [shittuf] between intellect and imagination is like the partnership between the angel and Satan." [MS. Oxford 1580 fol. 55b].

34. MS. Paris BN. 768 fol. 12a.

35. MS. Paris BN. 768 fol. 11b.

36. Incidentally, *Sefer 'Oẓar 'Eden Ganuz* is not an autobiography of Abulafia, as Shaḥar supposes (pp. 358-359), but a 200 folio work of which only one folio engages in autobiographical details.

37. See Idel, *Abraham Abulafia* pp. 25-26 and note 170.

38. I found no divergence between the concepts found in Abulafia's *Perush*

Sefer Yeẓirah and his other writings. Quite the contrary. His other works aid in understanding this work, as we have seen above. This contrasts with Shaḥar's claim that "portions of *Perush Sefer Yeẓirah* constitute a divergence not only from traditional Jewish doctrines, but also from Abulafia's other works" (p. 359).

Chapter 3

Abraham Abulafia on the Jewish Messiah and Jesus

During the Middle Ages, Jews and Cristians argued the question of the true faith in dialogue, polemics, and public religious debates. The most pressing and acute challenge to Judaism was the question of the identity of the Messiah whom the Christians claimed had already come in the person of Jesus of Nazareth. The most common answer among Jews—although the most dangerous, was absolute rejection of Jesus as the Messiah. This position had various literary expressions of greater and lesser subtlety. A literary parody found in *Sefer Toldot Yeshu*,[1] depicted Jesus as a magician. In face to face debates, however, the Jews did not dare mock Jesus, and limited their rebuttal to a refutation of the Christological interpretation of Scripture. These debates were forced upon the Jews who had no interest in an open confrontation with the dominant religion. R. Abraham Abulafia took a unique position on the question of Jesus and attempted to conduct a dialogue with Christians as well. In elaboration of this, I will first discuss the episode of Abulafia's visit to the Pope.

As early as the age of twenty, Abulafia left Spain, because "the spirit of God awoke me and moved me, and I left there and by sea, and on dry land came straight away to the land of Israel. It was my intention to go to the Sambation river."[2] This occurred in the year 1260. About ten years later, God appeared to him and commanded him to go and speak with the Pope. This revelation took place in the year 1270. His attempt to gain an audience with the Pope occurred on the eve of Rosh Hashana in the year 1280. Abulafia set the date of the End (the time of redemption) for the year 1290, and it seems that for Abulafia, these messianic events occurred every decade.

Now let us consider the circumstances of Abulafia's mission to the Pope. Close reading of a passage in *Sefer Ha 'Edut*[3] indicates that the date of the meeting with the Pope was possibly determined by a revelation that Abulafia had in Barcelona in the year 1270 (the year "El"—of God). The ninth year, following that revelation, would be the year 1280 approximately. In our opinion, the phrase, "as He commanded" at the end of the passage, may be understood to allude not only to the deed, but also to the time of its execution. If this interpretation is correct, it is useful to compare this passage to a section of the *Zohar*,[4] written in the 1280s, which describes the coming of the Messiah, and the death of the ruler in Rome.

> I shall see him, but not now [Num. 24:17]. Some of these things were fulfilled at that time, some later, while some are left for the Messiah. . . . We have learned that God will one day build Jerusalem, and display a certain star flashing with . . .[5] and it will shine and flash for seventy days. It will appear on the sixth day of the week, on the twenty-fifth of the sixth month, and will disappear on the seventh day after seventy days. On the first day it will be seen in the city of Rome, and on that day, three lofty walls of that city shall fall, and a mighty place shall be overthrown, and the ruler of that city shall die . . . . In that time mighty wars will arise in all quarters of the world.

Aaron Jellinek made a computation, and found that Pope Nicholas III died on the twenty-second of August 1280, which was the twenty-fifth of Elul 5040. It follows that the statement of the *Zohar* about the twenty-fifth day of the sixth month (that is, Elul)—the day on which the ruler of Rome would die—conforms to the day of the death of Nicholas III!

Abulafia's report of his mission parallels the above description in the *Zohar*. He attests that he went to the Pope "on the eve of Rosh Hashana" that is, on the twenty-ninth of Elul.[6] Bearing in mind that both sources concern events of messianic importance, one can assume that both sources, the *Zohar* and Abulafia, treat one and the same event: the death of Pope Nicholas III. It is difficult to determine whether the *Zohar* reflects a particular event, Abulafia's mission to the Pope. It is more than reasonable to assume that a Judeo-Spanish tradition about the date of the appearance of the Messiah on Rosh Hashana eve, in the year 1280, was the source of Abulafia's revelation, being known to Rabbi Moses de Leon as well. In his description, however, the author of the *Zohar* attributed the event to a future time.

Now let us return to the story of Abulafia's attempt to gain a papal audience. Abulafia went to Soriano near Rome, despite the extreme personal danger involved in his attempts to win a papal interview. He knew that the Pope had ordered that "they should take him outside the city, and burn him in the fire, and (for that) the wood was placed behind the inner gate of the city." In *Sefer Ha 'Edut*, Abulafia emphasized his willingness to endanger himself. The book was written "as a testimony between himself and God that he was ready to suffer martyrdom for the sake of the love of His commandment."[7] Abulafia interpreted the Pope's death[8] to be "a testimony of divine providence that He saved him from his enemy." In *Sefer Ha 'Ot*[9] Abulafia attributed the Pope's death to the actual power of the Divine Name. "His adversary died, unrepentant, in Rome by the power of the Name of the Living and Eternal God." On the same page Abulafia states, "His Name fashioned my tongue into a spear with which I killed them that deny Him, and I killed his enemies by a righteous judgement." This stands alongside Abulafia's report in *Sefer Ha 'Edut*[10] that "the Pope died suddenly . . . because of a plague." This event undoubtedly encouraged him and moved him to action.[11] In several books, we read of Abulafia's vigorous propaganda for his views. In *Sefer Ha 'Ot*[12] he writes, "And into the hand of Zakhariah, God gave the gift of grace and a portion of mercy. So he went about the lands of the Gentiles where Israel are dispersed and began to speak and concluded as he began, for he proclaimed the Name of God, the Lord of the world, from its beginning to end, and did not waiver to the left or the right.

Only a few of the sages of Israel were willing to listen to him speak the Wisdom of God, and the exalted degrees of its ways . . . and there arose those who denied the supreme wisdom, those who were smitten with the stroke of death, and they spoke grandly against the Lord and His annointed, and against all those who joined him." In *Sefer HaYashar*, Abulafia writes, "And Raziel said that in many places he called out to the people and abjured the holy people to sanctify the Name and to learn it properly."[13] In the introductory poem to *Sefer Ḥayyei Ha'Olam HaBa'* we read, "You shall revive a great multitude with the Name *Yah* and you will skip like a lion in every city and field."[14] When Abulafia realized that the Jews had turned a deaf ear to his word, he tried his luck at influencing the Christians. So he writes in *Sefer Ha 'Ot*, "And God commanded that he speak to the Gentiles of uncircumcised heart and flesh, and he did so. He spoke to them, and they believed in the message of God. However, they did not return to God, because they trusted in their swords and bows, and God hardened their impure, uncircumcised hearts."[15]

Abulafia's attempts to meet with Christians and to expound his religious conceptions did not lead to a softening of his criticism of that religion. An outstanding example of his uncompromising attitude to Christianity, and in certain measure also to Judaism, as understood by his Jewish contemporaries, is to be found in his version of the famous tale of the three rings. Abulafia was one of the first writers in Europe to employ it.[16] His version of this parable has been printed several times,[17] but only partially in each case. This discussion will be well served by quoting the complete version of the tale as it appears in Abulafia:[18]

> It is well known among the nations for some time that our people were the first to receive the Torah from God. No nation denies this, and what is acknowledged publicly by all does not need further proof. If so, that which originates in the Source of all is superior to its counterparts. Its language is superior to all languages. That He spoke to all that He said to this people in their particular language and that He commanded that all be written in their alphabet bear witness to this. Furthermore, what He wrote on the two tablets of stone was written in the holy language [Hebrew] which persists until this day as a living tradition. This remains true whether Scripture is to be understood both literally and esoterically or in only one of these two ways. If one will say, "It is true, but He says that that nation was unworthy of that high degree, and He exchanged them for another nation and changed their laws and commandments, and diminished their scripture." Behold! One who says this must admit of necessity to the exalted degree of that scripture, and to the exalted degree of its language, and alphabet. After he conceded the principal matter, he came to question its value, because he saw that it was lacking the three virtues mentioned before. We also will not contest the matter of that scripture's sensible deficiency, for if we were to deny the sensible, we would have to deny the intelligible. This is because the sensible precedes the intelligible in nature, although the intelligible precedes the sensible in degree[. . . .] However, we also will acknowledge the truth. Today, the [Hebrew] Scripture lacks those three virtues, but this is not because it has been exchanged for another. Rather, the matter resembles that of a man who had a beautiful pearl which he wanted to give as an inheritance to his son. While he was instructing his son in the matter of wealth, so that the son would recognize the virtue of the pearl, and would value it in the same way, the son came to anger his father. What did the father do? He did not want to give the pearl to another man, for if the son would repent and please his father, he would lose his inheritance. Rather, the father cast the pearl into a pit, for he said, "If my son does not repent, I do not want him to lose it. While he does not repent, the pearl will remain hidden in the pit. When he repents, I will immediately take it from there, and give it to him." All the while that the son did not repent, the servants of his father used to come to him and trouble him. Everyone would boast that his lord had given him the pearl, but the son did not pay attention to them, because he had no intelligence. After a while, they so aggrieved him

that he repented, and his father forgave him and brought the pearl out of the pit and gave it to him. The servants had to exert themselves and offer many words of apology. This has happened to us in the matter of those who say that God has taken them in exchange for us, for all the while that we do not make peace with God, as we have sinned. We have no mouth to answer them. However, when we will repent, and He will return our captivity, those who shame us now will be ashamed before us when they see that God has returned our captivity. They will see that their thought and image were figments of the imagination, and that we have been afflicted for our sins, but all have been absolved. As of today, we have not attained that exalted degree to which we expect to rise at any time. For this reason, the disputation continues about who is beloved of God and who has the truth, we or our enemies. This will persist until that Judge will come and take the pearl out of the pit and give it to His chosen, to us or to them.[19] Then the absolute truth will become perfectly clear, and the precious treasure will become radiant and return to its rightful owners, those worthy to inherit it, those who are called "sons of God." Jealousy and strife, disputation and hatred, will cease, and mere imaginations will be removed from the minds of men. Then, each and every man will consider his fellow man to be like himself, just as man can see every one of his limbs, and that every limb is himself, every part of every limb altogether is himself. Then many will go about and knowledge will increase; no longer will anyone instruct his fellow man and say, "Know God," for all shall know the Name from the greatest to the smallest, for the earth will be filled with the knowledge of God as the water that covers the ocean. Since the matter is so, all agree that for all time the chosen language is the holy tongue [Hebrew].

Close study of this passage indicates that Abulafia made unique use of this tale. Certain narrative elements that appear in most of the other versions are not to be found in his rendering. First, in most versions the story speaks of three identical rings, of which one is the original and the others are copies. Their identical appearance makes it impossible to distinguish between them. This, of course, resembles the condition of religion in the Middle Ages, when it was impossible to know which one of the three monotheistic religions was true. The tales of the three rings was composed in an agnostic and tolerant spirit. All three religions appear outwardly to have equal value, and no standard of measurement exists in the present to gauge their veracity. In opposition to this, Abulafia claims that there is only one pearl[20] and that the servants merely pretend to have the pearl in their possession. This variation alters the "liberal" spirit of the original story. Abulafia implies that Christianity and Islam are not even copies of Judaism. They are a vain pretense, having no theological basis at all. Second, in general literary tradition, the story speaks of three sons who are equal in their father's system. Other rings were made so as to prevent arguments. In Abulafia's version, there is only one son, and the servants are his rivals.[21] From the outset, Abulafia denies the possibility of an equal contest between the religions. Third, Abulafia's most interesting innovation in the story that none of the contestants has the pearl in hand, the pearl being hidden away all the time, is that three religions exist. In his view, even Judaism does not possess religious truth in its entirety.[22] However, the Jews are best endowed to attain this truth, because they are "the sons of God"—and not servants. When religious belief is cleansed of illusory opinions, Judaism will be the universal religion. This process will reach its conclusion with the arrival of the Messianic Age, when knowledge of the true God will break down the barriers between the religions.

In another context, Abulafia discusses the role of the Messiah who will effect the negation of the distinction between the religions and a recognition of the true God. In *Sefer Mafteaḥ HaShemot*,[23] he says of the three religions: "In the future . . . all three religions will know the supreme Name as it is said, 'For then I will turn to the people a pure language that they may all call upon the Name of the Lord.' [Ẓefaniah 3:9]. The great wisdom of the redeemer shall be the cause of this knowledge. Of him it was said [Isaiah 52:13] 'Behold my servant shall deal prudently [be intelligent], he shall be exalted and excellent, and shall be very high.'

In the *kabbalah* [tradition], it is said, 'He shall be more exalted than Moses, and more extolled than Abraham; and higher than the ministering angels; greater than any man.' " The statement, quoted here in the name of "kabbalah", can be found in several midrashim.[24] However, it is a more likely assumption that Abulafia drew the general idea from a passage, attributed to Naḥmanides, which has been preserved in several manuscripts. According to that source, the Messiah is superior to Abraham, Moses, and the ministering angels, because "none of them approached the true knowledge of God as closely as the Messiah . . . therefore Isaiah said that he will be of superior intelligence, for he will have great knowledge of the Holy Blessed One and will have an exalted and excellent knowledge of His Name, blessed is He, more than all that was created before him."[25] Naḥmanides refers to another virtue of the Messiah: "Furthermore, he will convert many nations to Judaism." It should be noted that this discussion of the Messiah by Naḥmanides is a theoretical one. Abulafia, however, undoubtedly had his own messianic activity in mind. This is evident in Abulafia's diversion from the typology which Maimonides determined as criteria for recognition of the true Messiah "The Messiah will not be wiser than Moses, but will only be similar to Moses." [*Code:* Laws of Repentance 9:2].[26] Did Abulafia consider himself to be wiser than Moses? In Abulafia's story of the pearl, he claims that the son is not yet in possession of the pearl, but that one day the son will receive it. According to the allegory, Abulafia saw himself making great innovations in religion which would lead to the perfection of all mankind.

Abulafia's position on the question of Jesus versus the Jewish Messiah clearly reveals his attitude toward Christianity. In *Sefer Mafteaḥ HaShemot*[27] he writes, "Similarly, the seal of the sixth day of the week is that of Jesus of Nazareth. However, the seal of the seventh day of the week, which is half of the Tetragrammaton is [that of]. . . the King Messiah." In the book, *Ḥayyei Ha'Olam HaBa'*, written several years before *Sefer Mafteaḥ HaShemot*, this idea appears in a slightly different form:

> However, the Name *Yah* [*Yud Heh*], which is found in many verses of the Hagiographa, and in a few places in the Prophets, and least of all in the Torah, is part of the entire proper Name of God. It is half of this Name, and it is at the beginning of the Name, and it is at its end. Now although half of the Name is as the whole Name, see that this half of the Name signifies the mystery of the King Messiah which is the seventh day, and rules over the body of the Satan whose name is Tammuz, as the verse, "the women weeping for Tammuz" [Ezekiel 8:14]. This was one form of idolatry, worshipped by the women of ancient times. The mystery of the season of the month of Tebet, known to the kabbalists, explains the matter of one half of the Name; the mystery of the season of the month of Tammuz explains the secret of the other half of the Name. The whole Name is indicative of the perfection of the season of the month of Nissan, and half of the whole Name is indicative of the season of the month of Tishrei. This is the secret of Aries and Libra. One is Tebet, and the other is Tammuz.[28]

The two passages contradict one another, for, in both, the Messiah is associated with the seventh day. Abulafia's connection of the two is based upon a *gematriah*—that both words have a numerical value of 453. The second quotation states that the Hewbrew words for the body of Satan and Tammuz, also have a numerical value of 453, the same as that of the word "Messiah". However, the relation between the Messiah and the body of Satan is one of ruler and subject, which, in Abulafia's opinion, expresses the relation between the Jewish Messiah and Jesus. In *Sefer Mafteaḥ HaShemot*, Abulafia describes the seals of the sixth and seventh days of the week, which correspond to Jesus and the Messiah. We learn about the nature of these seals in a composition by one of Abulafia's students, *Sefer Hakdamah*[29]: "Know that the sixth day has the numerical value *Henriẓ*, three hundred forty-five, and is the active force within the half of the Divine Name, *Yah*. However, the seventh day is signified by the half of the Name, *Vav-Heh*, and is the secret of the King Messiah who will come speedily in our days. All his activity will be founded upon the letters *vav-heh* and also upon the letters *yud-heh* which are the mystery of the sixth day. In the Messiah's days, the Name will be whole, and he [the Messiah] will complete all the work of creation, as the verse says, *"Vayekhulu ha-shamayim*—and the heavens were completed . . ." (Genesis 2:1). This quotation clearly states that the seal of the sixth day is the abbreviation *Yud-Heh.* The seal of the seventh day, however, is *Vav-Heh,* an abbreviation of the sentence above, from Genesis.

Now let us return to the passage in *Sefer Ḥayyei Ha'Olam HaBa'.* The reference to two halves of the divine name is to be understood to mean *Yud-Heh* and *Vav-Heh.* Further proof that this was the writer's intention can be found in the mention of the paired months, Nissan and Tishrei, Aries and Libra. In several places in his writings, Abulafia mentions that the "squaring" of the letters *yud-heh* is equivalent to 121 and represents the constellation of Aries.[30] As in the passage from *Sefer Ḥayyei Ha'Olam HaBa',* an analogy is made between the King Messiah and the letters *vav-heh.*[31] Therefore, one may assume that the letters *yud-heh* correspond to the body of Satan or Tammuz, and in consequence to Jesus of Nazareth. It is possible that Abulafia associated the crucifixion with Maimonides' remark in the *Guide of the Perplexed* (III:29), about the "strange death" of Tammuz. The description of the relationship between the Messiah and Jesus as that of a ruler and slave is supported by remarks in *Sefer Mafteaḥ HaShemot.*[32] "The Greek Christians call him Messiah. That is to say lord, (*adonei*) that man, an allusion to the verse, "The man, the lord (*adonei*) of the land, spoke roughly to us" [Genesis 42:30]. This means that he [the Jewish Messiah] shall stand up against him [Jesus]. He will inform everyone that what Jesus said to the Christians, that he is God, and the son of God, is completely false, for he did not receive power from the Unified Name. Rather, all his power depends upon an image, hung upon the Tree of Knowledge of good and evil, while the matter of the Messiah relies upon the Tree of Life. It is the pillar which upholds all. Jesus, however, was hung bodily because he relied upon a material tree, while a spiritual matter, which is divine intellect, gave the Messiah eighteen years of life and of these, two years remain."

The meaning of the section is clear: Abulafia, who had been the Messiah these eighteen years,[33] depends upon the Tree of Life, the divine intellect, or the Active Intellect. Jesus relied upon the Tree of Knowledge of Good and Evil,[34] and invented an imaginary religion[35] which speaks about matters of convention, good and evil. The superiority of Abulafia to Jesus resembles that of the intellect to the imagination or the body. Again, we read in *Sefer Mafteaḥ HaShemot,*[30] "The error of the Christians in our time concerns Jesus, son of Pantera; the hidden matter of Jesus is that he was a bastard, conceived during his mother's menstrual impurity. That blood is the mystery of primordial matter of which all created things are made and whereby they bear a common name." The meaning of this seems to be that Abulafia considered menstrual blood to be matter which can take on all forms;[37] again, Jesus is representative of matter in contrast with the spirituality of the Jewish Messiah. It seems to us that a similar polarity is to be found in another of Abulafia's works,[38] "the messiah, son of Joseph, was born in the physical realm, but the messiah, son of David, was born in the metaphysical realm." It can be assumed that Abulafia identified the Messiah, son of Joseph, who was born naturally with the body, and the Messiah, son of David, with the metaphysical intellect. In his book, *Ḥayyei Ha'Olam HaBa'*[39] Abulafia expresses this by means of *gematriah*—equations of terms whose Hebrew letters have an equivalent numerical value, for example, "David, Messiah, son of Jesse"; by the method of permutation, one realizes the secret teaching, "David son of Jesse is the messiah," and also "The messiah, son of David, is a lad" (*na'ar*). The latter is an allusion to the well-known identification of the Hebrew word *na'ar*—a lad, with the angel Metatron who represents the Active Intellect. It is possible that Abulafia considered the death of the body, parallel to the death of the Messiah, the son of Joseph to be a precondition for the appearance of the Messiah, and the son of David, who represents the intellect. If we go one step further, we can assume that Abulafia also had in mind the death of Jesus, whose father was named Joseph. In as early a source as *Tractate Sukkah*,[40] a parallel is drawn between the death of the Messiah, son of Joseph, and the death of the Evil Inclination. It is possible that Abulafia's statement contains an allusion to this Talmudic source. There is a parallel discussion of good and evil in terms of the dichotomy of body and soul in Abulafia's *Sefer HaMeliẓ*.[41] There, Abulafia's remarks concern Armilus,[42] the legendary adversary of the Messiah: "However, the sages said that the entire nation of King Armilus shall fall before you. So did God assure us that He would save him from his enemy. Armilus is the first king and is thirteen years his senior, for when Armilus begins to fall, he shall always fall.

The sages noted that the name Armilus signifies Satan, and is the name of the Evil Inclination which is the angel of death." The section describes the victory of the Messiah over Armilus. However, Armilus, the son of Satan,[43] becomes Satan himself. The war between Armilus and the Messiah becomes a war between the body and the soul. In the continuation of the above quotation, Abulafia writes, "and it is an allegory concerning the powers which at times are weakened, and the intellect. In any case, one must strengthen the powers of the intellect and remove anyone who in any way prevents the attainment of intellectual apprehension."[44]

In this connection it is proper to mention Abulafia's view that Jesus is "an alien god." In *Sefer Sitrei Torah*, he writes about Jesus, "That man founded a new religion, as evidenced by the remainder of the nation which is called until this very day by the name attributed to him by his and their consent. They are called Christians, annointed ones, because he named himself the annointed one, the Messiah. The Torah, however, called him 'an alien god.' Understand this well, for it is a great secret."[45] The intention here is that the numerical value of the word *Yeshu* (Jesus) has the same numerical value of 316 as the Hebrew words for an "alien god" (*elohei nekhar*). This is an explicit polemic against the Christian belief that Jesus is God. For Abulafia, Jesus is the body, the image of Satan, or an alien god. All told, these names have a clearly negative connotation. This assumption in no way restricted Abulafia's application of *gematriah* which he used in order to prove that Jesus is mentioned in the Bible. Later, Flavius Mithridates[46] and Paulus de Heredia[47] made the same claim, and it seems that they were influenced by Abulafia's works.[48]

Now let us return to Abulafia's statement in *Sefer Mafteaḥ HaShemot* about the King Messiah and Jesus of Nazareth. We have tried to prove that Abulafia's intention was to hint that, in degree, the Messiah is equivalent to the intellect, while Jesus is equated with matter. Ironically, this particular anti-Christian claim found its way into a Christian work of Kabbalah. The Christian author seems to have drawn upon the statement of *Sefer Hakdamah*, quoted above. The *Hakdamah* author seems to have been reluctant to reveal the superiority of the Jewish Messiah; before this passage, he writes, "Know that what I am to reveal to you is one of the most hidden things. God forbid if the nation of Edom were to know of it! This would constitute a great danger."[49] Ironically, what the author of *Sefer Hakdamah* wanted to conceal found its way to Johannes Reuchlin, one of the scholars of Edom. In his book, *De Arte Cabbalistica*, he writes, "*Scribitur in libro cabale Hacadma*(!), the secret of the King Messiah that he shall come speedily in our days and that by the letters *vav-heh*, and also by the letters *yud-heh* which are the mystery of the seventh day, all his activity will commence, and that His Name is whole, and that all the work will be completed by His hand."[50] Undoubtedly, *Sefer Hakdamah* was Reuchlin's source in spite of the slight corruption in the spelling of the title. It is surprising that Reuchlin ignored the anti-Christian meaning of the statement. Was he aware of this tendency, omitting it from his quotation, or was it missing in the source from which he drew? This quotation from *Sefer Hakdamah* is to be found in Ms., New York, JTS, 1887 (formerly Halberstamm 444). However, the words, "equals *Henriẓ*" and "the king of Edom" are missing.[51] G. Scholem has already ventured that Reuchlin had this manuscript before him.[52] The continuation of Reuchlin's discussion is worthly of attention, as he speaks of the transition from the sixth day to the Sabbath, which alludes to the passage from the active to the contemplative life.[53]

Notes to Chapter 3

1. This evaluation of Jesus is the subject of a recent study by Morton Smith, *Jesus the Magician* (London: 1978). Smith collected material from non-Jewish sources describing Jesus as a magician.

2. MS. Oxford, 1580 fol. 165a.

3. MS. Rome-Angelica, 38, fol. 10a; MS. Munich 285, fol. 36a. Abulafia's mission to the Pope had a messianic goal, and was perhaps motivated by a conception found in Naḥmanides' debate with Pablo Christiani. A. H. Silver has already taken note of this. See A. H. Silver, *A History of Messianic Speculation in Israel* (New York: 1927), p. 146. See also Scholem, *Major Trends*, p. 127f.

4. Zohar III, fol. 212b; in English translation: *The Zohar*, trans. M. Simon and H. Sperling, V, p. 322. See A. Jellinek, *Beyt HaMidrasch*, III, p. XXXVIIf.; A. Posnanski, *Schiloh* (Leipzig: 1904), p. 166, n.1; A. Geiger, *Nachgelassene Schriften*, III, p. 26n.

5. On the 'star of the Messiah', see *P.T. Ta'anit*, 4, halakha 6, and *Midreshei Geulah*, ed. Yehuda Even Shmuel (Jerusalem: 1954), p. 102.

6. See *Perek Eliyahu* in *Midreshei Geulah*, p. 52: "On the twenty-eighth of Elul, the Messiah whose name is Ynon shall emerge from the eternal mountains and will make war with the Ishmaelites." See *Midreshei Geulah*, p. 114.

7. MS. Rome-Angelica, 38, fol. 10a. In Naḥmanides' account of his disputation with Pablo Christiani, he writes that the Messiah "will come and will issue commands to the Pope, and to all the kings of all the peoples . . . and will work signs and wonders, and will have no fear of them at all. [J. D. Eisenstein, *Ozar Wikuḥim* (New York: 1928), p. 90]. See note 3 above, concerning the possible interconnection of Abulafia's mission to the Pope and this statement by Naḥmanides.

8. Abulafia never succeeded in meeting with the Pope. Therefore Israel Friedlander's claim that "Abraham Abulafia . . . in order to escape death, renounced his belief in the presence of the Pope," is completely unfounded! See Israel Friedlander, "Jewish Arabic Studies," *Jewish Quarterly Review* (n.s.) III (1912-13), pp. 287n., 428. Friedlander probably based his view upon that of Graetz who writes: "Possibly he told the Pope that he too taught the doctrine of the Trinity." Heinrich Graetz, *History of the Jews*, IV (Philadelphia: 1949), p. 7. Since Abulafia never met the Pope, it was impossible for him to tell the Pope about the existence of a doctrine of the Trinity. Rather, Abulafia thought that "The masters of the Kabbalah of *Sefirot* thought to unify the Name of God, and to avoid any belief in the Trinity. Therefore, they declared Him to be ten, for the Gentiles claim that He is three and

that three are one. I found that a few of the masters of Kabbalah believe this and say that the divinity is ten *Sefirot*, and that ten are one. Behold! They have rendered Him as multiple as possible, and have compounded Him as much as possible, for there is no multiple greater than that of ten." Abraham Abulafia, "Epistle," in A. Jellinek, *Auswahl Kabbalistischer Mystik* (Leipzig: 1853), p. 19. It seems to me that Graetz's error was caused by his reliance upon M. Landauer's attribution of a poem which begins, "'Ayaḥed El" ("I shall unify God according to the religion given by Him."), to Abulafia: See *Literatursblatt des Orients* 28 (1845), p. 473. In this poem the following line appears, "Why did he make ten sayings into three? Does the principle bough have a branch? . . . did he mention only three of His praises —and left unmentioned His scores of praises?" Had this poem been written by Abulafia there would be some truth to Graetz's proposal. However, the author of this poem is R. Asher ben David, a Provençal kabbalist who lived during the first half of the thirteenth century, and with whom Abulafia had no connection whatsoever.

9. Published by A. Jellinek in "*Sefer HaOt;* Apokalypse des Pseudo-Propheten, und Pseudo-Messias Abraham Abulafia," *Jubelschrift zum siebzigsten Geburtstag des Prof. H. Graetz* (Breslau: 1887), p. 67.

10. MS. Rome-Angelica, 38, fol. 10a.

11. In this context it is also worth mentioning another parallel between an episode in Abulafia's career with traditions about the Messiah—that is, Abulafia's detention in Rome after the death of the Pope. In *Sefer Ha'Edut*, MS. Rome-Angelica 38, fol. 10a, Abulafia states: "In Rome, the Minorities seized him, and he was held in their cloister for twenty-eight days." In *Sefer Zerubavel* (*Midreshei Geulah*, p. 73) we find the following: "He said to me: I am God's anointed one, and I have been imprisoned here at Rome until the time of the End."

12. Ibid., p. 78; "Zakhariah" is one of several appelations by which Abulafia called himself. "Raziel" is another.

13. MS. Rome-Angelica, 38, fol. 41a.

14. MS. Oxford, 1582 fol. 3a.

15. p. 76.

16. This parable is well documented in Islamic sources. See L. Massignon, "La Legende de *Tribus Impostoribus et ses Origines Islamiques*," *Opera Omnia*, I, pp. 82-85. This parable was well know in Italy during Abulafia's time. See Cecil Roth, "HaReka' Ha Histori Shel Maḥbarot Immanuel," *Assaf Festschrift* (Jerusalem: 1953), p. 455.

17. See M. Steinschneider, *Hebräische Bibliographie* IV (1861), p. 78, n. 7; *idem*, XII, p. 21; *Mose*, VIII (1885), pp. 359-361 (Italian translation). The Steinschneider version was copied by I. Zinberg, *A History of Jewish Literature* (New York: 1974), Vol. IV, p. 70n.

18. *Sefer 'Or HaSekhel*, MS. Vatican, 233, fol. 37b-39b.

19. See Steinschneider, *Hebräische Bibliographie*, IV, p. 78. The text reads: and they will give us." Undoubtedly, this version is a less than accurate rendering of Abulafia's words. See A. Berger, "The Messianic Self Consciousness of Abraham Abulafia—A Tentative Evaluation," *Essays on Jewish Life and Thought Presented in Honor of Salo Wittemayer Baron* (New York: 1959), p. 59f., n. 19.

20. Professor S. Pines has informed me that a similar parable, in which a "pearl" figures instead of a "ring" is to be found in a debate between a Nestorian patriarch and a Moslem at the end of the eighth century. See Timothy's *Apology for Christianity*, ed. A. Mignana (Cambridge: 1928). Woodbrooke Studies No. 2, p. 88f.; also S. Pines, "The Jewish-Christians According to a New Source," *Proceedings of the Israel Academy of Sciences and Humanities*, Vol. II (1956), p. 37f., n. 139.

21. The Gentile languages are also described as the "handmaidens" of the Hebrew language. In *Sefer Ha'Ot*, p. 71, ". . . two languages, Greek and Latin came into existence in order to serve the Jewish tongue. The power of both is interconnected above and below, for their power was hung and bound upon the cross, fastened with nails." This clearly indicates that Christianity also figures among the servants in the parable. See Abulafia's interpretation of the term *anti-christos* below.

22. One of Abulafia's disciples, the author of the book, *Ner Elohim*, differed with his master. In this parable of the pearl, Abulafia expressed his belief that in the Messianic Era, the ideal religion would make its appearance. "Pay no attention to the belief of every people that they alone serve God, and that all others are idolators, for all the sages of the other nations admit that God spoke to the prophets of that nation which is uniquely His and instructed that people, concerning the true way of divine worship. One who states otherwise is most certainly mistaken. However, this mistake shall not be corrected until the coming of Elijah who prophesied during the time of the prophets, and is still alive. He will reveal himself, and by prophecy, he will demonstrate who is in error, and who is not. Therefore, his name is Elijah (*Eliyahu*) the prophet (*ha-Navi*) for the letters of his name tell of the truth of his prophecy. For the two names contained within his name may be further divided into three: the first of two letters, and the one after that of four letters" (MS. Munich 10, fol. 156b-157a). The name Eliyahu ha-Navi (Elijah the Prophet) is subdivided into three names as follows: *El, YHWH, ha-Navi.* This mnemonic was already suggested by Abraham Ibn Ezra. See Y. L . Fleischer, "Rabbenu Abraham Ibn 'Ezra B'Ẓarfat," *Mizraḥ U-Ma'arav* IV, (1938), p. 358; also n. 33. See also Werblowsky, *Karo*, p. 270.

23. MS. New York, JTS 843, fol. 68b. A. Berger published a portion of this quotation in his "The Messianic Self Consciousness," but mistakenly attributed it to *Sefer Mafteaḥ HaḤokhmah.*

24. See *Midrash Tanḥumah* (Buber edition). I, p. 139, and the sources cited by Solomon Buber in n. 138.

25. See Neubauer-Driver, *The Fifty-Third Chapter of Isaiah According to*

the Jewish Interpreters (New York: 1969), Vol. I, pp. 76, 82.

26. Maimonides, however, describes the Messiah in terms approximating those of the Midrash. "When the true King Messiah will arise and will prevail, and will be excellent, and exalted . . ." (*Code*, Laws of Kings, XI:4). This passage has been deleted from most editions of the *Code.* Maimonides refrained from offering as detailed a description of the Messiah as found in the Midrashim, mentioned above in note 24; for example, whom the Messiah would excel, and above whom he would be exalted. This reticence was prompted possibly by Maimonides' desire not to rank the Messiah above Moses.

27. MS. New York, JTS, 843, fol. 80a. The passage is difficult to read in the manuscript.

28. MS. Oxford 1582, fol. 71b. This passage bears the marked influence of Maimonides' remarks about Tammuz in the *Guide of the Perplexed* III:29. See also the *Commentary on Ezekiel* of R. David Kimḥi (Ez. 8:14).

29. MS. Paris, BN 776, fol. 184b. When the letters of the name Henriẓ are rearranged, it becomes the word *Noẓri* (Nazarene, of Nazareth). Therefore, this is an allusion to Jesus. Undoubtedly, Abulafia and his disciples relied upon an earlier source which stated that the sixth day is signified by the letters *yud-heh*, and that the seventh day when "the heavens were finished" (Gen. 2:1) is signified by the letters *vav-heh* (*V*a yehulu *H*ashamayin). In *Sefer Meirat Eynayim* (MS. Munich 17 fol. 42b), R. Isaac of Acre writes, "This world was created by the letters *yud-heh*, that is the sixth day, *Y*om *H*ashishi, *yud-heh*, and the world to come was created by the letters *vav-heh*, *V*ayehulu *H*ashamayim (and the heavens were completed) whose initials are *vav-hah*." This statement does not appear in a messianic context. The homiletic also appears in *Sefer Get HaShemot*, Abulafia's first work (MS. Oxford 1658, fol. 90b): "That [the Tetragrammaton] is also divided into two names . . . after the likeness of the Merkavah which has two aspects, the sensible and the intelligible, as we have stated. These are indicative of two worlds which are this world and the world to come." Notably, the more common tradition speaks of the superiority of the Name, *yud-heh* to the Name, *vav-heh*. In *Sefer Oẓar Ḥayyim* (MS. Moscow-Günzburg, 775 fol. 226b), R. Isaac of Acre expressed the opinion that, "The Name YHWH contains both body and soul, both a simple and superior spirituality and a lower, compound spirituality. The first half of the Name, *yud-heh*, is certainly the secret of the superior simple substance which imparts efflux and the latter half, *vav-heh*, is undoubtedly the secret of the lower, compound, receptive substance. For this reason, the sweet singer of Israel, the anointed one of the God of Jacob, did not say, "Halleluhu Halleluhu" (Praise Him! Praise Him! lit. Praise *heh-vav*) but always said, 'Halleluyah' (Praise *yud-heh*). R. Isaac of Acre relied upon a tradition that he found in R. Abraham Ibn 'Ezra's work, *Sefer HaShem*, chapter VIII (Fiorda: 1834), fol. 19a, "How weighty are the words of our ancient sages of blessed memory who said that the upper world was created by half of the Divine Name." However, in chapter IV of *Sefer HaEmunah VeHaBitaḥon* of R. Jacob Ben Sheshet (printed in the collected writings of Naḥmanides, ed. Chavel, Vol. II, p. 363) we read, "I found an allusion to this and support for this in the verse,

'Let the heavens be glad and let the earth rejoice' (Ps. 96:11) in which the first letters of the words of the verse form the Name, YHWH. The verse attributed the Name, *yud-heh*, to the heavens and the Name, *vav-heh*, to the earth, and these correspond to the two worlds. Thereafter, I found that R. Abraham Ibn Ezra had mentioned the matter another time, in his liturgical poem for the *seliḥot* of the Day of Atonement. He wrote, ". . . the upper world with *Yud-Heh*, and the lower world with *Vav-Heh*."

30. See his epistle, *Sheva' Netivot HaTorah*, printed in A. Jellinek, *Philosophie und Kabbalah*, Vol. I (Leipzig: 1853), pp. 10, 18. It seems to me that the paired months Nissan and Tishrei have a significance beyond that derived from this numerical calculation (*gematriah*). Jesus was killed in the month of Nissan, while Abulafia went to speak with the Pope on the eve of Rosh Hashanah close to the month of Tishrei. However, this parallel presents a difficulty. Nissan—the month in which Jesus was killed has a numerical value in Hebrew of 121. This corresponds to the Name *vav-heh*, whose letters are the initials of the seventh day which symbolizes the messiah! It is also possible, of course, to connect the Name, *yud-heh*, to the sixth day of the crucifixion. According to most sources, this occurred on "Passover eve." In *B.T. Sanhedrin*, fol. 43a (cf. with *Dikdukei Sofrim*, IX, p. 126). There we read that "Jesus of Nazareth was a familiar of the king, and they hung him on Passover eve." If the word "eve" is understood literally, this means on the fifteenth of Nissan, which is equivalent to the letters *yud-heh*. 31. This analogy is also worthy of mention. The sixth day, the day of the crucifixion, is called "the accursed one" by Christians. In Hebrew, the words *Yeshu Hanoẓri* (Jesus of Nazareth) have the numerical value of 671, the same as the value of the words, *yom hashishi* (the sixth day). See N. T. Luke, XXIII: 54 and N. T. Mark, XV:42.

32. MS. New York, JTS 843, fol. 81b. This text is quoted in part by A. Berger in "The Messianic Self Consciousness," p. 57, n. 11. There is a play on words here. The word *adonei* (Lord) is read as *"anti"*. Abulafia means to say "anti-Christ."

33. *Sefer Mafteaḥ HaShemot* was written in the year 1289, exactly eighteen years after the revelation in Barcelona.

34. In the Middle Ages, it was commonplace that the wood of the cross came from the Tree of Knowledge of Good and Evil. See R. Nelli, "La Legende Medievale du Bois de la Croix," *Folklore* 20:4 (1957), pp. 3-12.

35. The Hebrew word *demut* (likeness) means the imagination, and is contrasted with the Hebrew word *ẓelem* (image) which denotes the intellect.

36. MS. New York, JTS 843, fol. 81a. In Hebrew, the words *Yeshu ben Pandera* have a numerical value of 713 which is the same as that of the words, *"Yesh mamzer ben hanidah"* (there is a bastard, conceived in menstrual impurity). On the meaning of the name Pandera, see J. Klausner, *Jesus de Nazareth* (Paris: 1933), pp. 20f., 23, and M. Smith, *Jesus the Magician*, p. 46f.

37. See *Igeret Sheva' Netivot HaTorah*, published by A. Jellinek, in *Philosophie und Kabbala, Vol. I* (Leipzig: 1853), p. 17. In *Sefer Gan Na'ul*, Abulafia

makes another connection between Jesus and matter: "And God appointed him over the land of Egypt (*Ereẓ Miẓraim*), and darkness fell upon Jesus of Nazareth." (MS. Munich 58, fol. 329b). Again, the words *Yeshu HaNoẓri* have numerical value equivalent to 671 which is the value of the letters of the words *Ereẓ Miẓraim*, the land of Egypt. On the land of Egypt as a metaphor for matter, see Idel, *Abraham Abulafia*, pp. 190-192.

38. *Sefer Oẓar Eden Ganuz*, MS. Oxford, 1580, fol. 102a. Cf. this is to the remarks of Rabbi Levi ben Abraham, a contemporary of Abulafia. In *Sefer Livyat Ḥen* (MS. Vatican 192, fol. 28a), R. Levi compared the messiah, son of Joseph, to the practical intellect and the messiah, son of David, to the speculative intellect. The opinion of R. Levi concurs with that of Abulafia, that the Messiah represents human intellect, developed to its greatest extent. See Vatican MS. 192, fol. 57b. On this particular conception of Abulafia, see Idel, (ibid.), p. 396ff. For the interpretation of the Messiah as "acquired intellect," see D. R. Blumenthal, "Was There an Eastern Tradition of Maimonidean Scholarship," *Revue des Études Juives*, 138 (1979), p. 64.

39. MS. Oxford 1582, fol. 67b.

40. *B. T. Sukkah*, fol. 52a. In the Middle Ages, the death of Jesus was identified with the death of the messiah, son of Joseph, mentioned in *Tractate Sukkah*. See H. Wirszubski, *Flavius Mithridates; Sermo de Passione Domini* (Jerusalem: 1963), p. 121, n. 4. Notably, Isaac Abrabanel considered the tradition about the death of the messiah, son of Joseph, to have been the source which influenced the formulation of the historical image of Jesus. See *Mashmia' Yeshu'ot* (1644), fol. 13c; *Ma'ayanei HaYeshu'ah* (1607), pp. 45, 74. The Sabbatean, Abraham Cardozo, compared Jesus to the messiah, son of Ephraim. He writes: "The first messiah, rooted in the shells [in evil] is Jesus of Nazareth who corresponds to the messiah son of Ephraim. Insofar as his [Jesus'] origin is with Samael, who so emanated upon him that he became a god, according to those who believe in him . . ." This text was published by G. Scholem in *Studies and Texts Concerning the History of Sabbatianism and Its Metamorphosis* (Jerusalem: 1974), p. 289 (in Hebrew).

41. MS. Rome-Angelica 38, fol. 6a-6b. MS. Munich 285, fol. 11a.

42. See Y. Dan, *HaSippur HaIvri BeYmei HaBaynayim* (The Hebrew Story in the Middle Ages) (Jerusalem: 1974), pp. 40-43, and notes.

43. Ibid., p. 40f.

44. MS. Rome-Angelica 38, fol. 6b; MS. Munich 285, fol. 11a. See also MS. Rome-Angelica 38, fol. 7b.

45. MS. Munich 341, fol. 160b. This passage has been deleted from several manuscripts; See MS. New York, JTS 2367, MS. British Library 757. In other mss. such as Paris 774, the words, "messiah" and "messiahs", i.e., "Christians" are missing.

46. See Wirszubski's remarks in *Flavius Mithridates, Sermo*, p. 40, n. 3.

47. F. Secret, "L'Ensis Pauli de Paulus de Heredia," *Sefarad* 26 (1966), p. 101.

Heredia mentioned Abulafia several times in this composition. See Secret's article, p. 98.

48. A *gematriah*, similar to the one mentioned here appeared in a work written before that of Abulafia. See M. Idel; "Two Notes on R. Yair b. Shabetay's Ḥerev Piphiot," *Kiryat Sefer* 53 (1978), p. 214, n. 14 (in Hebrew). See also Isaac Abrabanel in his *Maayanei HaYeshu'ah*, part XI, chapter 8.

49. MS. Paris, BN 776, fol. 184b.

50. In the 1517 edition, p. XVIII, and also in the Basle edition of 1587, p. 637. In the version which appears in Giovanni Pico della Mirandola's *Opera Omnia* (Basle 1557) Vol. I, p. 769, the word "three" appears instead of the word "perfect". See also F. Secret, *La Kabbale* (Aubier: 1973), p. 89f., where he translated Reuchlin's work. In addition to this attribution in Latin, Reuchlin quoted the text in its entirety in Hebrew. Reuchlin's quotation is comparable to the version found in *Sefer Hakdama.*

51. Fol. 12a.

52. G. Scholem, *On the Kabbalah and its Symbolism* (New York, 1969), p. 180. In Reuchlin, the end of the passage differs from that found in MS. New York. One must ask whether Reuchlin had another manuscript before him. Such a manuscript would be similar to MS. New York, but would have a wording closer to that of Reuchlin. The matter deserves investigation.

53. See Abraham bar Ḥiyya, *Megillat HaMegalleh*, ed. Poznanski (Berlin: 1924), pp. 57-58. On the one hand, Bar Ḥiyya speaks of the passage from the six days of creation to the Sabbath as the passage from this world to that of the Messianic Era, and on the other, as a passage from the creation of material bodies to the creation of the soul.

Chapter 4

The Influence of *Sefer 'Or HaSekhel* on R. Moses Narboni and R. Abraham Shalom

R. Moses Narboni was among the first of the Jewish philosophers who were influenced by Kabbalistic ideas. In his writings there are some allusions to the opinions of the Kabbalists,[1] and in some rare instances he enters into more extended discussions of those ideas, overtly indicating that they involve Kabbalistic issues.[2] It is worth noting the particular use that Narboni makes of *Sefer 'Or HaSekhel*, written by R. Abraham Abulafia.[3]

We find two citations of this book in the works of Narboni, where he quotes directly, almost verbatim, without mentioning a source. Furthermore, he relates these Abulafian ideas as his own opinions. These two citations appear in Narboni's commentary to *Kavvanot HaPhilosophim* (The Intentions of the Philosophers) by Abuḥamid Al-Ghazzali.[4]

Sefer 'Or HaSekhel
MS. Vatican 233 fols. 125a-b

A) And the level of attainment of the prophets who speak and who compose works is greater than the level of the prophets who

Commentary to *Intentions of the Philosophers*
MS. Paris BN 956 fol. 209a.[5]

A) Regarding the levels of attainment of the prophets, those who speak and compose works of prophecy are greater than those who keep their prophecy to themselves. And those who are sent on a prophetic mission are even greater. And those who change any aspect of the course of nature in order to verify that they were sent by God are of a higher order than all of the above.

keep their prophecy to themselves. And those who are sent on a prophetic mission are greater than the composers of works. And those who change the course of any aspect of nature to verify that they were sent by God are of a higher order than all of the above.

Ibid., fols. 113b-114a

B1) And when one's intellectual attainment includes all of the areas of intellectual pursuit under his domain, it is to be expected that he would receive abundant effluence from this attainment. Through this he will also be able to give partial form for a short duration to aspects of the material world, in the form of natural functions, within the domain of existence that arises and passes away. And because nature in and of itself continues to subsist, this person's effect on an aspect of the natural plane will last longer than the amount of time of that mental function of the prophet, which is not continuous with him. Therefore it is fitting to associate the function that changes nature in accordance with the mental function of the prophet, the One who is the first cause of this change, i.e., to God.

B2) And because the prophet would attain realization of God only through knowledge of the Name just as the consummate philosopher will attain knowledge of the Divine only through knowledge of His effects, therefore, we and those who came before us are in agreement in attributing the human enactment that differs from the usual function, to the Divine Power, and we say that it is with the Power of the Name that the prophet did what he did.

Ibid., fol. 208a

B1) And I say that because a human being is separate from the Active Intellect due to its being a partial intellect his being composed of a complex nature, and because his union with the Active Intellect is not permanent, therefore the operation of the prophet is different from the operation of an angel in that it is only partially effective due to aspects of the complex makeup of human nature that remains within the prophet and does not cleave to the Active Intellect. And the enactments of the human being will not continue to subsist like the manifestations of the partial forms enacted by the Active Intellect, which does not abide continuously with the prophet. Indeed it is the comprehension that is the reason for wonders, as indicated in the prophetic stories to where it is written: "And he fell upon his face" [Numbers 16:4], "and the Glory of God appeared to the entire nation" [Leviticus 9:23] . . . I do not know to where the Glory of God went when it departed from our Master Moses, when he ceased to contemplate the wonders and removed himself somewhat.

B2) And know that because the prophet will attain God through the ineffable Name, in accordance with the view of the Torahists, just as the philosopher attains knowledge of the Divine through observing His manifestations, therefore the Torahists attributed the particular manifestations in nature that differs from the usual mode, to the power of the Name of God, and they said that it is with the power of the Ineffable Name that the prophet enacted what he did. And we attribute this to the veritable union with the Divine.

As it is manifest prima facie, the first quotation is cited by Narboni almost verbatim. With regard to the second citation, the situation is different. The first section of the second quote from *Sefer 'Or HaSekhel* underwent partial changes in the hand of Narboni[6]. Yet, even in this section we find preserved some elements of the turn of phrase of Abulafia, such as "partial forms" (*ẓurot ḥelkiyot*), in place of "partial form" (*ẓurah ḥelkit*) of Abulafia,[7] or "the Active Intellect" which does not abide continuously with "the prophet" ("[*hasekhel hapo'el*] *miẓad shelo ya'amod sekhel hanavi' tamid 'immo*") in place of "the mental function of the prophet which is not continuous with him" ("*po'al sekhel hanavi' shehu lo ya'amod 'immo tamid*") in Abulafia.

The second section of the passage conveyed by Narboni with fewer changes from Abulafia's original version. A question therefore arises regarding the opening words of the second quotation by Narboni: "And I say that . . . " Is this simply a case of plagiarism, or is this designation justified, given the novel form the author uses to convey Abulafia's words (in other words, the designation "and I say" is not intended to refer to the second part of the second quotation)?

It seems to me that one answer to this question may be found in Narboni's commentary to Maimonides' *Guide of the Perplexed*, which was written after Narboni's book on *The Intentions of the Philosophers*. There, he says:

> And I say, that in the instance when the mind of the prophet is concentrated on partial forms, his (miraculous) enactment would take effect only on that part; as was the case with the splitting of the sea of reeds, where not all of the waters of the world were parted. In those instances of unstable cleaving, the intended wonder would likewise not stand nor would the sign (manifest be drawn). And when the Ineffable Name was to the prophets like unto a concise tablet corresponding to the First Form, the effects therefrom were attributed to what is called the "First Cause" among the philosophers, and it would be said that it was with the power of the Ineffable Name that the prophet enacted that which tore the pattern away from the natural cause.[8]

This quotation is essentially a summary of Abulafia's ideas, which Narboni used in his commentary to *Kavvanot HaPhilosophim*. Here too, Narboni presents ideas as his own when he uses the rubric of "and I say . . . " to convey those same ideas that appear in section 2 of quotation B. I would therefore conclude that this is an instance of plagiarism on the part of the author.

We may find other examples of this kind of "borrowing" from Abulafia on the part of Narboni. I refer, again, to Abulafia's *'Or HaSekhel* from the same page cited for quotation A. Here we are dealing not with tract borrowing, but with a reconstruction by Narboni based on the original.

'Or HaSekhel
MS. Vatican 233 fol. 125a

And when the previously indicated imaginary mental grasp ceases to exist, and her memory is erased from the hearts of those who feel and mentate then "He will swallow up death forever, and the Lord God will wipe away tears from all faces; and the reproach of His people will He take away from off all the earth; for the Lord has spoken it" [Isaiah 25:8]. In other words, the secret of the Intellect will be revealed after having been hidden.

Commentary to Kavvanot HaPhilosophim,
MS., Paris BN 956 fol. 201b.

And when the redemption, which is the true salvation, arrives, the prophecy designates that: "He will swallow up death forever, and the Lord God will wipe away tears from all faces; and the reproach of His people will He take away from off all the earth; for the Lord has spoken it" [Isaiah 25:8]. This is an allusion to the grasp of the Mind.[9]

Conspicuously, these two authors interpret the prophecy of Isaiah in a similar way; Narboni conceives the emergence of human intellect as the essence of salvation, while this conception is also critical to Abulafia's view of salvation. In another work Abulafia writes, "And the Messiah will be called the materialized human hylic intellect, and he is the redeemer."[10]

Similar borrowing of Abulafia's writing, appears in a work entitled *Neveh Shalom* by R. Abraham Shalom, a fifteenth-century Spanish thinker.

As other scholars have already noted, Abulafia and his work have been recognized by Abraham Shalom.[11] In addition, however, we can demonstrate that Abraham Shalom, like Narboni before him, made use of Abulafia's work without acknowledging the source.[12] A conspicuous example of this involves a passage already analyzed in the first essay of this volume.

'Or HaSekhel
MS. Vatican 233 fol. 115a.

The name [of God] is composed of two parts since there are two parts of love[13] [divided between] two lovers, and [parts of] love turn one [entity] when love became actuated. The divine intellectual love and the human intellectual love are conjuncted

Neveh Shalom
(Venice, 1575) fol. 87a-b.

And this is the power of Man, who can bind the lower aspect with the supernal in such a way that the lower aspect rises up and cleaves to the supernal, and the supernal descends and kisses that which rises, and this is the meaning of the verse "(the angels being one. Exactly so the name [of God] includes [the words] one one,because the connection of the human existence with the divine existence during the intellection—which is identical with the intellect in [its] existence—until he and he become one [entity].[14] This is the great power of man: he can link the lower part with the higher [one] and the lower [part] will ascend and cleave to the higher and the higher [part] will descend and will kiss the entity ascending towards it, like a bridegroom actually kisses his bride[15] out of his great and real desire, characteristic to the delight of both, from the power of the name [of God].

of God) ascending and descending on it" [Genesis 28:12]. For the intellects rise from the lower depths by way of the ladder of wisdom and the praiseworthy intellects descend towards them due to the true adoration, for the sake of their mutual pleasure, in the power of the Name. And in a similar mode, does the Divine Intellectual love, as he raises himself (!) from the base existence to the supernals. And the ascent to the supernal intellect consists of contemplating one's cause, and the descent to the human intellect is in a mode that is graspable to the baser existence and the function of the body.

Aside from the change in the order of sentences from the way it appears in *'Or HaSekhel*, Abraham Shalom modifies one of Abulafia's ideas in that the unity experienced by the bride and groom is absent from R. Abraham Shalom's words. In its place is the image of the ladder of wisdom. This indicates an intellectual flavor opposed to the ecstatic imagery exemplified by Abulafia.[16]

However, one motif important to Abulafia, that of the love between the Divinity and the human being, expressed as the love between the separate intellect and the human intellect, is identical in both Shalom's work and Abulafia's. The idea of the "Divine Intellectual Love" that turns towards man, and the "Human Intellectual Love" that turns towards God, is noteworthy. We have here an approach that differs from that of Crescas. The latter also speaks of the love of the Divine for the human, but he does not characterize it as "intellectual."[17]

A conception similar to that of Abulafia may also be found in Leone Ebreo's *Dialoghi d'Amore*, and we come across it in a modified form in the works of Spinoza.[18]

Notes to Chapter 4

1. Alexander Altmann: "Moses Narboni's Epistle on Shi'ur Koma" in Alexander Altmann, ed. *Jewish Medieval and Renaissance Studies* (Cambridge, Mass. 1967) pp. 242-253.

2. See Narboni's commentary to Maimonides' *Guide of the Perplexed*, Ya'akov Goldental, ed. (Vienna 1852) fol. 49a; also *Kavvanot HaPhilosophim* (Commentary to Al-Ghazzali's *Intentions of the Philosophers*) MS. Paris BN. fol. 178a and others. As Altmann pointed out in the article cited above, p. 243,

Narboni's sympathetic approach to Kabbalah changed later in his life, and in Narboni's commentary to Maimonides' *Guide*, he adopted a critical attitude.

3. For further bibliographical information, see Idel, *Abraham Abulafia* pp. 24-25.

4. For more information regarding this commentary, see Moritz Steinschneider: *Die Hebräischen Uebersetzungen des Mittelalters*, reprint ed. (Graz 1956) pp. 311-319.

5. This manuscript is a collection of philosophical writings brought together by the copyist, under the title *Sasson Limmudim* (The Joy of Learning). It was written during the last third of the fourteenth century. For more regarding this manuscript, see Georges Vajda *Sefer Tikkun HaDe'ot Le Yitzhak Albalag* (Jerusalem, 1973) pp. 10-11. The words of Abulafia also appear unaltered in various other manuscript editions of Narboni's *Commentary to the Intentions of the Philosophers*, among them, MS. Rome-Casanatense 156 fol. 130a; MS. Parma 2301, fols. 391a-b; MS. Paris BN. 908 fol. 162a, and others. Contrastingly, we find this text in different form, in many important details, in MS. Paris BN. 909 fol. 132b, where we read: "Said Moses (Narboni), the speakers among them, and the writers of books are of a higher order than those prophets who would (!) not compose books, who are not on as high a level as those who did compose books." It seems to this writer that the just-quoted version of Narboni's words is a reworking of the first quotation that occurs in the original text of Narboni. See below, note 9.

6. This version is found in identical form in manuscripts mentioned in note 5. It was already published by Colette Sirat "Pirkei Moshe LeMoshe Narboni" in *Tarbiẓ* vol. 39 (1970) p. 294.

7. The important novel idea that appears in Narboni's work, but not in Abulafia, in the first quotation of B, is the emphasis on the "partialness" of the human intellect. This "partial intellect" when it cleaves to the Active Intellect becomes transformed into the universal intellect. Because of this, at the moment of "Devekut" (union with the Active Intellect) one is able to change the course of nature. This idea, which is influenced by Ibn Sina is mentioned by Narboni just before the section quoted in B 1 (MS. Paris BN. 956 fol. 208b): "And according to Ibn Rushd (!) human nature derives from Angelic nature, and therefore, the partial intellect may, as Rabbi Abraham Ibn Ezra points out, when cleaving to All, enact in the hylic matter of the world." Apparently Narboni is alluding to Ibn Ezra's commentary to Numbers 20:8: "And when the part knows the whole he cleaves to the whole and initiates in the whole signs and wonders." See also Ibn Ezra, Numbers 22:28. It is worth noting that a similar conception to that of Abulafia's *'Or HaSekhel* may be found in *Sefer Ginzei HaMelekh* by R. Isaac Ibn Latif (published in *Kokhvei Yiẓḥak* 28 (1852) p. 12, chapter 4: "The nature of the human intellect is not to be actually complete and whole, but rather, when one perceives the forms of the world, in general and in particular, in a way congruent to one's mental grasp, then [he perceives] the whole, and the whole is in him. And thus, when one's knowledge extends [to] all of the particulars of existence, he is then to

be found within them all, when also, the natural forms and the abstract forms are engraved in his perception in a veritable way, then all is in him. And the completed person who holds them all in his mind, it may indeed be possible that through his agency a new form may temporarily manifest itself in existence, in accordance with the Divine Will, through miraculous means." Ibn Latif, and likewise, Abulafia after him, do not mention the partialness of the intellect and its transformation into the whole. See also C. Sirat (note 6 above) pp. 292-295; and Aviezer Ravitsky, "The Anthropological Theory of Miracles in Medieval Jewish Philosophy" in ed. I. Twersky *Studies in Medieval Jewish History and Literature* [Cambridge, Mass., 1984] vol. II pp. 246-248.

8. Fol. 38b. The phrase "tore the pattern from the natural course" is found in the writing of Al-Ghazzali, who writes (the following quotation is brought in Al-Ghazzali's name in *Sefer Hapalat HaHapalah* MS. Paris BN. 956 fol. 297b): "The signs that tear away from the natural course such as the transformation of a staff into a serpent."

9. This version is preserved in manuscripts mentioned in notes above. However, in MS. Paris BN. 909 fol. 157b and in MS. Paris BN. 347 fol. 113b we read (regarding the intellect and the imagination): "He is enclothed in falsehood, which is death. This is to say that the power of the imagination enclothes itself in death, which is the cause of the demise of the mind, for when one follows illusions, one negates one's going after true knowledge. Therefore, the prophet when he says, 'He will swallow death forever' means to say that at the time of the redemption this power of the imagination will disappear, and [only] the intellect will remain. This is the meaning of 'For the Lord has spoken it' or (the intellect) will occupy his place." In many ways, this version is closer to the spirit of Abulafia than the version preserved in most manuscripts.

Apparently, under the influence of Narboni, the anonymous author of *Sefer Toldot 'Adam* (Ms. Oxford 836 fol. 159a) writes: "And he should be concentrated on the separate intellect, and with the power of prophecy, the Divine Perceptions (!) are cleansed from all materiality and from the perception of imagination, which is the power of materiality. This is because 'he will swallow death forever'. In consequence, the great salvation will come; the true salvation and complete redemption, after which there will be no future exile." Regarding this work, written during the fifteenth century, see Idel, *Abulafia* p. 15, note 3; p. 118, note 93; idem, *The Mystical Experience* p. 224.

10. *Sefer HaMeliẓ* MS. Rome-Angelica 38, fol. 9a; MS. Munich 285 fol. 13a. Regarding Abulafia's opinion on this matter, see Idel, *The Mystical Experience* pp. 127, 140.

11. See Adolph Jellinek, *Auswahl Kabbalistischer Mystik* (Leipzig 1853), German section, p. 17, note 5, which refers to *Sefer Neveh Shalom*, discourse 5, chapter 4. Also Ḥayyim Michal, in *Sefer 'Or HaḤayyim* (Frankfort 1891) p. 117, which refers to discourse 5, chapter 9 and discourse 9, chapter 9. Also H. A. Davidson, *The Philosophy of Abraham Shalom*, (Berkeley and Los Angeles 1964) p. 15, note 164. It is important to note the fact that the quotation from Abulafia's

'Or HaSekhel occurs in the work of an author whose name is Abraham Shalom, since this book of Abulafia was dedicated to two disciples of Abulafia, one of them being R. Abraham ben Shalom Comti! Quotations from Abulafia's works in Spain are exception to the rule that this kabbalist is a banished person, and the occurence of a citation from *'Or HaSekhel* in the work of Abraham Shalom may be the result of a possible familiar relationship between the late thirteenth century follower of Abulafia and the middle fifteenth century Spanish author.

12. See discourse 5, chapter 4, fol. 65b, in addition to the quotation indicated on fol. 64b. Also, discourse 5, chapter 11 fol. 81a. This was almost entirely influenced by Abulafian ideas; these, in addition to the quotes brought with attribution from *'Or HaSekhel.*

13. This refers to the numerical value of "'ahavah" (love) = 13 + "'ahavah" (13 again) = 26; as well as "'eḥad" (one) = 13 + 'eḥad (13 again) = 26. 26 is the numerical value of the Tetragrammaton. This indicates the nature of the unity achieved by the cleaving through love of the human mind to the Divine. More on the erotic imagery used by Abulafia see Idel, *The Mystical Experience* ch. 4.

14. "He and he are one." This is the accepted version that expresses the unity between the human intellect and the Divine intellect in the writing of the Jewish philosophers. See above, essay I, and Idel, *The Mystical Experience* pp. 126-127.

15. Compare Abulafia, in *Sefer Ḥayyei HaNefesh* Ms. Munich 408 fol. 65b: " . . . The cleaving of all of one's attention to the Name of the Enactment is the secret of the bride and groom." In two places Abulafia indicates the numerical equivalence of "ta'anug" (pleasure) = 539 and "ḥatan vekalah" (groom and bride). See also the fragment that appears after *Sefer HaẒeruf* by a disciple of Abulafia, Ms. Paris BN. 774 fol. 35a.

16. The words of R. Abraham Shalom provide an interesting example of how the term "the ladder of wisdom" becomes "the ladder of ascension"—an almost ecstatic expression. Regarding these two terms and their history, see Alexander Altmann: "The Ladder of Ascension" in *Studies in Mysticism and Religion presented to G. G. Scholem* (Jerusalem 1967) pp. 1-32; on pp. 11-12 he makes a too sharp distinction between these two concepts.

17. Georges Vajda, *L'Amour de Dieu dans la theologie juive du Moyen Âge* (Paris, 1957) pp. 263-264.

18. See H. A. Wolfson *The Philosophy of Spinoza* (New York 1969) vol. 2, p. 304 ff; p. 310. It is worth noting the linguistic similarity between the expression "intellectual love of God" and the well-known expression of Spinoza *amor dei intellectualis.* To be sure, the implication of this expression in the works of Spinoza is different than its meaning in the writing of R. Abraham Shalom and Abulafia. With the latter two it refers to God's love of Man, whereas with Spinoza it refers to Man's love of God. However, like Spinoza, Abulafia associates love with intellectual perception. We bring here the words of Abulafia from his book

Sitrei Torah a commentary to Maimonides' *Guide of the Perplexed* (Ms. Paris BN 774, fol. 120b.): "For the word "ẓelem" (image, likeness) refers to the natural form, which is the species form. And this is the animating soul which is the human intellectual perception, and is similar to the Divine, and cleaves to her and is brought into existence therefrom. It tends to the Divine and preservation and existence are eternal." The "human intellectual perception" and the "Divine" correspond to the love between human and divine in *Sefer 'Or HaSekhel.*

Chapter 5

Mundus Imaginalis and *Likkutei HaRan*

The theory concerning the existence of a plurality of worlds is among the topics that, from the Kabbalah's conception, was considered to be of paramount importance. Relying on primarily neo-Platonic philosophical doctrines, Kabbalists developed complex theories that involved large numbers of "worlds." Clarification of the meanings and implications of these worlds was undertaken by G. Scholem. It is our intention here to concern ourselves with the concept of "*'Olam Hademut*" (which we translate, following Corbin's term, as "*Mundus Imaginalis*") and with the circle wherein this term appeared.

In two of his articles Scholem refers to the term "*Mundus Imaginalis*",[1] which appeared in a Kabbalistic work containing a list of the five worlds: "There are five worlds, which in descending order are: The World of Divinity, The World of the Intellect, The World of the Souls, the *Mundus Imaginalis*, and the World of the Senses." Scholem was baffled by the use of the term "*'Olam hademut*": in his opinion it occurs in the ontological position where the "World of Formation" would appear in the neo-Platonic scheme[2].

The language of the aforementioned quote makes a precise understanding of the concept underlying the term *Mundus Imaginalis* difficult. We will therefore attempt to render this term meaningful, by examining two discourses that have, as yet, escaped the attention of scholars. One of these is taken from *Likkutei HaRan*, a Kabbalistic collection where the above-mentioned quote appears. Immediately following this section, the text continues:

> And I came across a secret of supernal profundity. Know, that the world of the Divinity refers to the most highly exalted structure. The World of the Intellect represents the "Diadem" and although (all is, both are) one, this is the case only *in potentia*, for "womankind is a nation unto itself."[3] Understand this. The world of the souls corresponds to the supernal man, i.e. to Metatron, and the *Mundus Imaginalis* corresponds to Sandalfon, for he is the master of images and forms that confuse and frighten and cause trembling in the prophets and bring harm to the sons of man. The world of the senses is that which is perceived by the senses.
>
> Alternatively, the Divine World comprises the three supernals[4] for they are the secret of the world to come. The World of the Intellect is the androgyne [Male and Female]. In addition, I say that the World of the Divinity symbolizes that which is above the realm of pure thought, the World of the Intellect represents the three supernals,[5] the World of Souls, the androgyne, the *Mundus Imaginalis*, Metatron and Sandalfon, from one: good images, from the other: the contrary [i.e. the bad images]. The World of the Senses is that which is perceived (by the senses).[6]

In these collectanaea we read:

> From the Ran [an acronym of the author's name]: Regarding Moses, to whom God showed the entire land and all of the past and future up to the last day; this occurred through the agency of the secret of the enclothement of existence before him, before his eyes, within the *Mundus Imaginalis*. He who understands will understand.[7]

Elsewhere, in *Sefer Even Sappir*,[8] by R. Elnathan ben Moses Kalkish, we come across the term *Mundus Imaginalis:*

> No one can truly know Him [God] through that which is revealed, except that he separates Himself from the World of the Senses, removes himself completely therefrom, and turns his attention entirely to the supernal world. From these he rises up to the world of the soul. This realm is recognisable only after removing one's attention from the *Mundus Imaginalis*[9] and all of its aspects. Then one perceives the sustenance and everlastingness of the soul. And if one is graced with Divine assistance one can remove oneself above the World of the Soul and perceive the World of the Divinity. This is what the master of the prophets perceived.

If we compare the characteristics of the *Mundus Imaginalis* in the works we have quoted above, with those of the term "*'Alam Al-Mithal*", (i.e., the *Mundus Imaginalis* as it appears in Sufi texts), we find that before us we have a Sufi concept in Hebrew garb. The similarity is not only one of terminology, but also of conceptual content:

A. In both Kabbalah and in Sufism we find the *Mundus Imaginalis* in an intermediate position—a stage between the physical world and the spiritual world[10]. In at least one instance we can point to a correspondence between the Kabbalistic conception of the five worlds, and the Sufi conception of the World of Ideas, the World of the Intelligences (that are separated from matter), the World of the Souls, the *Mundus Imaginalis*, and the physical world.[11]

B. In *Likkutei HaRan* the demonic nature of the *Mundus Imaginalis* is clearly recognizable. They are "forms that confuse and frighten, and cause trembling in the prophets and bring harm to the sons of man." Sandalfon is the source of these negative manifestations, as the end of the first quote attests. According to Sufism, the *Mundus Imaginalis* was the source of demons, and it is there that sinful souls receive retribution[12].

C. The prophetic character of the *Mundus Imaginalis* is recognized in both *Likkutei HaRan* and in the words of R. Elnathan ben Moses. In Sufi literature we find the angels of the *Mundus Imaginalis* that materialize when they become revealed in this world[13].

In our opinion, these correspondences are a sufficient indication that conceptions common to both religious systems lie behind the meaning of the term. With both systems coinciding in time and place, we can assume that here is an example of Sufi influence, in that this system appears in Sufi literature already in the twelfth century, and was further developed by Ibn 'Arabi and his disciples during the thirteenth century[14].

We will now attempt to establish during which period, and in which circle of Kabbalists this Sufi term entered Kabbalistic literature. For this purpose we will analyze the identification of Sandalfon with the *Mundus Imaginalis* found in *Likkutei HaRan.*

The negative association of the *Mundus Imaginalis* vis à vis Sandalfon are not found during the Talmudic-Midrashic period. In the few sources from this body of literature where this angel appears, he is given both a positive and important function.[15] However, during the thirteenth century we find a change in the status of this angel, and this change is reflected in *Likkutei HaRan.*

In *Likkutei HaRan* and in the Talmudic-Midrashic sources as well, the identity of Sandalfon is related to that of Metatron. But Sandalfon is "Taller than his companion by a distance [of] [taking] 500 years [to traverse]",[16] and "stands behind the Chariot",[17] whereas Metatron is the Angel of the Countenance.

The first source where negative features are associated with Sandalfon is *Sidrei Shimmusha Rabba*, composed apparently during the second third of the thirteenth century:

> In the seventh hall is Sandalfon, pure and firm who works powerfully in heaven and earth. He created two great ones in the form of foetuses in the mother's womb. She gives them the spirit of life. It is he who brings death to the creatures of earth with a drawn fiery sword that is not consumed. And all creatures of earth and all who rule in the air of the firmament are under his domain. In his hand is the ability to enclothe the light of the Most High King, and to enclothe the prophets at the time of their prophecy, their spirits [enclothed] with the ray of the spirit, and their bodies, with the brightness of his body.[18]

Here Sandalfon is portrayed as both the Angel of Death, who bears a fiery sword, and as the source of the enclothement of the prophets. These two functions recall the first quote from *Likkutei HaRan* where we find that Sandalfon brings "harm to the sons of man." There he is also associated, albeit negatively, with the prophets. However, as in Talmudic-Midrashic sources, Sandalfon is "higher" than Metatron, who, according to *Sidrei Shimmusha Rabba*, is appointed on the Sixth Heavenly Hall.[19]

A clear conceptual change, regarding the standing of Sandalfon and Metatron, occurs during the second half of the thirteenth century, among Kabbalists who were close to R. Abraham Abulafia. In the commentary of *Sefer Yeẓirah* written by Abulafia's teacher, R. Barukh Togarmi, we read: "The intellect is Metatron, and the Ram [Aries] Sandalfon. Man is bull, the intellect [is the] [Divine Force] Shaddai. Man is the [young] ass, the intellect [and] the sense[s]."[20] This quote contains three groups, each having four components, and each of these groups contains the numerical value of 999: "the intellect is Metatron and the Ram Sandalfon" = "Man is the ox and the intellect Shaddai [Divine Force]" = "Man is the ass, the intellect, the sense[s]." The implication of these oppositions is explained by Abulafia's remarks regarding the relationship between Metatron and Sandalfon.[21]

In his opinion, Metatron, Angel of the Countenance, is the Active Intellect, whereas Sandalfon is the term denoting matter and Samael. In his *Sefer HaMelammed* we read:

> The imprint and seal that forms the human realm is called Sandalfon. He is called "'Ofan" [the wheel], when it is written (in the Bible) without the letter *vav* as it appears in the verse [Ezekiel 1:15] "I beheld and there was one wheel ['ofan] upon the earth," and it was explained [in the Talmud, *Ḥagigah* 13b] (that) this refers to Sandalfon whose head is in the firmament and whose feet are on the ground and he binds crowns for his Master.

And he is undoubtedly the mover of the body and his name is also Samael and from his power the living were created.[22]

A similar view may be found in Abulafia's work *Sefer Ḥayyei Ha-'Olam HaBa'*, where we read:

At the beginning the river is unified, and afterward it separates to different streams. And the river of nature is unified at the beginning, and is entirely one entity, truly with no separation. This is like unto the *prima materia*, which Ezekiel called "ofan" and of which our sages said that this is Sandalfon; he is the prime element and he is indeed the place of the body. Thus, our sages have said that his head is in the firmament and his feet are on the ground, and he binds crowns for his Master. This is because his Master is [the source of] his subsistence, for were he not to bind crowns he would be corrupted. Yet, from these crowns issues constant existense and because he is all, he is not corrupted and his body too is not corrupted. For "Sandalfon" has the numerical value of "body that is not corrupted" [guf velo' yipassed], whereas "his Creator" [kono] contains the numerical value of "and He is not corporeal" [ve-eino guf]. Indeed, Sandalfon, as the creator of the body is also in a certain way ['al panim] created [nif'alim, i.e. the same consonants as in 'al panim], as it is in the secret [of the prohibition] "ye shall have no other gods instead of ['al panay] Me." And his head is in the firmament and his feet are on the ground. This is the secret of the createdness of gods as "others," i.e., those who are not the preexistents of [all] the preexistents as am I, for I am the preexistent.[23]

In those two foregoing quotes, Abulafia establishes an association between separate concepts: the identification of Ezekiel's "wheel" (*'ofan*) with Sandalfon, in accordance with the Talmud tractate Ḥagigah, and an association of this "wheel" with Maimonides' interpretation of it as the "*Prima Materia*" (in *Guide of the Perplexed*, III, 2).[24] Thus, we have the identification of Sandalfon with the "wheel" and the *Prima Materia*. Being associated with matter, Sandalfon personifies all that is negative in nature, and therefore, Abulafia associates him with Sammael. In *Sefer Ḥayyei HaNefesh* Abulafia ways explicitly: "Metatron and Sandalfon are two ministering angels; one good and the other evil."[25]

In the works of Abulafia's disciples the polarization between Metatron and Sandalfon is expressed in a form similar to that of *Sefer Ḥayyei Ha-Nefesh;* in *Sefer Ner 'Elohim* we read:[26]

The southern point [pole] is always called the Angel of the Countenance, for there we find the head of the [astrological] dragon [Teli]. At the northern point [pole] is its tail, and her name is the Angel of the

Back. Those appointed over them are Metatron and Sandalfon respectively, or we may say, Michael and Gabriel[27]. The right handed attribute, compassion, is at the head and at the end is the attribute of Judgment, the Tail.

These words are no doubt influenced by Abulafia's doctrine. Rabbi Isaac of Acre writes:

Know that the words of Rabbi Eliezer regarding the two Seraphim serve to indicate the two Cherubim mentioned above. When it is said "from His right side" this indicates the attribute of compassion, who is Metatron; and in the supernal realm this refers to [one Sephira—attribute of] "Tiferet" [beauty]. When he said "from the left side" this refers to the attribute of Judgment, and its supernal aspect, the [sephira of the] Diadem ['Atarah].[28]

However, the most interesting discourse in this regard is in *Sefer Sha'arei Ẓedek* by an anonymous student of Abulafia.[29] There he writes:

The reason for those instances when we mention these Names and motivate them and yet, they do not function, is because [their function is] they are preceded by two causes: the first is the preparation; with regard to all of these forms, combining them to perfect harmony, in the essence of their formation. As they receive their nature from within the nature of Sandalfon, the Angel of the Back, therefore, when one attempts to remove one's thought from beneath his domain [and] the Divine assistance does not reach him, for this assistance comes from the side of Metatron, Angel of the Countenance. [This is the meaning of] what our sages said "the attribute of Judgement withholds," i.e., Sandalfon, who keeps the gate and binds and shuts all the supernal gates and sends his angels, who are sabotaging angels, etc. If this be the case, then if one's thought departs and is not accompanied by Divine assistance, and he cannot return to his natural state, that one would be in danger from evil spirits, demons and devils.

The general context of this quote from *Sefer Sha'arei Ẓedek* refers to the chanting of Divine Names in order to attain prophecy. According to the quote above, two possibilities avail themselves: first, that of Divine assistance, (i.e., the effluence of the intellect whose source is Metatron, the Angel of the Countenance who gives effluence to the prophet). This possibility corresponds to the "positive images" whose source is Metatron, according to *Likkutei HaRan*. The second possibility is a meeting between the soul of the prophet and the messengers of Sandalfon—demons and evil spirits—who are parallel to similar forms that confuse and frighten the prophets according to *Likkutei HaRan.* Another point that indicates a relationship between *Likkutei HaRan* and *Sha'arei Ẓedek* is the fact that the anonymous author of *Sha'arei Ẓedek* declares that he was familiar with Sufi techniques for attaining ecstasy.[30] Apart from these, we find a number of other characteristics shared by *Likkutei HaRan* and the school of Abulafia:

A) Abulafia and his disciples are characterized by their discussions regarding the relationship between the soul, or intellect, and the supernal world, and the erotic nature of this relationship.[31] This is also found in a section of *Likkutei HaRan*, where we read:

> We should not remove our thoughts from the Divinity, and our intellectual soul should always be longing and pining to perceive the Supernal, which is symbolized by the effluence of the Diadem. And one should be sweet to Her as one is sweet to a woman who receives effluence from her Man, who loves her with a powerful love. And if you act thus, she will cleave to you always in veritable union.[32]

In addition, among Abulafia and his disciples,[33] as well as in *Likkutei HaRan*, the effluence of the intellect is called the "seed." According to the author of *Likkutei HaRan*, Malkhut (the Diadem) is female in relation to the sefirot and "male in relation to the separate intellects and the souls of man, due to the fact that the effluence that comes from her to the intellectual soul is like the seed that comes from a man to the bowels of the woman, and as a man becomes older in years, so too, his mind which is suchlike effluence (?) grows with him."[34]

B) The mixture of philosophical concepts, numerology and letter combination, characterizes the writings of Abulafia and his disciples. These elements also appear in *Likkutei HaRan.* In a section published by G. Scholem we read:[35]

> When God gazed into Himself, from this gazing was found the primal intelligence, which is the binding that cleaves to the essence of created existence[36]. For He included [within Himself] the World of the Intellect, the World of the Soul and the World of the Senses, for He is the Great man [macroanthropos] who encompasses all of the present world. For the man of the senses is the microcosm and the man of the intellect is the macrocosm. His countenance symbolizes the entire World of the Intellect, the supernal world, and the World of the Separate Intelligences, and his feet symbolize the World of the Senses, the World of Combined Forms in general, the lower world, the natural world. His taking flight, as the verse states [Isaiah 6:2] "[he] shall fly" refers to the intermediate

world, the world of the heavenly bodies. Notice that (the word) ('shesh') [six: the number of wings] contains the same numerical value as the word "kesher", and the word "kenafayim" [wings] has the numerical value of the word "'eẓem" [essence]. Thus, "shesh kenafayim" [six wings] = "kesher 'eẓem" (binding with the essence) i.e., the primary intelligence that binds the essence of created existence, from the first created level to the last created level. These consist of three essences: one essence of the World of the Intellect, the essence of the World of the Soul, and the essence of the World of the Senses. Thus, three times (the word) "'eẓem" (essence) contains the numerical value six hundred, i.e., the word "shesh" (six) and the two letters that form the word "shesh" have the numerical value of three times the word "kenafayim" (wings).

The idea that "shesh kenafayim" (six wings) symbolizes the entire existence is found in the writings of Abulafia, in his *Sefer Sitrei Torah*, where he makes use of exactly these numerological devices to make his point: "shesh" = 600 = "kesher" (binding); "kenafayim" = 200 = "'eẓem".[37] What is missing in Abulafia is the neo-Platonic flavor found in *Likkutei HaRan*. Indeed, this neo-Platonism, together with the consideration of the sephirot (Divine attributes) as being (one with) the Divinity, although not present in Abulafia's writings, is a characteristic of *Sefer Sha'arei Ẓedek*.

C) In *Likkutei HaRan* we read:

Our teacher, the sage Ran: The Community of Israel [Knesset Yisrael] symbolizes the (ingathering, group) of the souls of the righteous of Israel, upon whom is drawn [Divine] mercy and Will [. . .] And not all of the souls of the body are indicated, but only the intellectual soul.[38]

Similar ideas are found in *Sefer 'Or HaMenorah* written within Abulafia's circle.[39] There we read:

As for the power of speech, which is the soul of speech that receives the Divine effluence, this is called "the Community of Israel" [Knesset Yisrael], whose secret meaning is the Active Intellect.

Like *Sefer 'Or HaMenorah*, Abulafia employs the term "Knesset Yisrael" to symbolize the whole, perfected person.[40]

D) The use of the word "demut" (image) as meaning "dimiyon" ([illusory] imagination) is widespread in the writings of R. Abraham Abulafia,[41] and is reflected in the Hebrew term for *Mundus Imaginalis* ('Olam hademut).

It seems to this writer that the parallels provided thus far indicate that the author of *Likkutei HaRan* was closely aligned with the circle of

R. Abraham Abulafia. We will now attempt to identify the author.

The first indication comes from the introductory sentence to the quotation cited at the beginning of the paper, regarding the five worlds: "I, YHC looked into the Kabbalah of Ran."[42] In my opinion, "YHC" indicates R. Isaac of Acre. In his work, *Me'irat Einayim*, the expressions "I, YHB SWR DITO"[43] or "and YHB/SNR/DITO"[44] occur quite often. We may assume that in the relatively late manuscript, wherein *Likkutei HaRan* is preserved, the letters "SNR DITO" are missing and the letter C (appears) in place of a *bet* for they look almost identical.

In order to strengthen the hypothesis that the compiler of *Likkutei HaRan* is R. Isaac of Acre, I will point to a number of themes that appear in both *Likkutei HaRan* and in the later writings of R. Isaac of Acre:

A. The first is the parable of the colored glass, which explains the variegated outcomes of the unified Divine effluence without indicating a change in the Divine Emanator.[45]

Likkutei HaRan
MS. New York JTS 1777
fols. 32b-33a

From our sage Ran: Know that the complete simplicity in the epitome of completeness is due to the veritable Existence of the Holy One. Blessed be He and as for the art of the construction [combining of complex forms], from the smallest of the small to the greatest of the great, none of them are as such, from the part of the Holy One and His Blessed Name, but rather, only from the part of the created beings who receive the effluence itself wherein there is no combination or construct whatsoever. All is simple in utter, complete simplicity. To illustrate this in a parable: observe the rays of the light of the sun, spreading on many partitions of glass [i.e. on various colors of glass], each different from the other. Then, the light will change with the change of the color of glass, and if the glass be red, you will see the color of the light as red, and if green, then it will appear green, and if saffron, then it will appear saffron, and if blue, then blue it will appear. And the change and combination occurs not on the part of the sun's rays, which are pure and not complex, not added to or reduced, the rays remain in simplicity, and

Sefer Ozar Hayyim
MS. Moscow-Günzburg 775,
fols. 176a-b

I saw a superlative parable to explain the secret of the unity of the effluence of the Unique Master, coming from within Him, and the unity of the Unique Master, unified in His effluence. This parable also applies to the secret of the rays of the supernal soul within a person and the unity of the soul in her rays. You may understand this based on what I heard from my master, of blessed memory, words which are to one's palate like the taste of good honey: A palace is made with many windows facing east and west, and within the windows are cut glass, and each piece of glass is its own unique color—this one all blue, this all black, this all red, this all green, this all saffron and this combining two colors, where one is unlike the other. Now when the light of the sun [passes through] them, the rays that strike the walls [of the palace] are variegated, with many colors, each different from the other, and none like the other, to the point that one who sees them will wonder and say that these differences are due to the light of the sun! And this indeed is not the case, for the change is due only to the receptors of the rays, i.e., to the many colored glasses the change is not in the light that passed through the glass; it is the glass alone that receives the change and the coming to be and passing away, not the sun at all. So too, in the case of the very nature of God, Blessed by He, who acts without being affected by another for He is the Primary of all Primaries.

that are set in the windows. So too we may understand the rays of the effluence of the Unique Master, One and unchanging, without addition or diminution. Indeed His works are variegated beyond investigation and infinite, all of them in accordance to the nature of the creatures which receive His effluence.

It is reasonable to assume that the "teacher" mentioned in *Sefer 'Ozar Ḥayyim* is the author of *Likkutei HaRan*, and thus, we are referring to the teacher of R. Isaac of Acre.

B. The particular designation of Sandalfon as "The master of images and forms that confuse and frighten and cause trembling . . . " also occurs in *'Ozar Ḥayyim* of R. Isaac of Acre: "Sandalfon is the secret of the fire that inflames and causes fear and trembling."[46]

C. In *Likkutei HaRan* we come across the acronym " 'ABYA' " twice (the Four Worlds: *'A*ẓilut—emanation, *B*eri'ah—creation, *Y*eẓirah—formation, and *'A*siah—action), and this acronym appears for the first time in Kabbalistic literature, in the writings of R. Isaac of Acre.[47]

D. The designations, "Supernal Man" referring to Metatron, Angel of the Countenance, and "The Man of the Senses" referring to man as microcosm recur in both *Likkutei HaRan* and *Sefer 'Ozar Ḥayyim*.[48]

These, and other indications, (see note 3) point to the identity of the compiler of *Likkutei HaRan*. I assume, after having studied *Sefer Me'irat 'Einayim* by R. Isaac of Acre, that the name of his teacher is contained therein.

As we know, R. Isaac often used acronyms in referring to his sources as well.[49] In the opening passage of a long discourse describing the descent of the Divine effluence and the ascent of the soul, he says: "From the mouth of Rabbi Nathan the Wise, I heard . . . "[50] We may thus reasonably assume that we can identify "Ran" as referring to the sage R. Nathan, and the acronym Moharan (MHRN) is deciphered as *M*ori *H*eḥakham *R*abbi *N*athan (my teacher, the wise Rabbi Nathan).

The analysis of quotations from *Sefer Me'irat 'Einayim* and *Sefer Shoshan Sodot* leads me to conclude that the opinions of R. Nathan are close in conceptual outlook to those of R. Abraham Abulafia, and we may assume that R. Nathan was the same person as Abulafia's close disciple, who he refers to as "Rabbi Nathan ben Se'adyahu".[51] A quotation from *Sefer 'Even Sappir* also points to the circle of R. Abraham Abulafia; therein, we find many discussions taken from the writings of Abulafia and his disciples.

The foregoing discussion informs us that within the circle of R.

Abraham Abulafia's disciples (i.e., in the writings of R. Nathan and in the anonymous work *Sha'arei Ẓedek*), there began to be closer association to Sufism. This is affirmed by the presence of Sufic meditation methods in the text of *Sha'arei Ẓedek*, and by our knowledge of the sources of some views expressed in *Likkutei HaRan*. The geographic range of the penetration of Sufism in ecstatic Kabbalah will be discussed in the following essay; it should be mentioned that this influence leaves its mark not only in the works of R. Nathan and the author of *Sha'arei Ẓedek*, but also in the works of R. Isaac of Acre,[52] who was one of the foremost Kabbalists of the fourteenth century.

Notes to Chapter 5

1. See G. Scholem "'Od Pa'am al Sefer 'Avnei Zikkaron," in *Kiryat Sefer* vol. 7 (1930-1931) p. 461; idem. "Hitpatḥut Torat Ha'Olamot BeKabbalat Ha-Rishonim," in *Tarbiẓ*, vol. 3 (1932), pp. 42, 46.

2. *Kiryat Sefer*, vol. 7, p. 461; *Tarbiẓ*, vol. 3, p. 46, where Scholem describes the *Mundus Imaginalis* as the world of the spiritual nature.

3. *Shabbat*, fol. 62b. This aphorism, as a reference to the last sephirah, referred to as 'Atarah or the Diadem, is also found in *Sefer 'Oẓar Ḥayyim* by R. Isaac of Acre, MS. Moscow-Günzburg 775 fol. 173b.

4. It is reasonable to assume that the source for the designation of the "three supernal (sefirot)" as the Divinity, is the *Book of Bahir*, paragraph 140, in the Margolioth edition, which offers a theosophical explanation of the word "'az" [then]: the *aleph* refers to the three supernals, and the *zayin* (numerical value of 7) refers to the seven attributes of construction. For a Christian explanation of this division, see Ḥayyim Wirszubski: "Pico's Companion to Kabbalistic Symbolism" in *Studies in Mysticism and Religion presented to Gershom Scholem*, [Jerusalem, 1967] pp. 358-361. See also *'Iggeret Ḥamudot* by R. Eliyahu of Genazzano (London 1912) pp. 29, 39 ff.

5. This conception already appears in the works of R. Azriel of Gerona; see Scholem's discussion of it in *Tarbiẓ* vol. 2 (1931) p. 431 and also in Moses Narboni's commentary to *Ḥai Ben Yoktan*, MS. Paris BN. 914, fol. 149b. See also the collectanaea of R. Yoḥanan Alemanno, MS. Oxford 2234 fol. 126b, ff.

6. MS. New York JTS 1777 (EMC 699) fol. 33a. *Likkutei HaRan* appears in this collection of Kabbalistic varia, on fol. 32a-34a, and a portion of this was published by Scholem in *Tarbiẓ* vol. 3, pp. 44-46. The quote brought in this article also appears in *Sefer 'Avnei Zikkaron* by R. Abraham Adrutiel, MS. New York JTS 1746 (EMC 651) fol. 3a-3b. However, Adruteil omits some important words regarding the *Mundus Imaginalis*. I quote this section from *Sefer 'Avnei Zikkaron:* "And the Divine World refers to that which is beyond the realm of pure thought. The

World of the Intellect refers to the three supernals, and the World of the Souls refers to the androgyne [Male and Female], and to the entire structure. The *Mundus Imaginalis* refers to Metatron, Angel of the Countenance, and Sandalfon. Alternatively, the Divine World refers to the three supernals, the World of the Intellect refers to the World of the Structure. Alternatively, the World of the Divinity refers to the construction, i.e., to the six sons to whom King David alluded in the verse [I Chronicles 29:11] 'To You, oh Lord, are the Greatness and the Power,' etc. The World of the Intellect refers to the Diadem ('Atarah i.e. the last Sefirah) and although they are all unified, this is only *in potentia*, not in actuality, because females are a nation apart. Understand if you are master of your soul. The World of Souls refers to the Supernal Man, Metatron, the Angel of the Countenance, and the *Mundus Imaginalis* refers to Sandalfon, who binds coronets for his Master. The World of the Senses is the sensible world."

7. Ms. New York JTS 1777 fol. 34a. On another instance of the occurrence of the view that Moses has received the capability to see the past and the future see M. Idel "R. Yehudah Ḥallewah and His 'Ẓafnat Pa'aneaḥ'" [Heb.] *Shalem* vol. 4 [1984] pp. 131-132 n. 32 and especially Pieter W. der Host, "Moses' Throne Vision in Ezekiel the Dramatist" *JJS* vol. 34 [1983] p. 28.

8. Ms. Paris BN. 728 fol. 14a. This interesting work, written in the middle of the fourteenth century, has not yet gained the attention of scholars. In studying it one finds that the author copied sections of various Kabbalistic works, without indicating his sources. Regarding this work, see M. Idel, in *Kiryat Sefer* vol. 51 (1977) p. 487. See also chapter VII n. 63.

9. Regarding this term, see Fazlur Rahman: "Dream, Imagination and 'Alam Al-Mithal" in *Islamic Studies*, vol. 3 (1964), pp. 167-180 (henceforth referred to as 'Rahman'). Also, H. Corbin: "La Resurrection chez Mulla Sadra Shirazi" in *Studies . . . G. Scholem* [n. 4 above], pp. 71-115 (henceforth, Corbin). See also Corbin's article "*Mundus Imaginalis* ou l'imaginaire et l'imaginal" in *Cahiers Internationaux de Symbolisme*, vol. VI (1964), pp. 3-26.

10. Rahman pp. 169-170 and note 7; also Corbin p. 109. For another occurrence of *'Olam hadimiyon*, a term closely related to the Sufic *'alam al-mithal* see the passage out of the Ḥallewah's *Ẓafnat Pa'aneaḥ* see Idel [n. 7 above], pp. 132-133.

11. H. Corbin: *L'imagination creatrice dans le Soufisme d'Ibn Arabi*, [Paris, 1958] p. 262, note 233.

12. Rahman p. 170 and note 8; Corbin p. 109.

13. Rahman pp. 170-171; Corbin p. 99.

14. Rahman p. 171ff; especially in Corbin, passim.

15. Gershom Scholem, *Jewish Gnosticism, Merkabah Mysticism and Talmudic Tradition*, [New York 1960] pp. 52-53, note 30.

16. *Ḥagiga* fol. 17b.

17. G. Scholem, *Encyclopedia Judaica* (1972) Vol. 14 col. 827-828.

18. G. Scholem, *Tarbiẓ* 16 (1945) pp. 202-203.

19. See also *Zohar* II fol. 202b. There we find Sandalfon appointed over the seventh firmament. However, in the Zoharic layer *Ra'ya Meheimna* we find Sandalfon as the source of judgments. See *Zohar* III fol. 29b: "And the animating soul (nefesh) that rules during the week, Sandalfon, issues from the Throne of Judgment."

20. Scholem *Abraham Abulafia* p. 236. The text published therein is faulty, and is corrected herein in accordance with MS. Paris BN. 770.

21. Some of the material that will be quoted in the course of this article was analyzed in Idel *Abraham Abulafia*, pp. 105-106.

22. MS. Paris BN. 680 fol. 307a "Po'el haguf" (the maker of the body) = 280 = "Sandalfon" (numerically). This section refers to the remark in the Talmud regarding Sandalfon, in *Niddah* fol. 25b. The division between the functions of Metatron and Sandalfon (Sama'el) is clearly noticeable in *Sefer Tikkun HaDe'ot* by R. Isaac Albalag, [Jerusalem 1973]. We read on p. 58: "It is said that Metatron is the Angel of Israel and Sandalfon is the Angel of Esau, i.e., their guides. Undoubtedly, both are appointed over the guidance of all people. The guidance of one inhibits the guidance of the other. The way that they guide the person is as follows: The natural energy is the primary completeness, it is the vitality function within which is the subsistence of the body. And the mental potency provides the final completeness. It is the consciousness, wherein lies the subsistence of the soul . . . and the natural aspect is called the evil inclination, and its function, i.e., the natural inclination, is the evil angel and the Satan who leads astray and causes harm, etc." See also ibid. p. 60. The distinction between Metatron as the source of intelligence, or of the soul, and Sandalfon—Sama'el as the source of the body, parallels well with *Sefer HaTemunah* [Lemberg, 1896] fol. 56a: "Metatron and Sandalfon: one rules from the earth to the heavens in their entirety, and he is Metatron, and one rules the earth and all that is upon her, and he is Sandalfon. One brings the souls to the body, Metatron, and one brings the [physical] imprint and form to the foetus and determines whether it be male or female, and he is Sandalfon." Sandalfon as the source of the material realm is also mentioned in *Sefer Tehillot HaShem* by R. Samuel Ibn Motot (MS. Vatican 255 fol. 54a): "The universal soul . . . is composed of two parts: the intellectual and rational part; the function of the soul that in and of itself, speaks, which the sages of the Kabbalah called Metatron, and beneath the quality of the soul is the level of the form from which issues the material realm, which they called Sandalfon." During approximately this same historical period we read from *Sefer HaPeliy'ah* [Korez 1784] fol. 16 col. c: Metatron and Sandalfon: two angels are the guides. "Metatron, Angel of the Countenance guides his sons and suffers their tribulations and pleads mercy on their behalf, and Sandalfon the Angel of the Back who is entirely composed of

judgment." It is reasonable to assume that the view of the author of *Sefer HaPeliy'ah* was influenced by the school of Abulafia, for in this work we find extended sections taken from two of Abulafia's works *Sefer Ḥayyei HaNefesh* and *Sefer Gan Na'ul.* The anonymous author of *Sefer HaMal'akh HaMeshiv* (MS. British Library 766 fol. 106a) we read: "Sandalfon is the powerful fire who sits near to the secret of the Shekhinah. He emits sparks of fire and flame which are all-consuming, and all are in fear of him." Regarding this work and its author, see Idel, "Inquiries," and also G. Scholem "HaMaggid shel R. Yosef Taitaẓak" *Sefunot* OS, vol. XI (1978) pp. 69-112, and *Tarbiẓ* vol. 5 (1934) p. 185, and note 1. It is likely that the term *Spiritus naturae* which appears in *Kabbala Denudata* by Knorr von Rosenroth, vol. I, pp. 261-262, and refers to Sandalfon also reflects the relationship between Sandalfon and the natural or material realm.

23. MS. Oxford 1582 fols. 25a-25b. This section is based on the numerological implications of 280: "Sandalfon = 280 = 'yesod haguf' (the element of the body) = 'guf velo' yipas'ed (the body is not corrupted) = 'guf lekono' (a body for his master) = 'po'al haguf' (the activity of the body) = ''al panim' (on the face of) = 'nif'alim' (the results of) = 'lekadmonim' (for the preexistent ones) = ''anokhi kadmon' (I am the uncreated); 'lekono' (for his creator) = 192 = 'ha'el 'eno guf' (God is not corporeal) = 'velo' ha'el koaḥ guf' (and God is not a corporal function); ''elohim 'aḥerim 'al panay' (other gods instead of Me) = 625 = 'elohim nif'alim 'aḥerim' (Alien and created gods).

24. Maimonides' words are left unexplained, but most commentators tend to explain the term ''ofan' as referring to primal matter.

25. MS. Munich 408 fol. 70a.

26. MS. Munich 10 fol. 130a. The north, which here is associated with Sandalfon, is associated with Sama'el in the writings of Abulafia. In *Sefer Get HaShemot* (MS. Oxford 1682 fol. 106a) he writes: "The left side refers to 'the northerly one,' who is the evil inclination." It is worth noting in this connection, the words of R. Isaac of Acre, who in *Sefer 'Oẓar Ḥayyim* (MS. Moscow-Günzburg 775 fol. 167a) writes: "And (the vowel note) Ẓere, which is written as two points, refers to the two anvils mentioned, Metatron, Angel of the Countenance, and Sandalfon."

27. The correspondence: Michael—South; Gabriel—North, is mentioned in Midrash *Genesis Rabba*, 1:3.

28. See paraphrase by R. Isaac of Acre, of a commentary on *Pirkei deR. Eliezer* published by G. Vajda: "Isaac d'Acco et Juda ben Nissim," *REJ* 115 (1956) p. 67. In *Sefer 'Oẓar Ḥayyim* (MS. Moscow-Günzburg 775 fol. 126a) we read: "The attribute of stern judgment and Sandalfon, who is the secret of the bull, and the secret of the forest, is the power of the night." See above, note 26.

29. Regarding this work, see G. Scholem: "Sha'arei Ẓedek—Ma'amar Be-Kabbalah Measkolat R. Abraham Abulafia Meyuḥas leR. Shem Tov (Ibn Gaon?)" in *Kiryat Sefer* vol. 1 (1924-25) pp. 127-139. We quoted from the Jerusalem MS.

8° 148 fols. 74a-74b. In MS. Milano-Ambrosiana, 60 we find a section containing material very similar to this work. There we read (ff. 42b-43a): "These are necessarily two opposites and they are called by two names based on their opposition: the aspect of existence, mercy, the right side, and the countenance, and he is called Sandalfon in the aspects of negation, stern judgment, the left side and the posterior." We may assume that the term "Metatron" is missing, and ought to appear between the words "countenance" and "and".

30. *Kiryat Sefer* 1 pp. 132-133.

31. Idel, *The Mystical Experience*, pp. 184-190.

32. MS. New York JTS 1777 fol. 33b.

33. Idel, *The Mystical Experience*, pp. 190-195.

34. MS. New York JTS 1777 fol. 33a.

35. *Tarbiẓ* 3, p. 45.

36. Compare with the words of R. Shem Tov Ibn Falakerah in *Sefer Moreh HaMoreh* [Presburg, 1837] p. 50: "And an ancient sage remarked that the perception of the Blessed Divinity in this world would bind this world with one rope so that it would not move or stray." Compare also with the words of R. Joseph Ibn Caspi, *Sefer Maskiyot Kesef* [Frankfurt au Main, 1848] p. 75.

37. MS. Paris BN. 774 fols. 134a-134b. The connections between this section of *Likkutei HaRan* and Abulafia's discussion of the subject of 'kenafayim' revolved around the idea of man-microcosm, cosmos-Great Man (macrocosm). This fact and the fact that both Abulafia and the author of *Likkutei HaRan* use identical numerologies, suggest that there existed a relationship, albeit perhaps only a literary one, between the two.

38. MS. New York JTS 1777 fol. 34a.

39. MS. Jerusalem 1303 fol. 28b. Regarding this work, see Idel, *Abraham Abulafia* p. 79.

40. Idel, *The Mystical Experience*, pp. 211-212.

41. Idel, *Abraham Abulafia*, p. 79.

42. MS. New York JTS 1777, fol. 33a. The beginning of this quote is omitted from *Sefer 'Avnei Zikkaron* by R. Abraham Adrutiel. See note 6, above. It is worth noting that the description of the MS. New York JTS 1777, apparently written by R. Yaakov Toledano, mentions R. Isaac of Acre; this refers, however, to a later section of the MS.

43. Pp. 44, 75. This acronym may be deciphered as follows: *Y*iẓḥak *H*aẒa'ir *B*en *S*hmuel N R *D*emin *A*cco *T*ibbaneh *V*etikonen (Isaac the Young, son of Samuel, may God guard him, of Acre, may it be rebuilt and re-established). It is worth noting that R. Isaac of Acre did not always make use of this particular

acronym to indicate reference to himself. He also used AHYDA (*A*mar *H*aẒa'ir *Y*iẓḥak *D*emin *A*cco) (said the youth, Isaac of Acre). See Gottlieb, *Studies* p. 232. Another acronym he used was VYHBDATO, which occurs in *Sefer 'Avnei Zikkaron* (occurring as well as in *Sefer Me'irat 'Einayim*). See G. Scholem 'Sefer 'Avnei Zikkaron' *Kiryat Sefer* 6 (1929-1930) p. 261.

44. Pp. 44, 50, etc.

45. This section is also quoted in *Sefer 'Avnei Zikkaron* MS. New York JTS 1746 (ECM 651) fols. 3a-b. A parable similar to these two versions is also found in the works of Steven bar Sudaili; see G. Widengren, "Researches in Syrian Mysticism, Mystical Experiences and Spiritual Exercises," *Numen* vol. 8 (1961) p. 195. Another parallel occurs in *Sefer Ḥovot HaLevavot* Sha'ar HaBeḥinah chapter 1, and also in *Sefer Ẓurat Ha'Olam* by R. Isaac ibn Latif (Vienna 1860, p. 40): "For the revealed light, depicted as whitening, does not actually change color for every individual, and does not receive any color from outside itself. Rather it is like the rays of the sun that reach glass lanterns, where the color of the light changes corresponding to the color of the glass; not that the light itself changes, for it does not receive color from anything outside itself." See S. Heller-Wilensky "Isaac Ibn Latif—Philosopher or Kabbalist?" in ed. Alexander Altmann *Jewish Medieval and Renaissance Studies* (Cambridge, Mass. 1967) p. 208 note 163. It is worth noting that in both 'Likkutei HaRan' and in Ibn Latif we come across the term 'nivra' rishon' (primal creation). I intend to focus on this term elsewhere. See also further in this article, note 52. The term "'eser mar'ot" (ten mirrors) was in general use amongst Kabbalists as a symbol for the sefirot, but without reference to different colors. See G. Scholem "Colours and Their Symbolism in Jewish Tradition and Mysticism" in *Diogenes* vol. 108 (1979) p. 98 and n. 44. The simile of the ten mirrors also appears in Kabbalistic varia from the school of R. Shelomo ben Abraham ibn Adret of Barcelona; see MS. Vatican 202 fol. 60a and MS. Parma 1221 fol. 110b. Later we find it in the writings of Moses Narboni, in his commentary to *Ḥai ben Yoktan*, see Vajda, *Recherches* pp. 379, 399. However, since the generation of the Expulsion from Spain, we observe a combining of the similes of the mirror and the colored glasses, due apparently to the influence of *Sefer 'Avnei Zikkaron* or its sources; See Gottlieb, *Studies* p. 422, note 77.

46. MS. Moscow-Günzburg 775 fol. 130b.

47. See G. Scholem in *Tarbiẓ* vol. 3 pp. 59-60. If we assume that the compiler of *Likkutei HaRan* was R. Isaac of Acre, then the source of the acronym 'ABYA' (the four worlds: 'Aẓilut [emanation], Beri'ah [creation], Yeẓirah [formation] and 'Assiah [action]) would seem to have been in Kabbalistic circles far from the Zohar and its various strata. Cp. however to G. Scholem in *ibid.* pp. 60-61, where he asserts that R. Isaac of Acre received the doctrine of the four worlds either from other Kabbalists "who were close in spirit to these authors (i.e. of the *Tikkunei Zohar*), or from the writings of Kabbalists of the generation of R. Moses de Leon, which are no longer extant." In the aforementioned article (p. 63, note 2) Scholem notes the use of the acronym 'ABYA' in *Likkutei HaRan*, but he was of the opinion that this work was composed during the fourteenth century.

48. MS. New York JTS 1777 ff. 32a-b, and MS. Moscow-Günzburg, 775 fol. 141b.

49. See Vajda, ibid., note 29 on p. 64.

50. *Me'irat 'Eynaim* p. 222: see Idel, *The Mystical Experience* pp. 133-134 and the pertinent footnotes.

51. Idel, *The Mystical Experience* p. 134. Scholem, (*Tarbiẓ* 3 p. 48.) cautiously chose not to decipher the acronym 'HaRan,' however, Georges Vajda, in his book *Juda ben Nissim Ibn Malka* (Paris, 1954) p. 79, note 2) speaks of R. Nissim as the author of *Likkutei HaRan*.

52. Regarding the similarities between R. Isaac of Acre and *Sefer Sha'arei Ẓedek*, see Gottlieb in *Studies* p. 233 note 7. I intend to bring additional material on this as well as on other issues in *Likkutei HaRan* in a critical edition of *Sefer Sha'arei Ẓedek*.

53. A brief survey of the connections between Kabbalah and Sufism may be found in G. Scholem: "A Note on a Kabbalistic Treatise on Contemplation," in *Melanges offerts a Henri Corbin*, [Teheran, 1977] pp. 665-670.

Chapter 6

Ecstatic Kabbalah and the Land of Israel

Although a number of Jewish mystics—Kabbalists—settled in Palestine in the thirteenth century, their presence did not contribute to the development of a Kabbalistic school of thought. We know almost nothing of the outcome of R. Jacob ha-Nazir of Lunel's decision to visit Palestine.[1] Naḥmanides, who exerted considerable influence among the Barcelona mystics, the followers of his Kabbalistic views, was nonetheless unsuccessful in motivating his disciples to settle in the Land of Israel,[2] and it would seem that his migration to Palestine did not lead to the creation of an independent Kabbalistic tradition. Similarly, R. Abraham Abulafia, who reached Palestine in 1260, left no imprint there. His principal aim was to search for the legendary Sambatyon River;[3] upon his reaching Acre, however, his search came to an end due to the war which then raged between the Mameluks and the Tatars in 'Ein Ḥarod ('Ein Jalud).[4] He thereupon retraced his steps, leaving no description in his works of Palestine and/or Acre.

In the early 1270s, Abulafia began the study of the "Kabbalah of names," disseminating this method among his students and followers, both personally and in writing. In 1287, while traveling through Sicily, he composed *Shomer Miẓvah*[5] at the request of "that fine and learned young man, R. Solomon ha-Kohen, son of the late Moses ha-Kohen of Galilee in the Land of Israel, who called upon me to compose a work on the procedures of the Priestly Blessing."[6] Abulafia testifies elsewhere that

R. Solomon had been one of his students: "and in honor of the aforementioned fine student R. Solomon . . ."[7] This is clear evidence that one of the rabbis of Palestine had learned Abulafia's Kabbalistic doctrines from Abulafia himself, as early as 1287.

Four years later, R. Isaac ben Samuel of Acre left for Spain, and an examination of this Kabbalist's writings reveals clear indications of the influence of Abulafia's mystical thought. These are especially apparent in *'Oẓar Ḥayyim*, a work which includes descriptions of R. Isaac's visions and mystical practices.[8] Furthermore, MS Sassoon 919, which contains material from *'Oẓar Ḥayyim*, makes mention of "the mystic sage R. Joseph ben Solomon of blessed memory of Galilee, of the province of Safed" (p. 50). The three authors we have mentioned are identified with Galilee, and two of them are associated with the thought of R. Abraham Abulafia.

To these we should add a fourth scholar—the author of *Sha'arei Ẓedek*.[9] The title page of this manuscript reads: "This book was written by R. Shem-Tov of Spain among his other works; he is of the city of Leon and is a great kabbalist. This work was written in Upper Galilee."[10] However, in a different manuscript of the same work—MS Gaster 954—we read: "This work of true kabbalah, inspiring of wisdom and understanding, was completed in the year 55 (*heh-nun*) in the month of Marḥeshvan in Hebron."[11] Whether the year (*heh-nun*) referred to 1290 or 1295 and whether we accept the location either as Upper Galilee or as Hebron, we are, in any case, provided with additional evidence concerning the ties between Abulafia and his Kabbalistic methods, and the Kabbalists of Palestine. In less than a decade—between 1287 when *Shomer Miẓvah* was written, and 1295—nearly all the evidence pertaining to the Kabbalah in Palestine is associated with the Kabbalistic methodology of Abulafia. This fact is particularly noteworthy in light of the minimal influence of Abulafia's mysticism among Spanish Kabbalists at the end of the thirteenth and the beginning of the fourteenth centuries. Here it is most probable that R. Solomon ben Abraham Ibn Adret's sharp attack on Abulafia and his "prophetic Kabbalah" deterred Spanish Kabbalists from following the path of "prophetic" mysticism.[12]

A more important question in the context of this discussion, however, is why the rabbis of Palestine were influenced by precisely this school of thought. It seems to me that at least a partial answer may be derived from a perusal of the works of R. Isaac ben Samuel of Acre and of the author of *Sha'arei Ẓedek*. These Kabbalists were greatly influenced by the teachings of Abulafia, but their writings contain a further characteristic lacking in Abulafia's thought—one that is of interest to us. In the writings of his Eastern followers in mysticism, the Kabbalah of Abulafia acquired a Sufic component.[13]

In practical terms, this phenomenon may be explained in two ways. The first holds that Abulafia's teachings reached Palestine and encountered various Sufic concepts. His students subsequently effected a synthesis between the two systems. The second possibility, however, seems to be the more reasonable; it assumes the existence of a Sufic-Jewish stream of thinking in the East prior to the dissemination of Abulafia's Kabbalah. When word spread of this school of mysticism—which is similar in several respects to Sufic and Yoga elements—scholars of Eastern lands sought ways to learn Abulafia's teachings. Consequently, R. Solomon ben Moses of Galilee went to Sicily to learn them. Thereafter, writers such as R. Isaac ben Samuel of Acre, and the author of *Sha'arei Ẓedek* emphasized Sufic fundamentals within works where Abulafia's influence is apparent.

The hypotheis that Sufic-Jewish tradition existed in the East, and likely also in Palestine, may well be supported by a series of studies undertaken in recent years which show clearly that an unbroken succession of writers in the Near East—principally in Egypt—were profoundly influenced by Sufic perceptions. S. D. Goitein[14] has shown that R. Abraham ben Moses ben Maimon and his colleague R. Abraham Ibn Abu-Rabiya he-Ḥasid joined an existing Pietist circle. Sufic influence extended into R. Abraham ben Moses ben Maimon's circle itelf,[15] and a clear mystic trend may be discerned in a work apparently written by R. Obadyah,[16] son of R. Abraham. Furthermore, an anonymous author who apparently lived in the fifteenth century continued to absorb Sufic influence.[17] We have, then, an unbroken chain of authors, all of Eastern communities, who developed a mystical trend under Sufic inspiration, starting from the first third of the thirteenth century. In this context, we should also mention *Perakim be-Haẓlaḥah* (chapters on Beatitude) attributed to Maimonides, that was composed apparently in the East,[18] and in which Sufic principles are recognizable.[19] Given this environment, there is no reason to wonder why Abulafia's ecstatic Kabbalah merited distribution and why Sufic principles were blended with his techniques.

A different question worthy of expanded discussion here is whether the Kabbalists we have mentioned absorbed Abulafia's views and superimposed them on Sufic concepts, each independently of the others, or whether there existed, in fact, a circle of Palestinian Kabbalists in which Sufic principles were blended with the Kabbalah of Abulafia. It would appear that there was indeed such a distinctive circle in Palestine and that we are not dealing with a number of individuals with a similar approach.

The geographic proximity of Acre, where R. Isaac ben Samuel received his education, and Galilee, home of R. Solomon ben Moses, and the close time-frame (as we have noted), tip the scales in favor of the assumption that there was a relationship between the two authors. If the evidence concerning *Sha'arei Ẓedek* having been written in Upper Galilee is correct, it points further to a concentration of Kabbalists in a relatively restricted geographic environment.

'Oẓar Ḥayyim, written by R. Isaac ben Samuel, and *Sha'arei Ẓedek* share certain similarities in several areas.

1. Ephraim Gottlieb has already remarked on an identical tale concerning Ibn Sina's use of wine, which appears precisely in these two works.[20]
2. Both works provide the same interpretation of the Talmudic dictum found in *Shabbat* 152b, concerning study of the Kabbalah after the age of forty.[21]
3. Both of these Kabbalists, unlike Abulafia, depict the danger of death while in a state of ecstasy, as if it were the experience of sinking into an ocean;[22] this may be a Sufic motif.[23] Abulafia, however, describes this peril in terms of being consumed by a great flame.[24]
4. As I have shown in the preceding essay, the Sufic-influenced Kabbalistic material available to R. Isaac of Acre, which is associated with his mentor, is similar to the approach in *Sha'arei Ẓedek*.[25]

Especially interesting evidence regarding the existence of the Kabbalistic circle in which R. Isaac ben Samuel of Acre participated, and which dealt with the teachings of Abulafia, appears in *'Oẓar Ḥayyim:*[26]

> And I heard from my late teacher . . . that "youth" is an appellation for the ancient one, for he is the eldest of all creatures, and should be so called, and not called a youth. And he said that this is but an appellation, for in Arabic they call the elder "shekh" [*shin* = 300, *khaf* = 20, totalling 320], and the secret of youth [*na'ar: nun* = 50, *'ayin* = 70, *resh* = 200, totalling 320] is also "shekh". One of the students asked: "Surely, however, in Arabic one says 'shekh' as if written with a *yod*—'sheikh'. And what is done with the remaining 'ten' [*yod*]"?

It is not Isaac's response that concerns us here, but rather the evidence that Abulafia's teachings were studied in a teacher-student framework.[27] Furthermore, while the teacher either knew no Arabic or accepted Abulafia's tradition by which "shekh" was written without the letter "*yod*,"[28] the students did know Arabic; one was the anonymous student who had posed the question, and the second was R. Isaac of Acre himself. R. Isaac's testimony does not hint at where this discussion took place; in theory, he could have learned Abulafia's teachings in Italy, while on his way from Palestine to Spain, or in Spain itself—though this possibility does not seem reasonable to me. I know of no evidence in relation to Spain concerning Abulafia's disciples' circulating his teachings there. Sicily, on the other hand, was Abulafia's bastion—but at present we have no evidence concerning his students' activities after 1291.[29] It is therefore more reasonable to assume that R. Isaac of Acre learned Abulafia's Kabbalah from one of his disciples in Palestine and not in Sicily. In this context, the fact that a possible son of R. Solomon ben Moses of Galilee—R. Joseph ben Solomon—is mentioned in a manuscript that includes material from *'Oẓar Ḥayyim*, may be significant.

One further piece of evidence should be added to the arguments we have cited as proof of the existence of Abulafia's Kabbalah in Palestine. In material belonging to R. Nathan (who was, in my opinion, R. Isaac of Acre's mentor and also, apparently, a disciple of Abulafia[30]) there appears a unique Sufic concept whose particulars are known to us only through Eastern Sufism. The first evidence concerning a system of five worlds, including one of the imagination—*'alam al-mithal*, or *'olam ha-demut* in the phrasing of the collections based on R. Nathan's work appear only in the thirteenth-century commentary of Abdel Rizak al-Kashani on a work of Ibn 'Arabi.[31] Thus R. Nathan's Hebrew material reflects a tradition put into writing in the East in the thirteenth century. It is difficult to assume that the synthesis between R. Abraham Abulafia's concepts and those of Sufism—which is undoubtedly of Oriental origin—found its way to the West within a short period of time and only there became known to R. Isaac ben Samuel of Acre. In my view, this Kabbalist served as the main conduit for transmission of the Kabbalistic-Sufic synthesis from the Orient to the Occident—a fascinating "migration" of Kabbalistic theory which was locked into a restricted circle in thirteenth-century Barcelona.[32] Abulafia, who absorbed the teachings of this group, conveyed these concepts to Italy and Greece and developed them over the 1270s and 1280s. By the end of the latter decade, his teachings had reached Palestine where they blended with the Pietist-Sufic trend of thought, and then returned in the 1290s to Spain. There, the Kabbalistic-Sufic synthesis had particular influence on the Kabbalistic doctrine of worlds—an influence discernible in the writings of R. Elnathan ben Moses Kalkish and R. Abraham ben Solomon Adrutiel.[33]

It seems, however, that Abulafia's doctrines continued to bear fruit in Palestine itself after the thirteenth century as well. The work *Baddei Ha-Aron*, composed in Palestine by R. Shem-Tov Ibn Gaon, contains a description of a vision of a Torah scroll in the form of a circle, a vision very similar to that witnessed by R. Isaac ben Samuel of Acre and described in *'Oẓar Ḥayyim*.[34] Abulafia's Palestinian Kabbalistic doctrines spread in an unprecedented fashion in the sixteenth century.[35] *Sulam ha-'Aliyah*, written by R. Judah Albotini in Jerusalem in the early sixteenth century, is based entirely on R. Abulafia's *Ḥayyei Ha'Olam HaBa* and on *Sha'arei Ẓedek*. Abulafia's influence is visible too in *'Even HaShoham* by R. Joseph

Ibn Ẓaiaḥ (Jerusalem, 1539). The greatest of the Kabbalists of Safed, such as R. Solomon ben Moses Alkabeẓ, R. Moses Cordovero, and especially R. Ḥayyim Vital were influenced by Abulafia's *Ḥayyei Ha'Olam HaBa'* and *'Or HaSekhel.* A sizeable collection of sections taken from Abulafia's mysticism, found in a manuscript copied by Menahem Papu (one of the Beit-El Kabbalists),[36] is but one source of evidence of the deep impact Abulafia's techniques had on the Beit-El group. In addition, traces of mystical-Sufic synthesis found in *'Oẓar Ḥayyim* are apparent in the writings of R. Judah Albotini[37] and R. Ḥayyim Vital, and in R. Elijah de Vidas's work, *Reshit Ḥokhmah.*[38]

It appears then that R. Abraham Abulafia's kabbalah underwent a turning point toward Sufism with its acceptance by the Kabbalists of Palestine in the thirteenth century. This development, and the extreme spiritualization of Judaism apparent in Abulafia's own writings, are apparently the factors responsible for the nearly total absence of discussion of the special status of the Land of Israel or of exceptional use of symbols linked thereto in prophetic Kabbalah. At first sight, this seems paradoxical; the Spanish Kabbalists and especially the book of *Zohar* develop the symbolism of the Land of Israel and locate the central work of Kabbalah there, while the mystics of Palestine itself seem to have nothing to say on the subject! We say "seem to," because the mystical systems which stress extreme ecstatic experience tend to downgrade accepted religious ritual, while objects associated with that ritual, such as the Torah, the Temple and its appurtenances, become, in the system of Abulafia, labels or symbols of internal events—stations in the spiritual life of the mystic.[39] This does not hold true in moderate mystical systems such as the Kabbalah of *sefirot* (Divine Emanations)—systems in which the mystic's spiritual life revolves around ritual, draws sustenance from ritual and strengthens it. One who feels in direct proximity to the Deity has no further need for any such means of ascent; at least, such a "journey" cannot be essential.[40] But if ecstatic Kabbalah did not make an important contribution to the enrichment of the concept of "the Land of Israel" as a mystical symbol—as did the *Zohar*—it is nonetheless true that the Land of Israel, Palestine, made a great contribution to this school of thought. This contribution, ironically, was nurtured by Muslim mysticism.

Notes to Chapter 6

1. See G. Scholem, "From Researcher to Kabbalist" (Hebrew), *Tarbiẓ* 6 (1935): 96-97.

2. R. Solomon ben Samuel Petit is an exception; he expounded Torah in the

yeshiva of Acre, though he left behind no Kabbalistic writings. Evidence of his mystical teachings may be found in R. Isaac of Acre's *Me'irat 'Einayim.* See H. Graetz, *History of the Jews* (Philadelphia, 1956), vol. IV, pp. 626-628.

3. See text published by A. Jellinek, *Beit ha-Midrash,* (Jerusalem, 1938) part 3, p. XL.

4. J. Prawer, *A History of the Latin Kingdom of Jerusalem,* 2 (Hebrew) (Jerusalem, 1971), pp. 420ff. Concerning Acre as a gateway for travellers at the time, see A. Grabois, "Acre as the Gateway of Jewish Immigration to Palestine in the Crusader Period," *Studies in the History of the Jewish People and the Land of Israel,* 2 (Hebrew) (Haifa, 1972), pp. 93-106.

5. It has been preserved nearly in its entirety in MS Paris BN 853, fols. 38a-79a. I have recently identified three pages belonging to this book from Geniza material (MS Cambridge T-S, Ar. 48.194) sent to me by Dr. Paul Fenton for identification. It seems reasonable to assume that the existence of the leaves of precisely this Abulafian work in the Geniza material is relevant to the subject of this article, namely our assertion that Abulafia's treatise was in the hands of Oriental—perhaps Sufi-biased—Jews. Details on this treatise may be found in Idel, *Abraham Abulafia,* p. 18.

6. MS. Paris BN 853, fol. 44b.

7. Ibid., 79a.

8. Concerning this work, see Gottlieb, *Studies* pp. 231-247.

9. Concerning this work, see G. Scholem, *"Sha'arei Ẓedek:* A Kabbalistic Essay of the School of Thought of R. Abraham Abulafia, attributed to R. Shem Tov (Ibn Gaon?)" (Hebrew), *Kiryat Sefer* 1 (1924): 127-139.

10. MS. Jerusalem 8° 148, fol. 18a.

11. See Scholem, MSS, p. 34.

12. See *Responsa of Solomon b. Adret,* part 1, sect. 548.

13. See G. Scholem, "A Note on a Kabbalistical Treatise on Contemplation," *Melanges Offerts a H. Corbin* (Teheran, 1973), p. 670, no. 3; Scholem (Note 9 above) p. 132.

14. N. Wieder, *Islamic Influences on Jewish Worship* (Oxford, 1947); S. D. Goitein, "Abraham Maimonides and his Pietist Circle," *Jewish Medieval and Renaissance Studies,* ed. A. Altmann (Cambridge, Mass., 1967), pp. 150ff.; S. D. Goitein, "R. Abraham Maimonides and his Pietist Circle" (Hebrew), *Tarbiẓ* 33 (1964): 181-197. Concerning Abraham Maimonides's relationship with Acre, see Grabois (above, n. 4), p.102-103.

15. For a summation, see G. D. Cohen, "The Soteriology of R. Abraham Maimuni," *PAAJR* 35 (1967): 75-98; 36 (1968): 33-56.

16. G. Vajda, "The Mystical Doctrine of Rabbi Obadyah, grandson of Moses Maimonides," *JJS* 6 (1955): 213-225; see now, Fenton (ed.), *The Treatise.*

17. F. Rosenthal, "A Judaeo-Arabic Work under Sufic Influence," *HUCA* 15 (1940): 433-484. Concerning two Jewish-Sufic manuscripts in Arabic, see Vajda (above, n. 16), p. 222; Fenton *The Treatise* p. 62 n. 89-90.

18. Ed. D. H. Baneth (Hebrew) (Jerusalem, 1939). On p. XXVII, Davidowich notes that Arabic and Hebrew manuscripts were written in "Syrian Mughrabi Rabbinic" hand. This work was little-known in the West. As Vajda has shown, of the two passages quoted by Steinschneider, only one (that of Don Benveniste ben Lavie, of the early fifteenth century) indeed parallels *Perakim be-Haẓlaḥah.* The second and later quotation was discovered by Vajda in R. Joseph Yaabeẓ's commentary on *Avot.* See G. Vajda, "Une Citation non Signalée du Chapitre sur la Beatitude attribué à Moise Maimonide," *REJ* 130 (1971): 305-306. Wieder (above, n. 14), pp. 45-46, assumed that R. Abraham, the son of Maimonides, is the real author of this treatise, whereas Fenton (above, n. 16), pp. 44-46, proposed R. 'Obadyāh—R. Abraham's son—as the possible author. The present author pointed to a certain affinity between the concept "world of imagination" in R. Natan's—R. Isaac of Acre's master—*collectanaea* and the view of the imaginative faculty in the Chapter on Beatitude, see Idel, "R. Jehuda Ḥallewah and his book Ẓafenat Pa'aneaḥ" (Hebrew), *Shalem* 4 (Jerusalem, 1984): 119-148.

19. *Perakim be-Haẓlaḥah* p. 11; see also notes 22-23 below.

20. Gottlieb *Studies* p. 233, n. 7.

21. See my article concerning the prohibition of study of kabbala before the age of forty, *AJS Review* 5, section B (1980): 8-10; see also the similar usage of the expression *adam katan* as microcosmos in Abulafia and R. Isaac of Acre, and the occurrence of the same phrase in *Sha'arei Ẓedek.* Cf. M. Idel, "The World of Angels in Anthropomorphic Shape" (Hebrew), *I. Tishby Festschrift* (Jerusalem, 1984), p. 57, n. 215; Idel, "Kabbalistic Materials from the School of Rabbi David ben Yehudah he Ḥasid" (Hebrew), *Jerusalem Studies in Jewish Thought,* II, 2 (1982-1983): 177-178, n. 40.

22. See *Sha'arei Ẓedek,* MS. Jerusalem 8° 148, fol. 65b, and *'Oẓar Ḥayyim,* MS. Moscow-Günzburg 775, fol. 161b; see also Gottlieb *Studies,* p. 237.

23. See *Perakim be-Haẓlaḥah,* p. 7, line 14. The meaning of *shekiy'ah* (sinking) to both these kabbalists, and in *Perakim be-Haẓlaḥah,* is that of *devekut* with the spiritual world, the universal intelligence or the universal soul. We may find similar application of this concept in Ibn Tufayl's *Ḥai Ben Yoktan.* See S. S. Hawi, *Islamic Naturalism and Mysticism* (Leiden, 1974), pp. 150-151.

24. Idel, *The Mystical Experience* pp. 120-121.

25. See chapter V above.

26. MS. Moscow-Günzburg 775, fol. 131b. Cf. the extant fragments of *'Oẓar*

Ḥayyim, MS. Sassoon 919, p. 217: "One day during this month, I, a young man, was sitting in the company of veteran students who loved wisdom"; afterwards, R. Isaac relates a discussion concerning the *golem*. We should mention here the description of R. Isaac's teacher in *'Oẓar Ḥayyim*, MS. Moscow-Günzburg 775, fol. 100a: ". . . as I have received from the paragon of his age in matters of modesty, kabbalistic wisdom, philosophy, and secrets of the combinations of letters, he was most won to instruct me in the ten *sefirot* of *belimah* and in the ways. . . . " This description, which is not in keeping with what we know about R. Abraham Abulafia himself—for he did not tend to deal in pneumatic contemplation of ten *sefirot*—is nevertheless in keeping with his theory, a blend of philosophy and combinations of letters. We should note that the addition of "kabbalistic wisdom" apparently refers to dealings in ten *sefirot*. Such study, in addition to philosophy and combinations of letters, is found in *Sha'arei Ẓedek*. In one surviving fragment of *'Oẓar Ḥayyim*, MS. New York JTS, 2263, fol. 14b, R. Isaac discusses a conversation between himself and "a genuine kabbalistic scholar (who) came from Damascus with kabbalistic wisdom"; this sage reveals to him a method involving combination of the letters of God's name.

27. Idel, *The Mystical Experience*, p. 134.

28. The discussion deals with a section of a work by R. Abraham Abulafia entitled *Ḥayyei Ha'Olam Ha-Ba'*. See MS. Oxford 1582, fol. 53a, and Idel, *The Mystical Experience*, pp. 116-118.

29. In that year, during which the traces of R. Abraham Abulafia were lost, R. Isaac left Palestine.

30. On this, see chapter 5 above.

31. H. Corbin, *Creative Imagination in the Sufism of Ibn 'Arabi* (Princeton, 1969), pp. 360-361, note 19.

32. In 1270/1271, R. Abraham Abulafia participated in a circle to which R. Baruch Togarmi belonged. It should be noted that R. Abraham ibn Ḥisdai had translated Algazali's *Mo'oznei Ẓedek* in Barcelona a generation earlier, and this work contains a brief description of Sufism. It is likely that Sufic concepts well-known in the West, such as in the quotations found in *Ḥovot HaLevavot*, contributed to a certain extent to the crystallization of "prophetic" kabbala in the early 1250s. The impression these concepts left, however, is rather weak. Concerning Algazali's description of the Sufis, see G. C. Anawati, L. Gardet, *Mystique musulmane* (Paris, 1961), pp. 186-187.

33. See chapter V above.

34. See Idel, *The Mystical Experience* pp. 109-116 and *'Even Sapir* by R. Elnathan ben Moses Kalkish, MS. Paris BN 727, fol. 10a. Concerning R. Shem Tov Ibn Gaon's dealings in kabbala of letter-combinations, see D. S. Levinger, "Rabbi Shem Tov ben Abraham Ibn Gaon" (Hebrew), *Sefunot* 7 (1963):17. Concerning a possible relationship between the commentaries of R. Shem Tov and R. Abraham

Abulafia on the dictum *min'u beneikhem min ha-higayon*, see Idel (above, n. 21), appendix, n. 17.

35. See G. Scholem, M. Beit Arié, *Introduction to the Book "Ma'amar Mesharei Kitrin" by R. Abraham ben-Eliezer ha-Levi* (Hebrew), (Jerusalem, 1978), pp. 15-16.

36. MS. Musajoff 30, film 22858, Institute for the Microfilming of Hebrew Manuscripts, JNUL, Jerusalem.

37. See Scholem, *MSS.*, p. 226, n. 2. On the influence of a Sufic view on the Safedian kabbalist R. Jehudah Ḥallewah, see my article (above, n. 18).

38. Gottlieb, *Studies* p. 238, n. 14, p. 246, n. 25; M. Pachter, *Homiletic and Ethical Literature of Safed in the Sixteenth Century* (unpublished doctoral dissertation, Hebrew, Jerusalem, 1976), p. 370, n. 48; and see below, n. 40. The unpublished section of *Sha'arei Kedushah* by R. Ḥayyim Vital mentions R. Isaac explicitly. See, e.g. MS. British Library, Margoliouth cat. 749, fol. 16b, in which the matter under discussion is the relationship between the soul and the Divine Presence. In his work *Sefer HaShemot*, R. Moses Zacut cites in the name of R. Ḥayyim Vital a tradition in the name of R. Isaac ben Samuel of Acre. See also R. Ḥayyim Joseph David Azulai's comments in *Midbar Kedemot*, part 8, section 17, item 11.

39. Idel, *Abraham Abulafia*, pp. 174-177. Concerning the Ka'aba and the well-preserved tablet of the Sufis, see G. C. Anawati and L. Gardet (above, n. 32), pp. 59-60; see also Corbin (above, n. 31), pp. 384-385.

40. We should mention here R. Isaac ben Samuel of Acre's commentary on the dictum "Prophecy does not dwell outside the Land of Israel": "The secret of 'outside of the Land' (Israel) and of 'the Land of Israel' . . . The 'Land' [*'ereẓ*] does not signify the earth of dust (i.e., the geographic land), but the lump of dust (i.e., the human body) in which souls dwell. The 'Land' is the palace of the souls; it is flesh and blood. The soul that dwells in earth [*ba-'areẓ*] which derives from Jacob's seed (i.e. stock) certainly dwells in the Land of Israel. Even if the soul dwells outside the Land (i.e., geographically), the Shekhina (i.e. the Presence of God) will rest upon it since it is definitely in the Land (i.e. earth) of Israel. But the soul which dwells in the Land (i.e., geographically) which does not derive from the seed of Jacob . . . who is Israel, our father, certainly dwells 'outside the Land' even if it is in the Land of Israel, inside Jerusalem. Neither will the Shekhinah dwell upon it, nor the spirit of prophecy, since it is certainly 'outside the Land'." (*'Oẓar Ḥayyim*, MS. Moscow-Günzburg 775, fol. 94a). Here, the Land of Israel has become an appellation for every member of the People of Israel; a Divine Presence capable of radiating only on these souls is a Sufic motif recurring in *'Oẓar Ḥayyim* (fol. 71b). See Werblowsky concerning the appearance of this motif in the kabbala of Safed and its connection with R. Isaac ben Samuel of Acre and with Sufism: Werblowsky, *Karo* pp. 58-59. See also Gottlieb, *Studies*, p. 242.

Concerning use of this Sufic motif in interpreting the Greek myth related by a Christian to R. Isaac of Acre, see Idel, "Prometheus in Jewish Garb" (Hebrew),

Eshkolot 5 (1980): 119-121; and above, n. 38. See also my article, "The Land of Israel in Medieval Kabbalah" *Land of Israel: Jewish Perspectives* ed. L. Hoffman (Notre Dame, IN: Notre Dame University Press, 1986), pp. 178-180.

Chapter 7

Hitbodedut as Concentration in Ecstatic Kabbalah

Individual and community in Jewish spirituality

Rabbinic Judaism, more than as the religion of a people, took shape as the religion of Jewish communities. From the time that the Temple cult ceased, those commandments applying to Israel as a nation ceased to have validity or contemporary force; the most significant religious-social framework that remained—and was even strengthened—following the destruction of the Temple was the community, whose focus was the synagogue. The common divine worship—prayer—was transformed into the center of religious life; it required the assembling of ten men as an essential precondition for the performance of many of its most important components. Halakhic thought made the gathering of the community a more and more essential part of the religious cult and rejected, directly or indirectly, tendencies toward individualistic separatism. Prayer, Torah study, circumcision, and marriage became understood as events which the individual performs within society and in which he must participate. Solitude, as a religious value or as a means of attaining religious ends, was preserved as a part of sacred history: the solitude of Moses on Mount Sinai, that of Elijah in the desert, and that of the high priest in the Holy of Holies became ideals that were part of the heritage of the past. The individual was no longer able to achieve perfection by separation from the company of other men: he was now required to join them in order to achieve religious wholeness.

This tendency, the literary expressions of which appear in the Talmud and the Midrash, was inherited by the Kabbalah. The very fact that several of its leading thinkers—the RABaD (R. Abraham ben David of Posquières, ca. 1125-1198), the RaMBaN (R. Moses ben Naḥman, 1194-1270), and the RaShBA (R. Solomon ben Abraham Ibn Adret, ca. 1235-1310)—were themselves Halakhic authorities, and simultaneously communal leaders, is sufficient proof of the need for continuity. The Kabbalists accepted the framework of the *miẓwot* as self-evident and fought for its strengthening and protection against challenges, both internal and external. The strikingly small number of original prayers composed by the Kabbalists, the exegetical nature of Kabbalistic literature from its earliest inception, and, above all, the nonexistence of separate Kabbalistic groups[1] or societies who separated themselves from the organized framework of the people as a whole, are all indirect evidence of a conscious and deliberate tendency to avoid turning the Kabbalah[2] into a focus of controversy and division among the members of the community. We thus find here an interesting phenomenon, different from analogous processes in Christianity and Islam, regarding the organization of groups with mystical tendencies.

In the latter two religions, mysticism is associated with the formation of brotherhoods or monastic orders, and most of the mystical literature, whether Christian or Moslem, is written within their framework. It follows from this that the full realization of the life of the spirit is connected, in both religions, with the choice of a way of life markedly different from that of most of their coreligionists. This way of life is sometimes characterized by separation from the life of the "lay" society; at other times the monk or devotee may continue to be active within society but will observe special norms and practices. These organizational forms are based upon the voluntary acceptance of limitations and obligations over and above those normally accepted as religious norms on the part of their members. The assumption is that these rules of behavior constitute a framework that makes the development of the life of the spirit possible.[3] Generally speaking, the establishment of organizations of this type is associated with the quest by these or other individuals for personal religious or spiritual attainments.[4] The "mobile" and nomadic character of both Christian and Muslim religious orders also stems from this.

At the time of its inception as a historical phenomenon, the Kabbalah did not know of any special organizational system; there were no specific practices or customs designed especially for the Kabbalists.[5] The spiritual life was generaly strengthened by intensifying the spiritual effort invested in the fulfillment of the *miẓwot*, which as such, were obligatory upon the entire people, or by deepening the understanding of the reasons underlying the *miẓwot*. At times, non-Halakhic means of attaining communion with God were set, but these were designed so as not to conflict even indirectly with the fulfillment of the *miẓwot*. Moreover, the carrying out of these practices was, in any event, extremely limited in time and was not intended to replace the Halakhic framework. Nor did they demand for themselves authority comparable to that of the Halakhah.[6] In practice, Kabbalah may be defined as a sort of *regula* of the Jewish religion: because of the broad scope of the Halakhic system, the fulfillment of the 613 commandments could be seen as a religious challenge which, despite its being normative, allowed for departure from the norm when the *miẓwot* were performed with Kabbalistic intentions. If the *regula* in Christianity was intended to add religious demands, expressed in both internal and external behavioral changes, the Kabbalah, generally speaking, was concerned with inner change and, at least in the beginning, did not tend to add or detract from the Halakhic norm. The external difference in behavior between the Kabbalist, the philosopher, and the Halakhist was far smaller than that between a monk and a lay Christian. If suffices to contrast the abstention from marriage as a decisive factor in the formation of monasticism or the special dress of both the monks and the Sufis with the total absence of anything of this kind among the Kabbalists. Put differently, the transformation of an ordinary Jew into a Kabbalist did not involve any discontinuity in his outward behavior, as opposed to what generally happened to one who joined a Sufi brotherhood or a monastic order.

Against the background of what we have said above, the appearance of the first discussions of the religious value of seclusion (*hitbodedut*) in medieval Jewish texts must be seen as indication of external influence. This is clearly the case in the discussions of the subject in the book *Ḥovot HaLevavot* (*Duties of the Heart*) by R. Baḥyah Ibn Paquda[7] (second half of the eleventh century), in which the Sufi influence is clear; this phenomenon reappears in the circle of Pietists (*Hasidim*) associated with R. Abraham Maimonides (1186-1237).

I wish to discuss here the specific meaning of the term *hitbodedut* within a particular Kabbalistic school, namely, that of prophetic Kabbalah founded by R. Abraham Abulafia[8] and the influence of that school upon the Kabbalah of Safed. I will analyze the texts in which the term *hitbodedut* has the specific meaning of "concentrated thought," as part of a clearly defined mystical technique. This meaning may have been influenced by the Sufi understanding of inner contemplation[9] or spiritual meditation or by the Sufi terms *taġrid* or *tafrid*, whose meaning approximates that of *hitbodedut* in some texts of ecstatic Kabbalah.

This meaning does not appear in any of the major Hebrew dictionaires. Nor have students of Jewish philosophy or of the Kabbalah discussed this meaning of the term, but there is no doubt that this understanding will contribute to a more exact interpretation of several important philosophic texts that until now have been differently understood.[10]

The Sufi background

The connection between pronouncing the name of God and *hitbodedut*, in the sense of seclusion in a special place, is already present in Sufism. The similarity of Abulafia's approach to this subject to the Sufi system is well known, and one need not assume that this is mere chance.[11] It is possible that he learned of this approach from his teacher, R. Baruch Togarmi, who was apparently of Eastern background, to judge by the name. Sufism may also have influenced Abulafia directly,[12] even though there is no evidence from his writings that he had any contact with Muslim mystics.[13] The precise way in which certain Sufi elements entered Abulafia's thought must remain an open question; however, it is appropriate to discuss here, in relation to *hitbodedut*, a description of the Sufi practice of *dhikr*, which was likely to have been known to Jewish authors from the mid-thirteenth century on: I refer to a passage in R. Abraham Ibn Ḥasdai's Hebrew translation of a work by the Persian Muslim theologian, jurist, and mystic, Abu Ḥamid Al-Ghazali (1058-1111), known as Moznei Ẓedek. The Sufi "path" is portrayed in the Hebrew version as follows:[14]

> I decided to follow this path, and I took counsel with an old teacher of the Sufi worship as to how I ought to behave regarding continual reading of the books of religion.[15] And he answered me thus: Know that the path towards this matter is to cut off and cease completely all of those things by which one is attached to this world, until your heart will not think at all of wife, or children, or money or home or wisdom or rulership. But bring yourself to a place such that their presence or absence becomes a matter of indifference. Then seclude yourself in a corner[16] and make do with the divine service of the commandments as ordered, and sit with a heart empty of all thoughts and worry, and let all your thoughts be only of the supreme God.[17] And accustom your tongue[18] to say the name of the living God, let it not cease to call upon the Lord continually, as in the saying of the prophet, "let them not depart from your mouth." And all this in order to understand God and to apprehend Him, until you reach the stage that, were you to allow your tongue to move by itself, it would run quickly to say this, because of its habit to do this thing. And afterwards accustom yourself to another thing, that is, to meditate in your heart and soul, in your thoughts alone, without any movement of your tongue. And then become accustomed to another thing, that there remain

> in your heart only the meaning of the words, not the letters of the words or the form of speech, but only the subject itself, abstract, firmly fixed in your heart, as something obligatory and constant. The choice is in your hand only up to this limit. After that there is no choice; you can but constantly remove the sickness of destructive lusts—but after that your own [free] will ceases, and yours is only to hope for that which may appear, of the opening of the gates of mercy, what is seen of Him to those who cleave to the exalted Name, which is a small part of what was seen by the prophets [. . .] but the level of those who cling to God cannot be told, nor their exalted qualities, and their imagination, and their [moral] virtues. These are the ways of the Sufis.

The final goal of the Sufi path, as described in this Hebrew text, is to cling to God. The essence of this clinging is discussed immediately before the passage quoted above:

> And to always hope and wait for God to open for him the gates of mercy, as these things were revealed to those who cling to Him and to the prophets, and their souls acquired that perfection of which man is capable—not through learning, but by separation from this world and *hitbodedut* and casting off all desires, and making his goal to receive God with all his heart and all his soul. And whoever shall be with God, God will be with him.

According to the Hebrew version of Al-Ghazali, the Sufis had a fixed path by which they attained communion with God, which involved several clearly delimited stages: (1) separation from the world; (2) indifference or equanimity; (3) solitude (*hitbodedut*); (4) repetition of God's name; and (5) communion with God. Despite the general similarity between certain of the various stations on the way toward *devequt* (clinging to God) in Al-Ghazali, and parallel steps in Abulafia, the difference between the approaches of these two mystics is clear. First, equanimity is mentioned neither in any of Abulafia's own writings nor in the book *Sha'arei Ẓedek*, which belongs to his circle. Second, in Al-Ghazali, *hitbodedut* refers to physical solitude in a secluded room, whereas in Abulafia it is sometimes understood in this way but at other times, where it is a precondition for pronouncing the names of God, it is understood in the sense of the concentration of one's mental activity. Third, the recitations in Al-Ghazali differ from those in Abulafia: Al-Ghazali proposes pronouncing the name with one's tongue, in one's heart, and fixing its meaning in one's thought; Abulafia proposes reading the name and combining its letters in writing, verbally, and in one's thought. From this, it follows that we cannot base his system upon that of Al-Ghazali, at least not directly and not in full.

Hitbodedut in the writings of Abraham Abulafia

Most of the discussions of *hitbodedut* that were written prior to Abulafia saw it as an activity engaged in by Moses, the prophets, and the pious men of ancient times. The approach of both Jewish philosophers and Kabbalists was based on the assumption that prophecy was a phenomenon of the past. For this reason, their discussions of this subject must be seen primarily as literary activity—exegesis of the Bible or of talmudic sayings—rather than as rules for actual practice.

This situation was radically changed in the writings of Abulafia. As one who saw himself as a prophet and messiah, he believed that his particular form of Kabbalah paved the way for mystical experience for all who would follow his path. For this reason, the tone of his writing is clearly practical; his writings, from which we shall quote below, are intended as guides to "prophecy" for his contemporaries, and the autobiographical hints therein leave no doubt that he himself followed these techniques and enjoyed their fruits. These two facts are clear signs of the actualization of the discussion concerning *hitbodedut*, whose effects are also felt among later Kabbalists, under the direct or indirect influence of Abulafia's writings.

In the commentary on his work *Sefer Ha'Edut*, written on the occasion of his abortive attempt in 1280 to meet with Pope Nicholas III, Abulafia writes:

> The Pope commanded all the guards of his house, when he was in Soriano . . . that should Raziel[19] come to speak with him in the name of the Jews, that they take him immediately, and that he not see him at all, but that he be taken outside of the city and burnt. . . . And this matter was made known to Raziel, but he paid no attention to the words of those who said this, but he practiced *hitbodedut* and saw visions and wrote them down, and thus came about this book.

The close connection between *hitbodedut* and revelation is better explained if we assume that Abulafia concentrated in order to receive an illumination which would guide him in this critical situation, when he was also pressed for time. From what we know, Abulafia arrived at the palace in Soriano right at the time he wrote these things, so that it is difficult to imagine that he found a house or room in which to seclude himself, as he advises in his other writings. It is clear that this is not a casual suggestion, nor a historical description of the prophets, but a first-hand account of the use of *hitbodedut* in order to attain revelation. *Hitbodedut* in the sense of concentration appears to have been part of a way of life, and not only a sporadic activity performed in times of trouble or danger. In an epistle known as *The Seven Paths of the Torah* (*Sheva' Netivot HaTorah*), Abulafia enumerates a long list of works which he learned, but which did not bring him to "prophecy":[20]

> But none of this brought me to apprehension of the Active Intellect, to the point that I could take pride in prophecy, that I could fulfill the verse, "For in this shall the proud man take pride . . ." [Jeremiah 9:23] until I received this apprehension in actuality, and I placed my soul in my hands according to the way of the Kabbalists, in knowing the Name alone. Yet nevertheless there were strong obstacles[21] against me because of my sins, and they held me back from the path[22] of *hitbodedut*, until the Holy Spirit left me, as is the case today.

Abulafia here states explicitly that it was only the actual practical use of the technique of combination of letters of the divine name which brought about these revelations. This technique is referred to as "the way of the Kabbalists," and it constitutes the particular Kabbalistic method advocated by him. The expression "the way of *hitbodedut*," may also allude to this, which is why it makes sense to assume that *hitbodedut* refers not to isolation from society but to the use of a Kabbalistic technique of combining letters,[23] for which mental concentration is indispensible. An alternative interpretation of this incident, that Abulafia was unsuccessful in isolating himself from society, seems to me to be incorrect: we know that he attempted to disseminate his teachings in public and that he was persecuted by his opponents, who certainly would not have objected were the prophet-messiah to abandon his public activity and withdraw to some isolated place to engage in his own private, peculiar form of Kabbalah. It seems to me that Abulafia's comments concerning "obstacles" are to be interpreted as referring to disturbances, whether internal or external, to his own powers of concentration.

Support for this understanding of Abulafia's comments may be found elsewhere in his epistle *Sheva' Netivot HaTorah*. In the description of the seven ways to interpret the Torah, he mentions, at the end of the fifth path:

> This path is the beginning of the wisdom of letter-combination in general, and is only fitting to those who fear God and take heed of His name. And the sixth path . . . is suitable to those who practice concentration (*hitbodedut*), who wish to approach God, in a closeness[24] such that His activity—may He be blessed—will be known in them to themselves.

It also seems to me that one may discern here the connection between the "practitioners of *hitbodedut*" and the "science of letter combination." In this passage as well, he speaks of closeness to God, but it is still only a stage preceding the seventh path (appropriate to prophets), through which there comes about the "apprehension of the essence of the Ineffable Name." It follows from this that the "path of *hitbodedut*" is an earlier stage in the process intended for the attainment of prophecy. It must be stressed that, despite the objective description of the practitioners of concentration, this is not only a theoretical discussion; the seven ways of reading or of interpreting the Torah do not refer to the distant past, but constitute a living option for the members of Abulafia's own generation, he having been the one to restore these older ways of reading. Abulafia saw himself as a prophet both to himself and to others—that is, as one who had undergone the final two stages along the path outlined in his epistle. For this reason, it seems that his words must be seen as an autobiographical testimony, from which point of view this text should be combined with the previous quotations, whose autobiographical character is quite evident.

A close relationship between letter combination and *hitbodedut* appears in the book *Ḥayyei Ha'Olam HaBa':*

> He must also be very expert in the secrets of the Torah and its wisdom, so that he may know what will occur to him in the circles[25] of the combination, and he will arouse himself to think of the image of the Divine prophetic Intellect. And when he begins to practice letter-combination in his *hitbodedut*, he will feel fear and trembling, and the hairs of his head will stand up and his limbs will tremble. (MS. Oxford, 1582 fol. 11b-12a.)

Here, *hitbodedut* designates the special concentration required by the Kabbalist in order to combine letters. This intense concentration involves physical side effects[26] that would be difficult to explain were they caused only by withdrawal from society.

In conclusion, we should emphasize the innovation involved in Abulafia's understanding of *hitbodedut* as concentration. According to extant Kabbalistic sources, he seems to have been the first Kabbalist to connect *hitbodedut* with a practical, detailed system to give the concept *hitbodedut* real content: essentially, the combination of letters and the vocalization associated with them. Later we shall see that the presence of an association between *hitbodedut* and letter combination or the recitation of divine names is likely to be a conclusive sign of the direct or indirect influence of Abulafia's Kabbalistic system.

Most of the texts to be discussed below were written in the Middle East, or by authors of Eastern origin. This striking fact is doubtless connected, first of all, with the relationship between Abulafia's system and

Sufism, a relationship acknowledged by the Kabbalists themselves. Second, as Abulafia's Kabbalah was subject to intense attack by the RaShBA[27], its influence within Spain itself was limited, which created an imbalance between the spread of prophetic Kabbalah in the East and its curtailment in the West. On the other hand, there is considerable discussion of *hitbodedut* among Jewish philosophers in Provence and Spain during the thirteenth to fifteenth centuries, albeit lacking in Abulafia's practical tone, in which classical prophecy is interpreted as a phenomenon attained through the help of *hitbodedut*, whether this is understood as concentration or as withdrawal from society. These discussions are likewise associated with Arabic philosophical texts, such as *Sefer Hanhagat HaMitboded* by Ibn Bajjah, or *Sefer Ḥay Ben Yoktan* by Ibn Tufail, and they later influenced the development of Kabbalah during the sixteenth century. On the other hand, the Spanish Jewish thinkers contemporary with the Kabbalists were influenced neither by Abulafia's doctrine of *hitbodedut* or that of his disciples nor by the Jewish-Sufic approaches of the school of Abraham Maimonides (1186-1237).

In the Abulafian Tradition

Among those works closest to Abulafia's system, one must include the book *Sha'arei Ẓedek;* this work, composed in Palestine in 1290 or 1295, clearly reflects knowledge of the Sufi approach. For our purposes, the anonymous author's comments concerning the influence of letter combination and *hitbodedut* are of particular significance: "And I, through the power of combination and of *hitbodedut*, there happened to me what happened with the light that I saw going with me, as I have mentioned in the book *Sha'arei Ẓedek.*"[28]

The experience of the "light," which occurs as a result of letter combination and *hitbodedut*, forms an interesting parallel to the Holy Spirit mentioned in the above quotations. Moreover, the author of *Sha'arei Ẓedek* also experiences "speech" as a result of the combination of the letters of the Holy Name.[29] This provides additional evidence of the practical use of *hitbodedut* in the sense of concentration. It seems to me that the term recurs in this sense in two additional passages in *Sha'arei Ẓedek.* One of these passages speaks of the progress of the philosopher beyond natural wisdom to divine wisdom and of the possibility that on some rare occasions the following might occur:

> He should greatly refine and draw downward the thought, and seek to concentrate on it, that no man should contaminate his thought . . . and he

will see that he has great power in all the wisdoms, for such is its nature, and he will say that a given matter was revealed to him as if a prophecy, and he will not know the cause.[30]

Hitbodedut is described here as a departure from the ordinary course of thought among the philosophers, which results in a revelation whose source no one can identify. In order to exemplify this path, the author relates a story pertaining to the Muslim philosopher Avicenna (980-1037):[31]

I found in the words of one of the great philosophers of his generation, namely, Ibn Sina, in which he said that he would concentrate while composing his great works, and when a certain subject or matter would be difficult for him, he would contemplate its intermediate proposition and draw his thought to it. And if the matter was still difficult, he would continue to think about it and drink a cup of strong wine, so as to fall asleep[32] . . . and the difficulty in that subject would be solved for him.

It seems to me that the preceding story does not refer to the withdrawal of that Arab philosopher from other people for two reasons: first, that *hitbodedut* and "drawing down of thought" are mentioned together in the first quotation from *Sha'arei Ẓedek*, which we quoted above; since *hitbodedut* is there connected with thought, it makes sense to assume that elsewhere too this anonymous Kabbalist would use this term in a similar or identical sense. Second, in another story parallel to the one quoted above, preserved in the writings of R. Isaac of Acre, who was apparently a contemporary of the author of *Sha'arei Ẓedek*, solitude is not mentioned at all.

The Evidence of Isaac of Acre

Traces of Abulafia's understanding of *hitbodedut*, together with other additions whose source is apparently in the Pietistic-Sufi environment within which he grew up, are found in the works of R. Isaac ben Samuel of Acre (late thirteenth to mid-fourteenth century).[33] In the book *Me'irat 'Einayim*, he writes:

He who merits the secret of communion [with the divine] will merit the secret of equanimity (*hishtawwut*), and if he receives this secret, then he will also know the secret of *hitbodedut*,[34] and once he has known the secret of *hitbodedut*, he will receive the Holy Spirit, and from that prophecy, until he shall prophesy and tell future things.

Separation from or equanimity toward worldly things, which is called *hishtawwut* (equanimity), makes possible *hitbodedut*, which here clearly refers to concentration. According to R. Isaac, a condition of *ataraxia*[35] ("absence of passion," a term used in the Cynic and Stoic tradition), is necessary for concentration, which leads, as in the case of Abulafia, to the Holy Spirit, and even to prophecy.[36] One should note here the introduction into the context of Kabbalistic thought of equanimity as a precondition of *hitbodedut*—an idea found neither in the writings of Abulafia[37] nor in *Sha'arei Ẓedek*. Its appearance in R. Isaac of Acre is another important addition based on Sufi influence. Further on in the same passage, the author quotes another Kabbalist who has not yet been identified by scholars, referred to by the acronym ABNeR:[38]

> R. Abner[39] said to me that a man who was a lover of wisdom[40] came to one of the practitioners of concentration, and asked to be received as one of them. They replied: "My son, may you be blessed from heaven, for your intention is a good one. But please inform me, have you achieved equanimity (*hishtawwut*) or not." He said to him: "Master, explain your words." He said to him: "My son, if there are two people, one who honors you and one of whom despises you, are they the same in your eyes or not?" He replied: "By the life of my soul, master, I derive pleasure and satisfaction from the one who honors me, and pain from the one who despises me, but I do not take vengeance or bear a grudge." He said to him: "My son, go in peace, for so long as you have not achieved equanimity, so that your soul feels the contempt done to you, you are not yet ready to link your thoughts on High, that you may come and concentrate. But go, and subdue your heart still more in truth, until you shall be equanimous, and then you may concentrate." And the cause of his equanimity[41] is the attachment of his thoughts to God, for cleaving and attachment of the thought to God cause man to feel neither the honor nor the contempt that people show him.

We have here two traditions concerning the interrelationship among cleaving and equanimity and concentration. R. Isaac's opinion, which places attachment to God in one's thought before equanimity,[42] appears in the first quotation, as well as at the end of the second passage, beginning with the words "and the cause"; this conclusion constitutes, in my opinion, R. Isaac's statement of his own view, which differs from that of R. ABNeR, who claims that equanimity is the condition for attaining *devekut*, and that concentration (*hitbodedut*) is only possible thereafter. All this indicates that R. Isaac had before him two traditions concerning this matter: one which he advocated and which was close to that of Abulafia, and the other that of the unknown Kabbalist, R. ABNeR. The appearance of the discussion concerning the connection between equanimity and concentration in R. ABNeR indicates that R. Isaac was in contact with Kabbalists who were influenced by Sufism. Since R. ABNeR is already quoted by R. Isaac at the beginning of his book *Me'irat 'Einayim*,[43] it makes sense to assume that R. Isaac was familiar with Sufi concepts even before he began writing this book, which is today considered his earliest work.

In his book *'Oẓar Ḥayyim*, R. Isaac again discusses the concept of *hitbodedut:*[44]

> I say that if a man does that which his soul [wishes] in the proper ways of *hitbodedut*, and his soul is immersed[45] in this light,[46] to look at it—then he will die like Ben Azzai[47] who "looked and died." And it is not proper to do this, for "precious in the eyes of the Lord is the death of His righteous ones" (Psalms 116, 15)] for whoever attempts to break through and to go beyond the Partition will be stricken, and a serpent shall bite him.

The expression "the ways of *hitbodedut*" is deserving of particular attention, recalling as it does the phrase we found above in Abulafia, *derekh ha-hitbodedut* (the path of *hitbodedut*). We noted there the close connection between concentration and letter combination. Despite the fact that the letter combinations are not mentioned in the passage from *'Oẓar Ḥayyim*, it seems to me possible that "the paths of *hitbodedut*" are in fact associated with them. Elsewhere in the same work, the author writes:[48]

> And by letter combinations, unifications, and reversals, he shall call up the tree of the knowledge of good and evil, righteous[49] and lying imagination, angels of mercy and angels of destruction, witnesses of innocence and of guilt, prosecutors and defenders, and he will be in danger of the same death as Ben Azzai.

It is difficult to avoid noticing the parallel between the danger of death connected with Ben Azzai in the two passages cited, and "the ways of *hitbodedut*" and "letter-combinations and unifications" as possible sources of danger. It follows from this that, as in Abulafia, *hitbodedut* in *'Oẓar Ḥayyim* is connected with the concentration needed to combine letters. Confirmation of this understanding of *hitbodedut* is found in another discussion in the book mentioned:[50]

> He who has been granted by God the spirit to concentrate and to engage in wisdom and in combination of letters and all its prerequisites, to separate himself from the objects of sensation and from physical pleasures, all of which are transient, and to pursue the Intellect and speak of it and of

spiritual pleasures, which are eternal life.

Here *hitbodedut*, that is, the ability to concentrate, is a gift from God, with the help of which one may progress in a process whose final end is clinging to spirituality. This process is connected with intellective soul overpowering the appetitive:[51]

> And live a life of suffering in your house of contemplation[52] lest your appetitive soul overpower your intellective soul, for by this you will merit to bring into[53] your intellective soul the divine plentitude, and in the Torah, that is to say, in the wisdom of combination and its prerequisites.

The purpose of meditation and letter combination is to bring the spiritual abundance into the intellective soul or the intellect; we learn this also from another source:[54] "The wise man, who comes to isolate himself and to concentrate and to bring down into his soul the divine spirit, through miraculous and awesome deeds . . . that itself is the divine spirit to attain the intelligibles."

Comparison of this passage with others quoted from *'Oẓar Ḥayyim* will aid us in establishing the meaning here of the verb *hitboded.* In all other passages, R. Isaac used this verb, or a noun derived from it, to refer to spiritual activity, for which reason the verbs *poresh* and *hitboded* should be seen as referring to two distinct activities: separation from society or from the objects of sensation, and intellectual concentration. This distinction applies also to this pair of verbs in other passages from R. Isaac:[55] "It is right in my eyes that those hermits (*perushim*) who practice concentration, who have removed from their souls the sensuous things, of which the holy spiritual poet R. Eliezer the Babylonian said . . ."[56] Again, "This is the secret of the modest hermit like practitioners of concentration who flee from the sensual things and cling to the intelligibles"[57]. The meaning of abandonment of the sensuous and clinging to the intelligibles, together with a quite detailed description of the process, appears in an extremely important passage attributed to R. Isaac of Acre, quoted in the book *Reshit Ḥokhmah* by R. Elijah de Vidas:[58]

> Thus we learn from one incident, recorded by R. Isaac of Acre, of blessed memory, who said that one day the princess came out of the bathhouse, and one of the idle people saw her and sighed a deep sigh and said: "Who would give me my wish, that I could do with her as I like!" And the princess answered and said: "That shall come to pass in the graveyard, but not here." When he heard these words he rejoiced, for he thought that she meant for him to go to the graveyard to wait for her there, and that she

> would come and he would do with her as he wished. But she did not mean this, but wished to say that only there (i.e., in death) great and small, young and old, despised and honored—all are equal, but not here, so that it is not possible that one of the masses should approach a princess. So that man rose and went to the graveyard and sat there, and devoted all his thoughts to her, and always thought of her form. And because of his great longing for her, he removed his thoughts from everything sensual, but put them continually on the form of that woman and her beauty. Day and night he sat there in the graveyard, there he ate and drank, and there he slept, for he said to himself, "If she does not come today, she will come tomorrow." This he did for many days, and because of his separation from the objects of sensation, and the exclusive attachment of his thought to one object and his concentration and his total longing, his soul was separated[59] from the sensual things and attached itself only to the intelligibles, until it was separated from all sensual things, including that woman herself, and he communed with God. And after a short time he cast off all sensual things and he desired only the Divine Intellect, and he became a perfect servant and holy man of God, until his prayer was heard and his blessing was beneficial to all passers-by, so that all the merchants and horsemen and foot-soldiers who passed by came to him to receive his blessing, until his fame spread far about. . . . Thus far is the quotation as far as it concerns us. And he went on at length concerning the high spiritual level of this ascetic, and R. Isaac of Acre wrote there in his account of the deeds of the ascetics, that he who does not desire a woman is like a donkey, or even less than one, the point being that from the objects of sensation one may apprehend the worship of God.

This story contains several of the concepts discussed above: communion in thought—"the attachment of the thought of his mind"—here precedes *hitbodedut*, that is, concentration, just as the secret of *devekut* precedes that of concentration in the *Me'irat 'Einayim.* Moreover, the graveyard alludes, as we can see from the story itself, to a situation of equality of opposites, and from this point of view there is an interesting parallel to the secret of equanimity mentioned in *Me'irat 'Einayim.* From a study of the story, one may assume that equanimity precedes communion and that the latter in turn precedes *hitbodedut*, so that we have here the order of the stages as presented by R. ABNeR. For a deeper understanding of the significance of this parable, let us turn to another passage from the *Me'irat 'Einayim:*[60]

> From the wise man R. Nathan, may he live long, I heard . . . that when man leaves the vain things of this world, and constantly attaches his thought and his soul above, his soul is called by the name of that supernal level which is attained, and to which it attached itself. How is this so? If the

soul of the practitioner of *hitbodedut* was able to apprehend and to commune with the Passive Intellect, it is called "the Passive Intellect," as if it itself were the Passive Intellect; likewise, when it ascends further and apprehends the Acquired Intellect, it becomes the Acquired Intellect;[61] and if it merited to apprehend to the level of the Active Intellect, it itself is the Active Intellect; but if it succeeds in clinging to the Divine Intellect,[62] then happy is its lot, for it has returned to its foundation and its source, and it is literally called the Divine Intellect, and that man shall be called a man of God,[63] that is, a divine man, creating worlds.

Here, as in the story of the princess, we read of a spiritual ascent, through which one becomes "a man of God." Both cases speak of *hitbodedut* and *devekut*, although in the latter case it is difficult to determine the exact relationship between the two concepts. Likewise, the supernatural qualities of the man of God are mentioned in both passages: here he is "a creator of worlds"; in the parable of the princess "his prayer is heard and his blessing is efficacious"; at the end of the first quotation from *Me'irat 'Einayim* it speaks about prophecy which enables the prediction of the future.

Examination of all of the sources relating to *hitbodedut* that we have quoted from the writings of R. Isaac of Acre indicates that its purpose was to remove the thought process from objects of sensation and to lift it up to the intelligibles or even to the highest levels of the world of Intellect. The final goal of this process of ascent is to commune with God Himself,[64] as is clear from the parable of the princess. This is even true in the quotation from R. Nathan, in which *devekut* to the Divine Intellect is mentioned.

One might well ask whether one can identify the exact nature of the princess in this story. She is portrayed there exclusively as an earthly substance, but this level of understanding seems insufficient. The conclusion, quoted from *Reshit Ḥokhmah* in the name of R. Isaac, states that "from the sensual one must understand the nature of divine service," in the context of "lust for a woman." Concentration on this desire causes the meditator to leave the world of the senses, that is, the physical form of the princess, and to cling to intelligibles, and afterward to God Himself. In *Me'irat 'Einayim* the author writes: "It is not like your thoughts in the objects of sensation, but it speaks of the intelligibilia, which are commanded by the '*a*[*tarah*]".[65] The letter *'ayin* is the initial of the word *'atarah* [crown], which corresponds to the *sefirah* of *malkhut*, which is the *Shekhinah*. It follows from this that R. Isaac identifies the intelligibilia with the *Shekhinah*. Furthermore, immediately following the passage quoted above he adds: "See the parable of the princess, etc., as explained in *Keter Shem Tov* [by Shem Tov Ibn Gaon]: 'the Torah [spoke here of] the unification of *'atarah*.'" The identification of the crown as the princess—referring to the *sefirah* of *malkhut*, which is in turn identified with the intellect—suggests a withdrawal from the objects of sensation, a distancing from the physical form of the princess, while attachment to the Intellect is seen as cleaving to the supernal, ideal princess—the *Shekhinah*[66]—and then to God Himself.[67] This clinging may be what is referred to as "divine service" by R. Isaac, and the practitioner of concentration who clings to God may be the "perfect servant." One may also go a step further and interpret the expression "man of God" (*'ish ha-'elohim*) in the parable of the princess in an erotic sense: the mediator is transformed into the likes of Moses, the husband (*'ish*) of the *Shekhinah*, symbolized here by the word "God" (*ha-'elohim*).[68] This is a common idea in Kabbalah, and such a possible interpretation should not be rejected out of hand. In the context of this discussion, we should mention the spiritual pleasures which, according to R. Isaac, accompany attachment to the Intelligibles.

As we stated above, there is a similarity between the parable of the princess and Diotima's statement in Plato's *Symposium;* however, in her speech, Diotima does not at all mention solitude, either in the sense of seclusion from society or in that of mental concentration. But these two forms of solitude are mentioned by the Muslim philosopher Averroes (1126-1198) in connection with Socrates' understanding of God:[69]

> And he who among them belongs to the unique individuals, like Socrates, who choose isolation and separation from other people and retreat into their souls always, until those of great heart believed that through this dedication and forced contemplation of the above-mentioned forms, one shall arrive at the first form that can be apprehended.

Here, as in the parable of the princess, it is possible to go from the intelligibles, or the forms, to the apprehension of God Himself, by means of solitude and mental concentration. Is the attribution of the practice of solitude to Socrates connected with the fact that he was the one to quote Diotima's comment in Plato's dialogue? In any event, Averroes's comment seems to reflect an older tradition concerning Socrates as a recluse, which was also cited by R. Judah Halevi (ca. 1075-1141).[70]

We saw above that *hitbodedut* was part of a technique of concentration and attachment of the human soul to God. However, according to R. Isaac of Acre, *hitbodedut* is, in addition, able to serve as a means of drawing the divine pleroma down into the human soul:[71]

> When man separates himself from the objects of sensation and concentrates[72] and removes all the powers of his intellective soul from them, but gives them a powerful elevation in order to perceive Divinity, his thoughts shall draw down the abundance from above and it shall come

> to reside in his soul. And that which is written, "Once in each month" is to hint to the practitioner of *hitbodedut* that his withdrawal from all objects of sensation must not be absolute, but rather "half to God and half to yourselves," which is also the secret of the half-shekel, "the rich man should not add, nor the poor man subtract, from the half-a-shekel" [Exodus 30:15], whose esoteric meaning is "half of one's soul," for *shekel* alludes to the soul.[73]

This evaluation of *hitbodedut* is already referred to in Abraham Ibn Ezra's commentary on Exodus 3:14 (long version) and in Abulafia, but R. Isaac of Acre seems to emphasize this approach more clearly and fosters its inclusion in the later Kabbalah.

Shem Tov Ibn Gaon and his *Baddei Ha'Aron*

The approach of R. Shem Tov ben Abraham Ibn Gaon (late thirteenth to fourteenth century) to *hitbodedut* should be understood within the context of Abulafia and of R. Isaac of Acre. His book *Baddei Ha'Aron*, which was written at least partially in Safed, contains an interesting discussion of *hitbodedut*:[74]

> He should concentrate his mind until he hates this world and desires the world to come. And he should not be surprised that they [the Sages] said that one who is engaged in the secrets of the Chariot need not stand before a great man or an elder. . . . And he will see that there is no end to his intellect, and he shall delve deeply into the secrets of the Chariot and the structures of Creation, to the place where the mouth is unable to speak and the ear is unable to hear. Then he will see visions of God, as one who dreams and whose eyes are shut, as it is written, "I am asleep but my heart is awake, the voice of my beloved knocks. . . ." [Song 5:2] And when he opens his eyes, and even more so if another person speaks to him, he will choose death over life, for it will seem to him that he has died,[75] for he has forgotten what he saw. Then he will look into his mind as one looks at a book[76] in which are written these great wonders.

By the power of his mental concentration, the Kabbalist turns to his inner self[77] and discovers there amazing things, written as in a book; this situation of introspection is an extremely sensitive one, which may easily be disturbed by any outside stimulus. Note the use here of the expression "visions of God," which is indicative of a revelation that may be associated with the previous mention of the secrets of creation or the secrets of the chariot. According to R. Shem Tov, this inner revelation is transformed into a source of the writing of this book:[78]

> When he has no friend with whom to practice concentration as he would wish, let him "sit by himself and be silent, for He has come upon him" [Lam. 3:28]. And he shall begin to write what he sees in his mind, as one who copies from a book that is written before him, black fire on white fire,[79] in the true form of a sphere,[80] like the sun, for the light has come upon him at that hour,[81] and all the seas would not suffice for ink, nor all the rushes of the swamps for quills, as in the parable of the Sages,[82] until the heavens be revealed to him as a book.

Here, unlike in the first quotation, the Holy Spirit seems to move within the one meditating, and he must seek a companion with whom to practice concentration. It is also possible that these represent a series of different levels of events; the first passage speaks of one's attempts to reach the stage of mystical experience, from which it follows that *hitbodedut* also here means concentration; the second passage describes the experience itself, during which the meditator requires human company; this stage is described in some detail further on in R. Shem Tov's description:[83]

> And they [i.e., the Kabbalists, "those who receive the truth in each generation"] did not have others with whom to practice concentration properly, for the spirit of their bellies disturbed them, and they secretly opened their mouths in wisdom, and they conversed with [their quills] of reed and marsh.

We find here a unique understanding of the function of *hitbodedut:* companionship makes it possible for the meditator to relieve himself of the burden of his mystical experience; without him, the Kabbalist would have to write down his words and "speak with the reed," something which may later bring about disaster: "and it is possible that it will afterwards come into the hands of unworthy people, and strangers will husband Him, which is not as the law."[84] R. Shem Tov goes so far as to say that even the meditator himself is likely to become confused in his later understanding of the things revealed to him during the mystical experience:[85]

> [These contents] do not help a man nor does he understand them, unless he received a tradition by word of mouth. Even those who themselves write it may at times not understand it well at that time, and when the revelation [i.e., the appearance of the Holy Spirit] passes, he will look at them and not understand them, and even when they are explained, he will be unable to conceptualize them.

The passages quoted above appear between two discussions concerning letter combination; the first discussion opens with this sentence:[86]

> And he shall arouse through his wisdom the thought, which is dormant in the sea of darkness, and say in his heart: "As I knew the form of the letters and they were inscribed on my heart, one next to its companion, I will examine each letter, in its combinations and its vocalizations, and its combination arising from the combination of letters, to levels without end, of levels of the letters, even though these also are without end."

This indicates that the mental concentration (i.e., *hitbodedut*) mentioned in the first passage from the book *Baddei Ha'Aron* begins with an arousal connected with letter combination; this approach approximates the prophetic Kabbalah of Abulafia and his school. After the discussions of *hitbodedut*, R. Shem Tov again mentions the combination of letters, and adds the advice that one deal only with the combinations of vocalization marks. At the conclusion, he says:[82]

> But if he will understand the things which I have written concerning the thirty-two paths and the letters, one above the other, at once visible and invisible, and imagine them in his mind after receiving them verbally, and the light appears above him, or from fire, "for it is a spirit in man" [Job 32:9] that he shall know the hidden letters.

It is clear that R. Shem Tov advises here a system of letter and vocalization combination in order to attain the experience of appearance of the light and of speech—"it is a spirit in man." This experience is very similar to the descriptions connected with *hitbodedut*, as quoted above. But these do not seem to be merely suggestions; the Kabbalist writes further: "I also saw hidden and sealed mysteries, worthy of concealment, but the spirit pointed them out, and I could not go by without a hint to those who pay heed to the language of the dotted letters."[88]

It makes sense to assume that this is a description of an experience of R. Shem Tov himself, who, as is known, dealt with the textual tradition of the Bible and, as a result of this particular involvement, almost certainly arrived at an experience of light and spirit that obligated him to write down some of the things which are in *Baddei Ha'Aron*. This teaches us that the Kabbalah with which he was involved was not only a matter of theory, or confined to the distant past,[89] but a current practice in fourteenth-century Safed. The fact that the book *Baddei Ha'Aron* was written in the Galilee, where R. Isaac of Acre was also educated and where the anonymous author of *Sha'arei Ẓedek* also almost certainly stayed, teaches us that R. Shem Tov might have continued an ecstatic Kabbalistic tradition that already existed in the land of Israel. In any event, in his first Kabbalistic work, *Keter Shem Tov*,[90] there are no traces of the ecstatic Kabbalah, such as we find in his later work.

To conclude our discussion of the work *Baddei Ha'Aron*, let us return to the opening of the first passage we cited from this book and quote it in its fuller context:[91]

> And do not be astounded by what the Sages said [b. Sukk, 28a] concerning Jonathan ben Uziel, namely, that when he was engaged in the study of the Torah any bird which flew overhead was immediately consumed by fire. And he should concentrate in his mind . . . and he should not be surprised that they [the Sages] said that one who is engaged in the secrets of the Chariot need not stand up either before an elder or a great man. And he should understand the words of R. Akiba to Ben Zoma,[92] "From whence and to where" and their answers to one another, in which the second word was written without the *yod.*

Involvement in Torah and involvement in the secrets of the chariot are understood here as stages advancing mental contemplation. The meaning of involvement in Torah is explained above as profound involvement in the combinations of letters and vowels. The nature of the involvement in the secrets of the chariot according to R. Shem Tov is not clear. We already saw above, in the writings of R. Isaac of Acre, that the practice of *hitbodedut* is compared to the path of Ben Azzai and R. Akiba when they entered into *pardes.* It is possible—and this requires proof—that involvement in the secrets of the chariot refers also to the science of combining letters; support for this interpretation may be found in the approach of Abulafia, who sees in the secret of the chariot the combination of holy names. If this is so, *hitbodedut* depends upon involvement in the secrets of the chariot.

Sulam Ha'Aliyah of R. Judah Albotini

We read in another work that represents a loyal continuation of the path of prophetic Kabbalah, *Sulam Ha'Aliyah*, by R. Judah Albotini (d. 1519):[93]

> By this he shall ascend to the level of equanimity, as that sage[94] said to his student who asked him: "Will you teach us the secret of the Chariot?" He answered: "Have you achieved equanimity?" And the student did not understand what he was saying to him, until he explained the matter to him, namely, that all attributes are equal to him. And this was what he said to him, "If a man insulted you, and took away that which was yours, would you be angry and strict with him over this? And if he did the opposite,

namely, to honor you and to give you many gifts, would you rejoice over this and feel it? And would you feel in your soul that you were affected by these two opposites?" Then his master said to him, "If so, then you have not yet acquired the quality of equanimity,[95] that is, that it should be equal to you whether it be honor or its opposite. And since such is the case, how can you ascend to the level of *hitbodedut*, which comes after you have achieved equanimity?

The parallels between this story and that told by R. Isaac of Acre in the name of R. ABNeR in his book *Me'irat 'Einayim* are clear; nevertheless, one may not necessarily assume that this book is the direct source of R. Judah's words here for several reasons: first, in Albotini equanimity (*hishtawwut*) immediately precedes *hitbodedut*, as it does in R. Isaac's view, whereas in R. ABNeR *hitdabbekut* (communion with the divine) comes between them. Second, despite the similarity in subject matter, this is not an exact quotation from the version in *Me'irat 'Einayim.* Elsewhere in this book there are direct quotations from the writings of Abulafia and from the book *Sha'arei Ẓedek*, but all of them are identified with appropriate references. Third, the attitude toward the activity of Ben Azzai differs in R. ABNeR and in Albotini: only the latter emphasizes this personality's high level. Fourth, *Sulam Ha'Aliyah* quotes the Talmudic saying concerning the teaching of the secret of the chariot, which is absent from *Me'irat 'Einayim.* The addition of the expression "secrets of the chariot" (*ma'aseh merkavah*) in the specific context of this story indicates that this subject was seen as related to *hitbodedut.* According to Albotini, or his unknown source, R. Eleazar ben Arakh was referring to *hitbodedut* when he used the phrase "secret of the chariot."[96] However, in place of the preconditions mentioned in the Talmud, which emphasize wisdom—that is, "a wise man, who understands by himself"—*Sulam Ha'Aliyah* stresses the trait of *hishtawwut.* This change, which is not accidental, relates to the tendency of the Sufis to diminish or even to negate completely the value of intellectual wisdom and learning. It is worthwhile to compare this approach to *hishtawwut* with that of R. Joseph Karo:[97]

He should have concern for nothing in the world, except for those things which pertain to the service of God, but all the things of this world should be equal in his eyes, everything and its opposite. For this is the secret of the wise man, who was asked by one who wished to practice union:[98] "Have you achieved equanimity?" For the truth is that one for whom the good things of this world and its ills are not equal cannot practice union in a complete manner.

According to R. Werblowsky this is a quotation from Ibn Paquda's *Ḥovot HaLevavot.* However, this passage seems even closer to Albotini: first, because both Karo and Albotini speak of a "sage" who answers the question, whereas Baḥyah refers to a *ḥasid* (pious man). Second, the use of the term *shaweh* (equanimous) is common to the two Kabbalists but is absent from Baḥya. Third, the expression "from honor and from its opposite" is close to Karo's "a thing and its opposite." Despite this, we may not assume that Karo was influenced by the version in *Sulam Ha-'Aliyah,* since he completely ignores the importance of *hitbodedut.* Moreover, as one can learn from their continuation, Karo's words were written outside of Palestine, and it seems unlikely that Albotini's work came there and was used without being cited by name. The similarity in the details between the two sources is indicative of a common source that was different from the version in *Ḥovot HaLevavot.*

Let us now return to the book *Sulam Ha'Aliyah.* Albotini was apparently the first to state, in an unambiguous way, that *hitbodedut* differs from solitude:[99]

> For the welfare of the body,[100] that is, solitude brings about purity of the potencies and cleanness of qualities. Equanimity brings one to concentration of the soul, and concentration brings about the Holy Spirit, which brings one to prophecy, which is the highest level. If so, one of the necessary prerequisites for your path in concentration is that you first have the quality of equanimity, that you not become excited by anything.

We find here another case in which a Talmudic saying is incorporated in the discussion of *hitbodedut;* this use gives the two spiritual levels—*hishtawwut* and *hitbodedut*—a privileged place within the sequence of stages bringing about the Holy Spirit in the Talmudic tradition, and it indicates that these Sufi concepts were understood as matching—or even explaining and interpreting—the ancient Jewish tradition. However, this harmonistic claim has a harsh ring, from the standpoint of the Talmudic tradition. Although *hishtawwut* is claimed to fit a certain statement in the Talmud, at the same time it opposes certain central Jewish attitudes. The previous quotation continues:[101]

> On the contrary, he must have joyfulness of soul and be happy with his lot, and think in his heart that he alone is one and rules over this entire, low world, and that there is no person, near or far, who will concern himself over him,[102] nor anyone who can do him any evil or damage or harm or trouble, nor any good, for all the good of this world and its wealth is in his hands, and he needs nothing. Of this, the Sages said: "Prophecy does

> not dwell save upon one who is wise, courageous and wealthy" [*Shabbat*, 92a] And "Who is wealthy? He who rejoices in his lot.

"Joy in one's lot" is here given a far-reaching interpretation from a Jewish point of view: it is taken to mean a feeling of total independence and separation from one's environment. This matches R. Shem Tov Ibn Gaon's approach to the contemplative's relationship to the members of his family,[103] but it is certainly a far-reaching step compared with what is stated in the book *Baddei Ha'Aron.* For R. Judah Halevi, separation from the world constitutes a psychological state preceding ecstasy, for which reason—one may assume—it is more fixed and continues for a longer period than the separation caused at the time of *devekut* itself, according to R. Shem Tov. The state of *hitbodedut* is attained by letter combinations, just as it was by the Kabbalists of the school of Abulafia:[104]

> who was expert in the wisdom of *ẓeruf* and that of *dillug*. . . . Afterwards, let him perform this means of *hitbodedut*, in combination with the verse that he wishes to use from the Torah, and he should repeat this many times, or for a month, more or less, as he wishes, until he sees that he is perfect in that path, and so he shall further persist in this *hitbodedut*."

The various systems of letter combination are understood here as means of *hitbodedut*, or among its paths. We have here a system of intellectual exercises whose purpose, according to Albotini, is to prepare the soul to receive the Holy Spirit.

R. David Ibn Abi Zimra

One should note the influence of the interrelationship among *hitbodedut*, Holy Names, and the attainment of the Holy Spirit upon the approach of R. David ben Solomon Ibn Abi Zimra (RaDBaZ, 1479-1573). This Kabbalist, who was acquainted with the system of Abulafia, writes in his book *Magen Dawid:*[105] "I have already seen one who wrote that, through the concentration on the Holy Names in holiness and in purity, one may reach the stage of the Holy Spirit, even in our times, and this is a matter with which the enlightened man will not be in doubt about the matter of the Holy Names."

The author goes on to develop this idea more fully elsewhere; but, as opposed to what is said in this passage, which sees the acquisition of the Holy Spirit as possible in the present, the RaDBaZ explains the phenomenon of the Urim and Thummim as reached by means of *hitbodedut:*[106]

> The matter of the Urim and Thummim . . . is that one of the Holy Names, known to the priest, was contained in the folds of the breastplate, and the priest would direct his attention and thought and intentions towards that name and concentrate upon it, and be adorned with the Holy Spirit by that same name, and it would be pictured in his mind.

According to him, this phenomenon resembles prophecy: "For at times the prophet would direct his thoughts and contemplate, and with a slight arousal would understand the intentions of God, even in a mysterious metaphor or parable. And at times he would not be ready, and he would concentrate and see the vision and the parable." The prophet was required to concentrate and to meditate in order to decipher for himself the contents of his vision: "For were the intention of your thoughts towards prophecy in great concentration, you would know by yourself and would not need to ask the meaning of the parable."[107]

Hitbodedut in the writings of R. Moses Cordovero

As we have seen, several motifs relating to *hitbodedut*, which originated in the circle of R. Abraham Abulafia, reappeared at the beginning of the sixteenth century in the writings of two Kabbalists who were among the exiles from Spain and Portugal, R. Judah Albotini and R. David Ibn Zimra; both lived and were active in Jerusalem. One must ask whether it is merely coincidence that interest in *hitbodedut* reemerged in sixteenth-century Palestine, after it was associated with Kabbalists active in the late thirteenth and the early fourteenth century who had a certain relationship to the land of Israel.[108] This question becomes more serious in the light of the fact that the Spanish Kabbalists of the fourteenth and fifteenth centuries almost completely ignored the teaching of Abulafia, and even during the generation of the Expulsion he was still regarded as the "black sheep" of Kabbalah in the eyes of many Spanish Kabbalists. The renewed interest of Palestinean Kabbalists of Spanish origin in the Kabbalah of Abulafia and its offshoots, points toward their encounter with the Eastern Kabbalistic heritage, which combined ecstatic Kabbalah with Jewish-Sufi pietism.[109] The presumption that such a Kabbalistic tradition, whose traces were lost for a period of slightly less than two hundred years, did exist may also explain the interest of the Safed Kabbalists during the latter half of the sixteenth century in Abulafia's and Acre's doctrine of *hitbodedut*.[110] I would conjecture that we are speaking here not only of the preservation and study of Abulafia's writings but also of a living Kabbalistic tradition—which may explain the origins of Albotini's *Sulam Ha'Aliyah* and the centrality of *hitbodedut* and letter combination among the Kabbalists of Safed from the middle of the sixteenth century on. In contrast, Spanish Kabbalists on the eve of the Expulsion, such as the circle of the author of *Sefer ha-Meshiv*, were much involved with techniques of revelation, including incantations for dream questions and formulas for automatic writing—concerns that were continued in the Kabbalah of Safed. However, as opposed to Abulafia, they did not emphasize the relationship between *hitbodedut* and letter combination. In the writings of R. Moses Cordovero, we hear for the first time of an integration of Abulafia's doctrines within an overall summary of Spanish Kabbalah—namely, in his book *Pardes Rimmonim*. As opposed to the comprehensive work of R. Meir Ibn Gabbai, which is based almost entirely on Spanish Kabbalah,[111] Cordovero includes themes and quotations from the writings of Abulafia, giving them a standing unknown among the Spanish exiled Kabbalists who were active outside the land of Israel. This incorporation is quite clear in the discussion of *hitbodedut*, and its implications for the development of Kabbalah will be treated later in our discussion. There is no doubt that the Safed Kabbalists had copies of several of the most important writings of Abulafia and his disciples. Thus, for example, we read in R. Moses Cordovero's commentary on the *Zohar* passage known as "the *Sabba* (the elder) of *Mishpatim*":[112]

> And as *'ADaM* (man—i.e., the letters *'DM*) follows alphabetical order, [its letters symbolizing] world [location], year [time], soul [personhood], until he attaches himself to the secret of *neshamah, ruaḥ, nefesh* [the three levels of soul], that is *NRN*, the secret of *'ShN*, in the secret of the letters which are transmuted in his mouth, and the secret of the vocalization signs, and the secret of the *hitbodedut* brought down to man by them, as is written in the book *Sha'arei Ẓedek*[113] by R. Abraham Abulafia, author of *Sefer Ḥayyei Ha'Olam HaBa'*.[114]

This passage indicates that Cordovero had before him two of the principal works of prophetic Kabbalah; from them he learned, among other things, the secret of *hitbodedut*, which, as we have seen above, is connected with the combinations of letters and of vowels. Through *hitbodedut*, the soul becomes attached to the supernal hypostases known as *neshamah, ruaḥ, nefesh.* We have here a neo-Platonic formulation of the understanding of *devekut*, influenced not a little by the approach of the author of *Sha'arei Ẓedek.*[115] A closer examination of the meaning of the word *hitbodedut* in this text would be worthwhile. It is clear that the stage portrayed here is one reached by the practitioner of concentration after the process of *ẓeruf* and not before it, which differs from the texts discussed until now. Here, *hitbodedut* is transformed into the final stage before *devekut*. One should compare Cordovero's unique use of this term with that of his disciple, R. Ḥayyim Vital, who writes in the book *Sha'arei Kedushah*, apparently in the name of his teacher:[116]

> "The sons of prophets, who had before them drum and pipe, etc." for by the sweetness of the sound of the music, *hitbodedut*[117] rests upon them, by the pleasantness of the sound, and they cast off their souls. And then the musician ceases his playing, but the prophetic disciples remain in the same supernal state of *devekut*, and they prophesy.

In this quotation from Vital, as in Cordovero, *hitbodedut* occurs as a result of the use of a certain technique,[118] and in the wake of this concentration the soul attains the state of *devekut*. This intermediate situation may signify a kind of abnegation of the senses[119] or isolation of the soul from objects of sensation, which enables it to attach itself to a higher level.

In *Pardes Rimmonim*, Cordovero paraphrases a very important passage from Abulafia's book *'Or HaSekhel*,[120] defining *hitbodedut* as retirement to an isolated room and letter-combination. However, beyond these quotations one finds here an interesting discussion based upon the doctrines of Abulafia's school:[121]

> Several of the early ones explained that by the combination and transmutation of the seventy-two-letter holy name[122] or the other names, after great *hitbodedut*, the righteous man, who is worthy and enlightened in such matters, will have a portion of the Divine Voice (*bat qol*) revealed to him, in the sense of, "The spirit of God spoke in me, and His word was on my lips" [II, Samuel 23:2]. For he combines together the potencies and unites them and arouses desire in them,[123] each to its brother, as the *membrum virile* of man and his companion [i.e., the female], until there is poured upon him a spirit of abundance—on the condition that he be engaged in this thing, as a vessel prepared to and worthy of receiving the spirit, for if such is not the case, it will become cruel[124] to be turned into "a degenerate wild vine."

Thus *hitbodedut*, in the sense of concentration, advances the process of letter combination,[125] whose purpose is the attainment of the holy spirit, in the spirit of Abulafia's Kabbalah. The conclusion of this quotation favors the approach of R. Isaac of Acre, in which combination enables the soul to receive the abundance or the spirituality. This expression is interpreted elsewhere as well in connection with *hitbodedut*:[126] "The prophets, of blessed memory, used to acquire, by means of those letters, through great concentration and by virtue of their pure soul, that spirit embodied in the letters." The letters combined by the Kabbalist are transformed here into a sort of talisman, which absorbs the supernal abundance.[127] After the spirituality is absorbed by means of the letters, it becomes attached within the soul, which is prepared for this by concentration.[128] *Hitbodedut* is described as a process by which the soul is transferred from the world of matter to the world of spirit, or as a technique of spiritual elevation, through contemplation of sensory data and its stripping away, in order to understand the spiritual element within it. The mystical aspect of *hitbodedut* is clearly expressed in another book by Cordovero, namely, *Shi'ur Komah:*[129]

> The sons of the prophets, when they used to prepare themselves for prophecy, brought themselves [to a state of] joy[130] as in the verse, "Take me a musician, and when the musician plays . . . [II, Kings 3:15]. And they would concentrate in accordance with their ability to do so, in attaining the wondrous levels and casting off the material, and strengthening the mind within the body, until they abandoned matter and did not perceive it at all, but their mind was entirely in the supernal orders and subjects. Ane they concentrate, and cast off the physical, and go away—and this matter is man's preparation on his own part.

According to Cordovero, the "sons of the prophets," that is, the ancient Jewish mystics, had special methods of concentration: "according to their knowledge of concentration," which showed them how to cast off materiality and to prepare the dematerialized mind to apprehend the structure of the *sefirot:* "the sublime levels," "those supernal levels." We learn about the necessary transition between the physical and the spiritual from *Sefer 'Or Yakar:*[131]

> If one wishes to take pleasure in the understanding of his Creator, let him concentrate according to the accepted premises which he has learned, and let him look at a particular physical form, so that he may learn from it that which is alluded to in the spiritual worlds, and he will see the detailed organs of it, and the varied matters, and its lights. And from there he will come to understand the innermost secrets of the spirituality of that form, and he shall attain *devekut.* Such was the way of Adam in the garden of Eden. Now, if the cherubim were physical-spiritual beings, he may gaze at them and come to contemplate and to apprehend from what is pictured here, in terms of the visual, that which makes sense to the mind—[proceeding] from the physical to the spiritual.

The Kabbalist is able to acquire "knowledge of his Creator" through contemplation of the form of his own physical organs, by means of *hitbodedut.* This statement reminds us of R. Isaac of Acre's story of the princess, which was quoted in the work of Cordovero's pupil, R. Elijah de Vidas. Furthermore, according to Acre, "from the sensory you shall understand the intelligibilia, for from your flesh shall you know God [after Job 19:26]." We have here a Kabbalistic variant of the saying "Know yourself and know your God,"[132] according to which concentration[133] plays a central role in the transition between one's self—that is, one's body—and the Divine. *Hitbodedut* is a means of uncovering the supernal source of material being; the cessation of *hitbodedut* is likely to bring about a distorted understanding of phenomenon. Thus, we hear of Moses that:

> Because he turned his heart away from prophetic concentration, in fleeing from the Creator's mission, turning his head in thinking that it was Amram, his father, who was calling him at that moment. For had he concentrated at that time, he would have understood how that voice was descending from the [cosmic] world of Creation to that of Formation, and from that of Formation into that of Action. . . . And the same happened to Samuel, at the beginning of his prophecy, that he did not concentrate, to understand the way of the voice, even though he was worthy of prophecy. So he thought that that voice was a human voice, that is, that of Eli, until he finally said, "Speak, for your servant hears"—that is, that he concentrated and apprehended the stages of prophecy, and understood the descent of the divine voice.[134]

Here, *hitbodedut* is understood as a combination of concentration and meditation at the same time; it is the means enabling the human intellect to restore the essence of things to their supernal source, by apprehension of their essence. This is the way by which one turns to the upper world:

> There are two aspects of *ḥokhmah:* the supernal aspect is turned towards the divine crown (*keter*), which aspect does not face downwards. . . . The second, lower aspect turns downwards. . . . Likewise man has two aspects: the first is that of his concentration upon his Creator, to add and acquire wisdom, and the second that by which he teaches others.[135]

It seems important to me to dwell upon a certain change in the use of the term *hitbodedut* in Cordovero's thought: concentrated thought enables one to uncover the hidden essence of the object of contemplation, through which one comes to understand the supernal source and the way in which the spiritual emanates down into the material world. According to Cordovero, the human intellect must cast off its physicality only in order to penetrate, by means of its concentration, beyond the physicality of other things, to uncover their spiritual nature[136] and to arrive in the final analysis at God Himself. According to another text, Cordovero seems to state that there are certain subjects whose apprehension cannot be guaranteed even by *hitbodedut:*[137]

> For the Torah is the secret of the upper Being which has come into existence below, and is not separated from the *sefirot*, but it nevertheless is present for those who exist below, while connected to the spiritual existence of the *sefirot*. When man concentrates in order to understand this mystery, he shall be astonished and be silent to his mind and not find it, for the Torah is not a separate being below.[138]

We find here an interesting approach, reminiscent of Isaac of Acre's opinion that the mystic is unable to penetrate the secrets of the Torah.

Safed and the dissemination of *Hitbodedut*

The penetration of the concept of *hitbodedut*, in the sense of intellectual concentration, into the writings of R. Moses Cordovero, sometimes combined with a technique of letter combination and bore important implications beyond the absorption of ecstatic Kabbalah within the framework of theurgic Spanish Kabbalah. This fact facilitated the dissemination of a number of elements associated with the technique of letter combination in Kabbalah generally; but no less important was the enhanced importance of *hitbodedut* in texts written by Cordovero's disciples. I refer particularly to the major works of Kabbalistic *mussar* written during the last third of the sixteenth century. As we have already seen above, R. Elijah de Vidas used R. Isaac of Acre's parable of the princess in his book *Reshit Ḥokhmah*. Elsewhere in his book, parables mentioning *hitbodedut* in the sense of seclusion from society also reappear.[139] But it seems to me that de Vidas knew more of *hitbodedut* from his teacher than what survived in his writings. In *Sha'arei Kedushah*, R. Ḥayyim Vital tells us:

> R. Elijah de Vidas, the author of the book *Reshit Ḥokhmah*, of blessed memory, told me in the name of his teacher, R. Moses Cordovero, of blessed memory, the master of *Pardes* [*Rimmonim*], that whoever wishes to know whatever he wishes should accustom himself to holiness . . . and after he recites the *Shema'* on his bed he should concentrate in his mind somewhat.[140]

This indicates that traditions concerning the importance of *hitbodedut* were transmitted orally, and it is likely that Cordovero himself also had traditions that he did not put down in writing. This assumption makes sense also on the basis of examining the extensive material concerning *hitbodedut* in the unpublished portion of Vital's *Sha'arei Kedushah.* This section is filled with quotations from the writings of Abulafia and Isaac of Acre, as well as from unidentified material dealing with *hitbodedut.*

The third work from Cordovero's circle, R. Eleazar Azikri's (1533-1600) *Sefer Ḥaredim*, in which Isaac of Acre is also mentioned, discusses the practical implication of *hitbodedut* at some length. For our purposes, it is worthwhile to examine two passages in which, in my opinion, there is noticeable Sufi influence. The first appears in Azikri's mystical journal:[141]

> It is written, "I have always placed God before me." It is written in the book *Ḥovot HaLevavot*, that it is inconceivable that a master and a slave, one being contemptible in the eyes of the other, or those who honor and those who despise him, should be equal in his eyes, as the *ḥasid* said to the man who wished to [mentally] concentrate, "You cannot do so unless you practice humility and, [receiving] insults, until you achieve equanimity." . . . And there are three conditions in this verse, *shiwiti*[142] ("I placed" —literally, "I made equal"), that is, that I make everything equal before me, my praisers and my condemners, for I am a worm.

It seems to me, despite the explicit mention of *Ḥovot HaLevavot*, that one ought not to see in this work the direct source of Azikri for the following reasons. First, Baḥyah does not mention *hitbodedut* in connection with *hishtawwut*. Second, Baḥyah does not mention here any interpretation of the verse from Psalms. Third, the language of the two passages differs in many details. Thus, one may assume that Azikri had in front of him an additional source, possibly one of the writings of Isaac of Acre written under Sufi influence.[143] Elsewhere[144] Azikri quotes R. Isaac ben Solomon Luria (ha-ARI, 1534-1572) as stating that *hitbodedut* "is helpful to the soul seven times more than study, and according to a man's strength and ability he should concentrate and meditate one day a week. . . ." This exaggerated valuation of *hitbodedut*, stated by Luria when he first started his own path as a contemplative,[145] reflects the Sufi understanding of the supremacy of *hitbodedut.*[146]

It should be noted that, despite the fact that, in these texts the term *hitbodedut* does not appear in conjunction with the discussion of letter combination or the uttering of divine names, one must assume that these constitute a technique used by Azikri when he practiced *hitbodedut.* In his mystical journal, he writes:[147] "And at every moment he unites His names with joy and trembling, and he flees from society as much as is possible, and is completely silent,[148] in a brilliant flame, alone, fearful and trembling, and the light[149] which is above your head, make always into your teacher, and acquire a companion." An interesting parallel to this appears in *Sefer Ḥaredim*, which was, as is known, a very popular and widely known book:[150] "But be enlightened in your mind, in the enlightenment of these matters (i.e., the *sefirot*) and imagine the letters of the names, that this is left to you, but to imagine more than the letters is tantamount [to arriving] at a corporeal conception. And visualizing the letters in the mind . . ." We find here a technique that is not identical to that of letter combination, but a visualization of the letters of the Divine Name, and this already appears in Abulafia and in Isaac of Acre,[151] and one may assume that the influence of these Kabbalists in these matters is also reflected in Azikri.

The incorporation of the concept of *hitbodedut* in the ethical writings of Cordovero's disciples constitutes the final stage in the process of penetration of *hitbodedut* into Jewish culture as a practical teaching. Abulafia's writings constituted the beginning of the process of absorption of the Sufi outlook within Kabbalah; however, his books were intended only for special individuals, and even though his writings were circulated in manuscript form, their influence was largely confined to Kabbalistic circles. The incorporation of the concept of *hitbodedut* into Cordovero's writings was an important step toward its dissemination among a far wider public, both because of the influence of the book *Pardes Rimmonim* and because of the incorporation of *hitbodedut* as a religious value in the Safed *mussar* works. However, although Cordovero still maintained the connection between *hitbodedut* and letter combination, his disciples removed the instructions pertaining to the combination of letters. The fourth section of Vital's *Sha'arei Kedushah*, containing detailed instructions for letter combination, was never printed. Azikri no doubt knew of the use of Divine Names in connection with revelation and made use of it, but he speaks little of this matter, whereas the connection between *hitbodedut* and letter combination is entirely absent from de Vidas. It is certain that the relatively popular character of these *mussar* works was the reason for the concealing of this part of Abulafia's Kabbalah, but its other element—*hitbodedut*—continued, together with R. Baḥyah Ibn Paquda's views on the subject, to constitute a source of inspiration for the guidance of Jewish mystics. The influence of the views sketched above may be traced through the writings of the Hasidic mystics and possibly even in the writings of R. Moses Ḥayyim Luzzato.

In conclusion, we should discuss the place of the texts quoted above within the general framework of Jewish mysticism. The drawing of a new and detailed path was not a purely theoretical matter; one may assume that most of the Kabbalists quoted above underwent mystical experiences after taking the steps described above: mental concentration and letter combination or the pronouncing of Divine Names. It should be mentioned that approaches which could be described as *unio mystica* appear in the writings of Abulafia, Isaac of Acre, Albotini, and de Vidas, or, as in the case of Azikri, coupled with ecstatic states. Therefore, the preceding discussion can serve as a kind of introduction to the more detailed analysis of one of the central subjects in the study of Jewish mysticism: the penetration of *unio mystica* into Kabbalistic thought and practice.

Hitbodedut and the Shutting of Eyes

One of the practical techniques advocated by the Kabbalists in order to attain a state of concentration—that is, *hitbodedut*—was the shutting of one's eyes.[152] This technique is well known to us from Sufism[153] and in connection with achieving *kawwanah* (direction, concentration) in prayer[154] and for purposes of contemplating colors which become revealed in one's consciousness among the Kabbalists.

An anonymous Kabbalist saw "the essence of *hitbodedut*" in the act of closing one's eyes:[155]

> And what is the essence of *hitbodedut*? By closing the eyes for a long time, and in accordance with the length of time, so shall be the greatness of the apprehension. Therefore, let his eyes always be shut until he attains apprehension of the Divine, and together with shutting his eyes negate every thought and every sound that he hears.

The connection between shutting one's eyes and *hitbodedut* here is in the shutting off of the person from the senses. This enhances concentration and facilitates the possibility of apprehension: the meditator enjoys Divine providence in accordance with the degree or level of comprehension. This connection between apprehension and providence indicates a possible influence of Maimonides's approach (*Guide* 3:51) to the relationship between them. At the beginning of the sixteenth century, R. Judah Albotini wrote in his book *Sulam Ha'Aliyah:*

> Those who practice concentration, when they concentrate upon some subject or some profound interpretation, close their eyes, and nearly obliterate their own powers, in order to remove their hidden mind from potential into actualization, and to make that interpretation firm and to hew it out and impress it upon their souls.[156]

Here, as in the anonymous quotation, the shutting of the eyes is associated with those who practice concentration, on the one hand, and the capability of apprehension, on the other. Elsewhere Albotini adds the following sentence to the material copied from Abulafia's *Ḥayyei Ha'Olam HaBa'*: "Then, in that situation, he shall strongly shut his eyes and close them tightly, and all his body shall shake, with trembling and fear, and his knees . . ."[157]

The practice of preceding the concentration necessary for apprehension by closing one's eyes found its way into one of the most famous works of R. Ḥayyim Vital, namely, *Sha'arei Kedushah.* According to the author, the fourth and final stage of the process of purification, whose ultimate purpose is the attainment of prophecy, includes seclusion in a special house:[158]

> And he should shut his eyes, and remove his thoughts from all matters of this world, as though his soul had departed from him, like a dead person[159] who feels nothing. . . . And he should imagine that his soul has departed and ascended, and he should envision the upper worlds, as though he stands in them. And if he performed some unification—he should think about it, to bring down by this, light and abundance into all the worlds, and he should intend to receive also his portion at the end. And he should concentrate in his thought, as though the spirit had rested upon him, until he awakens somewhat. . . . And after a few days he should return to meditate in the same manner, until he merits that the spirit rest upon him.

We find here a bold step, compared with its predecessors: the purpose of closing one's eyes in *hitbodedut* is now to merit the Holy Spirit, and no longer merely a realization of the intellect. Vital again suggests this practice for the purpose of *yiḥud*, along the lines of Lurianic Kabbalah:[160] "At the beginning you must shut and seal your eyes and concentrate for one hour, and then concentrate upon this—namely, the name MeTaTRoN—and divide it into three portions, each portion consisting of two letters, thus, *MeT TeR 'ON.*" Again, in a magical formula in the possession of R. Ḥayyim Vital, or written in his hand, we read:[161] "To ask [a question] while awake: Enwrap yourself in *ṭallit* and *tefillin* and shut your eyes in concentration and recite: blessed memory . . ."

One may clearly argue on the basis of these quotations that the suggestion of closing one's eyes to enable one to concentrate was adopted for various and peculiar reasons, which characterize systems of thoughts remote from one another. It is possible, by its means, to augment the intellect, to receive the Holy Spirit, or to ask waking questions or to perform mystical unifications.

In contrast to the understanding of *hitbodedut* a concentration and the shutting of the eyes as an earlier stage, which repeats itself in R. Ḥayyim Vital, one finds also the opposite outlook in this Kabbalist. He advises:[162]

> Meditate in a secluded house as above, and wrap yourself in a *ṭallit*, and sit and close your eyes and remove yourself from the material world, as if your soul had left your body, and ascended into the heavens.[163] And after this casting off, read one *mishnah*,[164] whichever one you wish, many times, time after time, and intend that your soul commune with the soul of the *tanna* mentioned in that *mishnah*.

In another formula, which appears immediately thereafter, Vital advises:[165]

> Meditate in a secluded house, and close your eyes, and if you wrap yourself in a *ṭallit* and wear *tefillin* this shall be better, and after you turn your thoughts completely and purify them,[166] then do combinations in your thoughts, using any word that you wish in all its combinations. For we are not strict as to which word you combine, but in whichever one you wish, for example: *'RẒ, 'ẒR, R'Ẓ, RẒ', Ẓ'R, ẒR'*. . .

These descriptions of *hitbodedut* fit in many details the technique suggested by Abulafia: that is, concentration in a secluded place, the wearing of *ṭallit* and *tefillin*, shutting one's eyes,[167] and letter combination. However, there is no doubt that to these details were added later approaches, including the attachment of the soul of the meditator to the soul of the *tanna* connected with the *mishnah* which is recited, or the ascent to the heavens. Despite this, we can state that Vital's descriptions give evidence of a continuation, with some changes, of the prophetic Kabbalah of the school of Abulafia. As this statement also holds true of other suggestions, which precede shutting one's eyes to concentrate, one may conclude that, with regard to *hitbodedut*, Vital was influenced by the various different versions of prophetic Kabbalah. His discussions of this subject, together with the material we have described in R. Moses Cordovero, indicate an impressive penetration of ecstatic Kabbalah into theurgic Spanish Kabbalah, which had come to Safed without having been previously markedly influenced by Abulafia's teachings.

On R. Moses Cordovero and R. Abraham Abulafia

We have already analyzed the history of Jewish solitary meditation which we defined as a specific form of intentional mental concentration. Its history from the period of Abulafia to the Kabbalistic *floruit* of Safed in the sixteenth century was delineated. We indicated a connection between the Kabbalah of Abulafia and his disciples and the Kabbalah of Cordovero and his disciples with evidence based on quotations from their works as well as from those of the anonymous author of *Sha'arei Ẓedek*. More specifically we examined the role of concentration and its connection with the technique known as letter combination (*Ẓeruf 'Otiyot*).

Despite the tendency among the Safed Kabbalists to quote from the writings of Abulafia regarding mystical practices, we have yet to provide evidence to prove that the Safeds actually used these practices. If we were to assert that they did, we would then have a framework with which to understand the function of Abulafia's ecstatic Kabbalah in the mystical life of the core group of Safed Kabbalists.

It appears to me that such information can be demonstrated through a further examination of the writings of Cordovero's disciples and admirers who spent time in Safed. I refer specifically to the writing of the sixteenth-century Italian Kabbalist, R. Mordekhai Dato[168] who, in his *'Iggeret HaLevanon*,[169] describes the Kabbalistic practices of Cordovero, his teacher, in the following words:

> The occupation of our ancestors, shepherding sheep (*Ro'ei Ẓon*),[170] contains a secret meaning. It actually refers to the vocation of Ẓeruf *'O*tiyot *N*ekudot, the combination of letters and vowel points.
>
> For the sage versed in the True Wisdom cares for the self by means of the secret of the combination of the holy letters and vowel points, for they are exceedingly great.
>
> Zeganzagel was the [angelic] teacher of Moses.[171] In gematria, this name has the numerical value of the word "Me'ayin,"[172] and this word is actually hidden[173] in Moses' name, when the letters of his name are fully spelled out thus: Mem *Mem* Shin *Yod Nun* He *Alef*, forming the word "Me'ayin."
>
> Know that the man, Moses Cordovero, took for himself the vocation of letter and vowel combination. He practiced it successfully and successfully trained others in this art.

This portrayal of Cordovero bases itself on ideas taken from Abulafia's *Hayyei Ha'Olam HaBa'*,[174] where he claims:

> These three principles, *'O*tiyot (letters) Ẓeruf (combination) and *N*ekudot (vowel points) forms *'OẒN*, whose letters may be rearranged to form the word Ẓon (sheep) which is used as an acronym for the above. This is what is denoted by "and Moses was a shepherd of sheep" (*'U Moshe Ro'e Ẓon'*). Thus, a person when he attains perfection become a shepherd.[175]

In another section of the same book we read:

> The secret name of Moses is Me'ayin.[176]

When we compare these words by Abulafia with the preceding portrayal of Cordovero by Dato, we cannot doubt that Dato saw his teacher as one occupied with practices that exemplify the Kabbalah of Abulafia.

Indeed, the quote from Dato contains other hints as well. From the beginning of the quote it is implied that the ecstatic Kabbalah was regarded as the "vocation of our ancestors." Such a designation not only adds to the prestige of this Kabbalah, but it may also imply that Cordovero inherited a Kabbalistic tradition from his own forebears or teachers. That Cordovero practiced this form of meditation is conspicuous; the fact that he was "successful" implies that he attained the mystical experiences that the "ecstatic Kabbalah" was intended to impart as designated by Abulafia. The successful training of "others" refers, no doubt, to Cordovero's own disciples.

Considering the implications of this portrayal, it is no wonder that the Abulafian Kabbalah figures so prominently in the fourth portal of the "Portals of Holiness" (*Sha'arei Kedushah*, written by R. Ḥayyim Vital),[177] for the book was written to guide the way for Vital's contemporaries to attain the prophetic or ecstatic experience.[178]

There is an interesting allusion, again, in the writings of Dato[179] regarding the relationship between the practice of letter and vowel combination and mystical experience:

> This spiritual shepherding in the secrets of the Alpha Beta, from the letter Alef to the letter Tau, through the different letter and vowel combinations forms the Divine Speech of the Torah and through it God speaks to His prophets.
>
> This [is the meaning of the verse:[180] "And he led his flock"] to the farthest end of the wilderness (ahar hadmidbar), where we read the word "midbar" (wilderness), which is written with the same letters as the word "Miyddaber", as in the verse,[181] "And I heard a voice 'speakingly' (miyddaber) to me." This refers to the Divine Speech that only the prophet can hear.
>
> This is further explained in the verse[182] "The spirit of the Lord spoke by me and His word was upon my tongue." For the words themselves were of the Holy Spirit that was placed within the mouth of the prophet. The prophet didn't speak them of himself.[183] And because the sage R. Moses Cordovero . . .

This passage indicates that Cordovero, like Moses, attained to prophecy, and that this was due to the spiritual shepherding of the Ẓon (letter and vowel and combination).

Abulafia writes that: "The differences between people are constituted in their different understandings of the way of the letters. The more one understands their secrets the greater one is in the eyes of God. It is through the letters and the understanding of their ways that God grants abundant wisdom."[184] From this we see that the practices involving the letters provide a path for the attainment of Divine Wisdom. These Kabbalistic techniques are depicted in the writing of Dato in a most interesting way. In another passage, Dato says,[185]

> There is a danger involved in embarking upon the wisdom of Kabbalah, lest it happen to one what happened to Ben Zoma, who "gazed" and was stricken with madness, or to Ben Azzai, who "gazed" and was struck dead, or to Elisha Aḥer who "gazed" and began to "uproot the shoots."
>
> When the four entered the "Pardes" (mystical orchard) only Rabbi Akiva entered in peace and left in peace. Among those who enter into the wisdom of the Kabbalah very few are rescued from error, and even an unintentional mistake in this wisdom is regarded, Heaven Forfend, as if it were intentional.
>
> That is so in this path. However, there is another path (to wisdom) that is not as dangerous. With it one may be confident as regards the danger. It is the path of the principle traditions of wisdom, which brings a person to knowledge without error.

Immediately following this passage Dato explains the principles of Abulafian Kabbalah. We may therefore conclude that the above-mentioned "path of the principle traditions of the wisdom, which brings a person to knowledge without error" refers to the Abulafian Kabbalah. However, it is difficult to identify the "dangerous Kabbalah" that may bring one to error. Is Dato referring to the Kabbalah regarding the *sefirot*, which was the classical Kabbalah of both the Spanish and Portugese Kabbalists before the Expulsion? If so, we again see an example of Abulafia's influence. For Abulafia, the Kabbalah of the *sefirot* is "beginner's Kabbalah," and there even "exist Kabbalists who (mistakenly) believe in the sefirot in the same manner as the Christians who believe in the Trinity."[186] Abulafia regards them as people who "added (to the true unity of God) to the extent that they made Him ten, and regarded the One as composed of multiple forms."[187] In contrast to this, Abulafia sees in his own Kabbalah a wisdom that surpasses the Kabbalah of the *sefirot*,[188] and a path that brings a person "easily"[189] to the prophetic state, namely, ecstasy.

An additional indicator regarding Cordovero's occupation with the Abulafian Kabbalah may be found, I believe, in Cordovero's magnum opus, *Pardes Rimmonim*. According to Cordovero,[190] there are "four categories of [the study of] Torah: (a) the simple narrative level, the material enclothement of the Torah; (b) the study of the Law and Midrashic lore, in their literal sense; (c) the study of the 'pleasant Kabbalah' such as the secrets explicated by the Zohar . . . for all of the Midrashim and Mishnayot as well as all the laws and commandments contain inner secrets and pleasant secrets;[191] and (d) the spirituality of the letters,[192] their essence and combination, one within the other."

From this we see that, according to Cordovero, the most sublime form of Kabbalah is not the study of the *sefirot*, which originates in the Zohar, among other places, but rather, it is the Kabbalah of the letters and their combination. However, "this Kabbalah is almost unavailable . . . and in its place we find the Divine Names, their functions and combinations, as they are derived from Biblical verses, together with the knowledge of their functions; how they derive power, and their place in the supernal *Merkavah* (Divine Chariot). This knowledge is almost unavailable . . . and an introduction to it will be found in these three gates (in *Pardes Rimmonim*), the Gate of thc Letters, the Gate of the Vowel Points and the Gate of the cantilation notes."

An understanding of the "fourth category" of Torah study as the field of letter and vowel combination concurs with what we quoted earlier from Dato. We cannot, however, categorically maintain that it refers exclusively to the Abulafian Kabbalah, for in addition, it undoubtedly also refers to the magical Kabbalah of *Sefer Berit Menuḥah*[193] as well as to *Sefer HaMeshiv*,[194] for therein we also find employed techniques that are clearly language-oriented. However, it is also clear that Abulafian Kabbalah occupied a central place in the corpus of advanced Kabbalah studies.

It stands to reason that, in the eyes of Cordovero, at least, if not among the Safed Kabbalists at large, the Kabbalah can be seen as a graded system containing two levels: 1) the lower level, consisting of the Kabbalah of the *sefirot*, which is derived from the Zohar, and 2) the higher level, the ecstatic or "Prophetic Kabbalah" of Abulafia. This gradation of value was to become crucial to the development of the linguistic mysticism of Ḥasidism.[195]

Notes to Chapter 7

1. Gatherings of Kabbalists and common study were evidently common already during the thirteenth century; it seems probable that the Zohar describes contemporary Kabbalistic practices in its own peculiar way, projecting contemporary customs into the distant past—particularly in reference to the gatherings of the *Idra*. However, the Kabbalists did not separate themselves from society for this reason, and, more important, participation in the *minyan* (quorum of ten for prayer) was of great significance for them both Halakhically and theurgically. It is worth emphasizing that the symbolic-theurgic stream in Kabbalah, represented by the Zohar, saw a source of great power in the joint efforts of a number of Kabbalists,

unequaled elsewhere. See Y. Liebes, "The Messiah of the Zohar" (Heb.), in *Ha-Ra'ayon ha-Meshiḥi be-Yisra'el* (Jerusalem, 1982), pp. 128-165, 175-191. Compare the legend concerning R. Joseph dela Reina and his disciples, who attempted, through their joint efforts, to defeat the forces of evil. See Idel, "Inquiries," pp. 226-230, 244-248. In contrast with Arab and Christian magic, in which the individual magician is at the focus of magical activity, here the group of Kabbalists act in concert. On the other hand, the individual meditation of those Kabbalists who belonged to the school of Prophetic Kabbalah foregoes the element of theurgic activity, being modelled after Sufi mysticism, as we shall see below.

2. Both here and below, my remarks refer to Kabbalah only in the narrow sense of the word: Sefirotic and Ecstatic Kabbalah. I do not intend to discuss the phenomena associated with Ashkenazic Hasidism (see note 3 below) or the Jewish-Sufic pietism of the school of Maimonides. On the problem of the *ḥavurah* (group or community) in Hekhalot literature, see Ira Cherus, "Individual and Community in the Redaction of the Hekhalot Literature," *HUCA* vol. 52 (1981), pp. 253-274. It must be noted that, despite the individualistic tendencies characteristic of some Hekhalot texts, we do not find there instructions concerning *hitbodedut* as a condition for descent to the Merkavah.

3. On this question, twelfth- and thirteenth-century Ashkenazic Hasidism differed from Spanish and Provencal Kabbalah of the same period. On the separatistic tendency among these *ḥasidism*, see: Ivan G. Marcus, *Piety and Society—The Jewish Pietists of Medieval Germany* (Leiden, 1981). For our purposes, it is significant that the religious demands of this pietism—whose historical activity continued for a relatively brief period—were later transformed into a kind of ideal, but were not codified within the Halakhah.

4. See Trimingham's remarks: "Early Sufism was a natural expression of personal religion in relation to the expression of religion as a communal matter. It was an assertion of a person's right to pursue a life of contemplation, seeking contact with the source of being and reality, over against institutionalized religion based on authority" (*Sufi Orders*, p. 2).

Within Christianity, the terminology used in connection with monasticism is sufficient indication of the personalist nature of the phenomenon. The terms *monozonos* and *monachos*—i.e., "individual"—are indicative of this.

5. The situation changed later, in the mid-sixteenth century in Safed, when the Kabbalists created special *hanhagot* (behavior patterns). However, these customs in turn rapidly spread beyond Safed, as a result of the initiative of the Kabbalists themselves, gradually becoming transformed into part of normative Jewish practice.

6. Of particular interest in this connection is the fact that Abulafia, who saw in the attainment of "prophecy" the supreme religious goal, did not "sanctify" the mystical techniques which he advocated for the achievement of this goal. In his writings, the various techniques are described in great detail, indicating that they were not understood as having religious worth in and of themselves. However, the

fact that neither Abulafia nor Acre—whose views concerning *hitbodedut* will be discussed later—wrote works explaining the Kabbalistic interpretation of the *mizwot* is worthy of note. This indicates that Prophetic Kabbalah by its very nature did not have an independent interpretation of the *mizwot*. While R. Isaac Acre's writings do contain some comments on the Kabbalistic meaning of the *mizwot*, particularly in regard to prayer, there is no systematic discussion of the subject. This is in striking contrast to the extensive literature of *ta'amei ha-mizwot* written at the end of the thirteenth and the beginning of the fourteenth century by the Kabbalists who followed the *sefirotic* system. Furthermore, R. Judah Albotini, one of the major later figures of Prophetic Kabbalah, wrote a commentary to Maimonides' *Mishneh Torah* containing considerable Kabbalistic material, but making no use at all of Abulafia's approach!

7. See Georges Vajda, *La theologie ascetique de Baḥya ibn Paquda* (Paris, 1957); Naftali Weider, "Islamic Influences on the Hebrew Cultus" (Heb.), *Melilah* 2 (1946), pp. 37-120; Rosenblatt, *Abraham Maimonides*, I, pp. 48-53; Fenton, *Treatise*, pp. 1-23; etc.

8. The term appears in the sense of "concentration" in the writings of Abraham Ibn Ezra, Maimonides (see note 130 below), and other Jewish philosophers, and in the Kabbalah of Gerona, but these texts, which antedate Abulafia, shall be discussed elsewhere.

9. See Rosenblatt, *Abraham Maimonides*, II:390: "ah-ḥalwa albatina" and in his *Commentary to the Torah* ed., Weinsberg, (London, 1958), p. 365. Compare also the term *ḥalwa ruḥania* to *ḥalwa gashmania* in R. Baḥya Ibn Paquda, *Al-Hidaya 'ila Fara'id al-Qulub*, ed., A. S. Yahuda, (Leiden, 1912), p. 396.

10. The understanding of *hitbodedut* as concentration in many texts minimizes their "separatist" character and strengthens the assumption that even the Kabbalists were less interested in the emphasis upon separation from the community than would appear from the frequent use of the term *hitbodedut*.

11. For a detailed description of the room or house in which one secludes oneself to pronounce the divine names, according to Abulafia, see Idel, *The Mystical Experience*, p. 38. The subject of the "concentration" or "seclusion house" reappears often in R. Isaac of Acre. See note 52 below.

12. He visited Acre for a very brief period in 1260 or 1261, and it is not impossible that he might have encountered the Sufi approach there. However, this possibility seems to me unlikely, as for several years thereafter he was preoccupied with the *Guide of the Perplexed*, and only after 1270 is there any mention of the beginning of his revelations and of his Kabbalistic studies. See Idel, "Abulafia and the Pope," p. 2, n. 3.

13. Despite this, Abulafia did not refrain from mentioning his contacts with Christians: see Scholem, *Major Trends*, p. 129. Scholem's formulation, "non-Jewish mystics," is inaccurate, as in the case of Abulafia, it refers to contacts only with Christians. On the other hand, his anonymous disciple, the author of *Sha'arei*

Ẓedeq did not hesitate to portray the Sufi system or mention Avicenna's practice of *hitbodedut*, discussed below. Fenton's emphasis, (*Treatise*, p. 21) on the fact that Abulafia must have definitely had contact with Sufis during the course of his many years of wandering in the East is unsupported by the available evidence. His statement there giving the estimated date of Abulafia's death as 1295 must also be corrected.

14. Ed., Jakob Goldenthal (Leipzig-Paris, 1839), pp. 49-51. The Arabic source of this passage is found in the work *Yiḥya 'Ulum el-Din*, (Cairo, 1933), III: 16-17. This is among the most widespread texts describing the *dhikr*, which has been repeatedly used by students of Sufism. See esp.: Louis Gardet, *Themes et Textes Mystiques* (Paris, 1958), pp. 145-148; G. C. Anawati-L. Gardet, *Mystique Musulmane* (Paris, 1961), pp. 186-187.

15. Compare with the statement in *Sefer Moznei Ẓedek*, p. 48:

> While in terms of wisdom there is a distinction between the path of the sect of the Sufis and that of those who delve into the way of wisdom, as the Sufis do not see [any need to make] efforts to pursue wisdom, nor to spread the teachings, nor to understand what was written by the authors who searched out the truth of these matters. But the way was . . . to receive the face of the Shekhinah with all one's heart and one's soul . . . for those who commune with Him and the prophets had all these things revealed to them, and their souls acquired perfection . . . not by learning, but by separation from this world and by concentration.

Compare to our discussion below of the statements of R. Isaac Luria, quoted by R. Eleazar Azikri.

16. In the original, *zawyah.* The literal meaning of this word is "corner," but the term became a standard Sufi term for a room or group of rooms set aside for meditation. See Trimingham, *Sufi Orders*, pp. 18, 176-179. The Jewish translator chose here the literal meaning, in translating it as *zawit.*

17. The attachment of thought to God precedes the final communion with God, in which God is with the one communing and the one communing is with God; communion with God (*devekut*) clearly returns later in R. Isaac of Acre. See note 42 below.

18. This is the *dhikr* of language. See Idel, *The Mystical Experience*, pp. 24-28, 30-37. In the original, written *allah allah.*

19. This refers to Abulafia, who designates himself in this way. Its numeric value is 248, i.e., *Avraham.*

20. Published in Adoph Jellinek, *Philosophie und Kabbala* (Leipzig, 1854), I: p. 21. On prophecy as a real option in medieval literature, see A. J. Heschel, "On the Holy Spirit in the Middle Ages (until the time of Maimonides)" (Heb.), *Alexander Marx Jubilee Volume* [Hebrew Section] (New York, 1950), pp. 117-208.

21. The nature of these obstacles may be alluded to in the book *'Oẓar 'Eden Ganuz:*

> And my spirit was enlivened within me, and the spirit of the Lord moved my heart, and a spirit of holiness stirred me, and I saw many awesome and marvelous and terrible sights, by wonders and signs. And among them were jealous spirits who gathered around me. And I saw fantastic and deceptive things, and my thoughts were confused, for I did not find there any other human beings who could teach me the path by which I ought to go. And so I was like a blind man at noon for fifteen years, and the Satan stood at my right hand to tempt me, and I was crazy because of the vision of my eyes. (MS. Oxford 1580, fol. 166a)

The need for a teacher or companion for guidance or assistance is also alluded to by R. Shem Tov Ibn Gaon in *Baddei Ha'Aron*, quoted below in the text, near note 83. Compare also Abulafia, in *Mafteaḥ HaḤokhmah*, MS. Parma 141, fol. 32a: "and it was revealed to us by it that the generation prevents this (the indwelling of the Shekhinah) from above during the times appropriate for it."

22. It seems probable to assume that Abulafia's use of the term *derekh* in various contexts: *derekh mekubbelet* (the accepted way), *derekh hitbodedut* (the way of concentration), *derekh ha-shemot* (the way of the names)—was influenced by the corresponding use of the term *tariqa* in Sufism; see Trimingham, *Sufi Orders*, p. 312, s.v. tariqa. Compare also the use of the expression, "this is one of the ways of prophecy," in the early kabbalistic work *Sha'ar ha-Kawanah*, published by G. Scholem, who claims that its author was R. Azriel of Gerona; see: Gershom G. Scholem, "The Concept of Kavvanah in the early Kabbalah," in *Studies in Jewish Thought*, ed. Alfred Jospe, (Detroit, 1981), p. 172. In my opinion, this text was composed during the late thirteenth or early fourteenth century. See Scholem, *Les origines de la Kabbale* p. 442, n. 119. The term *derekh ha-nevu'aḥ* (the path of prophecy) already appears in Maimonides, *MT, Yesodei ha-Torah* 7:4.

23. Abulafia speaks of both letter-combinations and of pronouncing divine names in connection with *hitbodedut*. Despite the fact that the two subjects differ in theory, in practice there are quite a few discussions in which they are connected by Abulafia. See Idel, *The Mystical Experience*, pp. 22-41. These two subjects were well-known in Jewish mysticism even before Abulafia. See Idel, *ibid.*, pp. 14-17. However, the Ashkenazic sources in which the mention of names and letter-combinations appear are unrelated to concentration or seclusion!

24. Compare the Sufi concept of *qurb*—mystical closeness to God. This concept was particularly dominant in Al-Ghazali's *Mozney Ẓedeq*, and might have influenced Abulafia. The practitioners of concentration are defined as "prophets for themselves," as opposed to those prophets who reach the seventh level, who are "prophets to others," in Maimonidean terminology.

25. This refers to the use of concentric circles, on whose perimeters are written the letters which the Kabbalist wishes to combine, the combination then being performed by using one of the circles. Compare *Sefer Sitrei Torah*, MS. Paris BN. 774, fol. 130b, "when you turn around the circle of the letters."

26. Similar phenomena are also mentioned by the anonymous author of *Sha'arei Ẓedek*—see Scholem, "Sha'arei Ẓedek," pp. 134-135; *Major Trends*,

p. 151—and by R. Eleazar Azikri, in a text to be quoted below from Pachter, "the Life", p. 135, which is also parallel to Azikri's statements in *Sefer Ḥaredim*, p. 256. The seriousness of the bodily phenomena associated with the ecstatic state, as described by Abulafia, does not correspond to the description of such phenomena as self-hypnosis, as argued by Bowers and Glasner. See Margaretta K. Bowers and Samuel Glasner, "Auto-Hypnotic Aspects of the Jewish Cabbalistic Concept of Kavanah," *Journal of Clinical and Experimental Hypnosis*, 6 (1958), pp. 4-9, 11-12, 16.

27. See *Teshuvot ha-RaShBA*, vol. I, no. 548, and R. Judah Ḥayyat, in his introduction to *Minḥat Yehudah*. Elsewhere, I shall discuss in greater detail the polemic between these two Kabbalists and its implications for the subsequent development of Spanish Kabbalah.

28. The quotation is from *Sefer Shoshan Sodot* by R. Moses ben Ya'akov of Kiev (Korzec, 1784), fol. 60b. See the corrected version published by Gershom G. Scholem, "Eine Kabbalistische Erklärung der Prophetie als Selbstbegegnung," *MGWJ* 74 (1930), p. 287. On p. 288, Scholem translates the term *hitbodedut* as "einsamen Meditation," which approximates the sense of "concentration."

29. See MS. Jerusalem 8° 148, fol. 66b, translated in Scholem, *Major Trends*, p. 152. On this work, see Scholem, "Sha'arei Ẓedek," pp. 127-139.

30. MS. Jerusalem 8° 148, fol. 59b, Scholem, *Major Trends*, p. 148. Scholem translates the term *wa-yitboded* as "retiring into seclusion."

31. MS. Jerusalem 8° 148, fol. 60a-60b; Scholem, "Sha'arei Ẓedek," p. 133.

32. This may be parallel to a technique of dream-questioning, which includes, among other things, *hitbodedut*, that is, concentration prior to sleep. Compare note 140 below.

33. On Isaac of Acre see also essays V-VI. Cf. *Sefer Me'irat 'Einayim*, ed., Goldreich vol. II: p. 218.

34. See Scholem, *Major Trends*, pp. 96-97, in which the term *hitbodedut* is translated as "loneliness," while in his *Kabbalah*, p. 174, the same passage is translated by the term "solitude," which he explains as "being alone with God." Fenton, *Treatise*, p. 63, n. 94, translates the term as "solitary devotion"; in his view, the term *hitbodedut* in R. Isaac is analogous to the Sufi concept of *ḥalwa*. Further support for the term *hitbodedut* as mental concentration may be found in the statement of R. Isaac in *Me'irat 'Einayim*, pp. 239-240, in which he depicts the situation in the sixth and seventh millennia as follows:

> And the apathy of people towards their bodily needs will grow, and *hitbodedut* and men's efforts concerning the needs of their souls will be strengthened . . . Those who practice concentration and those who separate themselves will increase in numbers, until prior to the end of the seventh millennium man and beast will disappear from the entire world, because through the great strengthening of soul over body, all objects of bodily sensation will be nullified, and even during his lifetime man will

> be like a soul without a body because of his intense communion with God, may He be blessed and praised, even while he is still in his home, bound with chains.

Hitbodedut is here connected with "the needs of the soul," for which reason it makes sense to assume that this activity is connected with the spiritual element in man. On the diminution of men associated with the doctrine of cycles (*shemitot*), see also *Sefer HaTemunah* and, in greater detail, *Perush Sefer HaTemunah* (Lemberg, 1892) p. 56b. Cf. Gershom Scholem, *Sabbatai Ṣevi, The Mystical Messiah, 1626-1676* (Princeton, 1973), p. 814. The entire subject is deserving of more detailed discussion.

35. See Scholem, *Major Trends*, p. 96-97; Werblowsky, *Karo*, pp. 161-162. Hebrew literature contains other examples of the concept of *hishtawwut* in which the term itself is not mentioned. In Maimonides' letter to R. Ḥasdai, he writes:

> And it happened once that a sage and a great philosopher were traveling on a ship and sat in the place of the refuse, until one, that is, one of the people of the ship, came and urinated on him on the place of the refuse, and he lifted his face and laughed. And they asked him: "Why do you laugh?" He answered them: "Because is it now absolutely clear to me that my soul is on the highest level, because I did not at all feel the disgrace of this thing." . . . And the philosophers have said that it is very rare to find a man whole and complete in both ethical qualities and in wisdom, and if he is to be found, he is called a divine man, and certainly such a one as this is on the highest level.

The expression "man of God" also appears in the book *Me'irat 'Einayim;* see our discussion below, and in note 63. It seems to me that the approach here to *hishtawwut* approximates that of the Stoic *apatheias*, which sees equanimity of the soul as a goal in itself. A parallel to this story appears in Maimonides' *Commentary to the Mishnah*, Abot 4:4, and in R. Joseph ben Judah ibn 'Aknin's *Tib el-Nufus;* see Abraham Halkin, "Classical and Arabic Material in Ibn 'Aknin's 'Hygiene of the Soul,'" *PAAJR* 14 (1944), pp. 66-67, who cites the Sufi sources of this incident, on p. 67, n. 1. It is worthy of note that neither Maimonides nor ibn 'Aknin use the term *hishtawwut—istiwah.* (Dr. Paul Fenton drew my attention to Halkin's discussion of this subject) It is also instructive to note that in the version of the story found in Elijah de Vidas' *Reshit Ḥokhmah*, Sha'ar ha-'Anawah, Ch. 3, the "philosopher" or "*ḥasid*" is portrayed as one who wished to concentrate:

> And now I shall tell you what was related concerning one of the pious men (*ḥasidim*). Once a *ḥasid* was asked, "Which was the happiest day of your life?" He answered; "Once I was travelling on a merchant ship, carrying the richest merchandise, and in order to concentrate on my Creator I went down to the bowels of the ship and lay down there in the lowest place. And one of the young merchants came and shamed me in his eyes, and spat on me and uncovered me and urinated on me. I was amazed at his arrogance but, by the life of God, my soul was not pained by his action at all, and when he went away from me, I rejoiced greatly that my soul had reached this stage of humility, for I knew from it that it had "ways among those that stand" [after Zech. 3:7], for this quality so ruled me that I did not feel at all.

This version is closer to Maimonides' account in the *Commentary* to Abot, but nevertheless there is no reason to assume that it was copied from there.

36. Compare what is told about R. Ḥayyim Vital, in *Sefer Sha'arei Kedushah*, MS. British Library 749, fol. 15b:

> The story is told of a man who fasted most of his days, and who did many righteous deeds and married off several orphans, but who pursued honor. And he came to those who practice *hitbodedut*, who had reached the level of prophecy, and said to the greatest among them: "Sir, in your kindness let me know the reason why it is that, after I have performed all these good deeds, that I have not yet merited the level of prophecy, to tell the future as you do." He answered him: "Take a purse full of figs and nuts and hang it around your neck, and go to the main street of the city before the great and honorable people, and gather together some youths and say: 'Do you wish that I should give you figs and nuts? Then hit me with your hand on my neck and on my cheek.' And after you have done this many times return to me, and I will guide you in the way of prophecy." He replied: "Sir, how can an honorable man such as myself do such a thing?" He answered: "Is this a great thing in your eyes? This is naught but the lightest task that you must perform if you wish that your soul see the light of truth." Then he stood up and left with downcast soul.

There is no doubt that this story is an interesting parallel to the story told by "R. ABNeR," and it is probable that Vital found this story in one of the lost writings of R. Isaac of Acre. See also the passage from R. Eleazar Azikri printed by Pachter, "The Life," p. 140, to be discussed below; and see also our discussion of *Sefer Sulam Ha'Aliyah*. One should also note Elijah de Vidas' quotation in the name of R. Isaac of Acre, who in term claims to have received it from R. Moses, the disciple of R. Joseph Gikatilla, linking the indwelling of the Shekhinah in a person with extreme humility, without mentioning *hishtawwut* or *hitbodedut*. See MS. British Library 749 fol. 15a, which is parallel to *Reshit Ḥokhmah, Sha'ar ha-'Anawah*, Ch. 3. Comparison of the statements of Gikatilla's disciple with the latter discussion of R. Isaac of Acre is extremely revealing and indicates, in my opinion, the great difference between the "Spanish version" of Prophetic Kabbalah taught by Abulafia in Spain, in which *hishtawwut* plays no role, and that form taken in the East, incorporating far more Sufi influences—in our case, *hishtawwut*. See the discussion below on *hishtawwut* in R. Judah Albotini.

37. The closest that Abulafia comes to discussing *hishtawwut* is in *Sefer HaḤeshek*, MS. New York, JTS 1801 (EMC 858) fol. 2b: "He who knows the truth of existence will be more modest and humble of spirit than his fellow." It is worthy of note that Isaiah Horowitz, *Shenei Luḥot HaBerit* (Amsterdam, 1698), fol. 371a, quotes the story concerning *hishtawwut* from *Ḥovot HaLevavot*, but interprets *hishtawwut* as modesty! See also Pachter, "Devekut," p. 117, no. 264; and compare also Isaac of Acre's description of one of his teachers, "the greatest man of his generation in his modesty and his wisdom of the Kabbalah and philosophy and in the wisdom of letter-combination" (MS. Moscow-Günzburg 775 fol. 100a). This seems to be a series of adjectives: modesty—perhaps meaning

hishtawwut—followed by engagement in various wisdoms.

38. *Me'irat 'Einayim*, p. 218. See also Gottlieb's straightforward comments in *Studies*, pp. 236-239.

39. Scholem, *Major Trends*, p. 372, n. 59, points out the similarity between what is told by "R. ABNeR" and a passage in Baḥya Ibn Paquda's *Ḥovot HaLevavot*, V:5. However, it must be emphasized that R. Baḥya does not mention *hitbodedut* in this connection, for which reason R. Abner's remarks should be seen as a development beyond that found in R. Baḥyah and possibly independent of it. Cf. note 40, below. For possible sources of Baḥya, see Vajda, "Observations," p. 130 and n. 3.

40. Fenton, *Treatise*, p. 63, n. 94, relates to "virtuous man" rather than to "lover of wisdom." He also suggests a Sufi source, Al-Maki's *Kuṭ Al-Kulub*, as a possible source for R. Isaac's story, although he does not reject the alternative possibility that it may be *Ḥovot HaLevavot.*

41. In Vital, MS. British Library 749 fol. 17b, the continuation of the text differs on several points, worth mentioning here: "*Hishtawwut* will come about because of the attachment of the thought to God, blessed be He, which is called 'the secret of *devequt*,' as noted, because the attachment of his thought to God envelopes that man, so that he will not look at one who honors him nor at insults." Vital apparently used here the material quoted above from *Me'irat 'Einayim*, using the expression, "the secret of *devequt.*" Later, Hasidism was influenced by the understanding of *hishtawwut* as the result of *devekut*, and not by the approach of R. Baḥya: compare Schatz, *Ḥasidut*, p. 153. Cf. note 90 below.

42. In my opinion, one must distinguish two different stages of communion with God, according to R. Isaac. In the first, one attaches one's thought to God, as a result of which one merits *hishtawwut*, which is a precondition of continued progress towards attachment of the soul to the Infinite, in other words, towards *unio mystica.* The quotation from *'Oẓar Ḥayyim* to be cited below (n. 67) contains a description of the purification of thought and its embodiment in spirit as one of the conditions of meditation. See the text in *'Oẓar Ḥayyim*, MS. Moscow-Günzburg 775 fol. 100a: "and I see my soul attached to the Infinite," while on page 111a it reads, "'And he shall cleave to his wife and they shall be as one flesh' [Gen. 2:24]—when the *hasid*, the enlightened one, allows his soul to ascend, to commune with the secret of divinity to which she [the soul] has been attached, it swallows him." Compare Gottlieb, *Studies*, pp. 236-238. Communion in thought appeared in Jewish literature, and was particularly important in the thought of Naḥmanides. See Scholem, "Devekut," p. 205. Naḥmanides alludes to both of these stages in his commentary both on Lev. 18:4 and on Deut. 13:5, but he restricts the attachment of the soul (*devekut ha-nefesh*) to select individuals, using such phrases as "in the matter of Elijah" or "and this is possible among people of a [high] level." It would seem that, in the school of Naḥmanides, "attachment of the thought" or "attachment of knowledge" (*da'at*) was considered as the more easily attained level; see the quotation from *Me'irat 'Einayim* below, n. 66, and there, p. 240, and in the

words of R. Isaac in *Sefer 'Oẓar Ḥayyim*, below, n. 67, where they speak of "attachment of thought." Cf. note 59 below. Like Naḥmanides, R. Isaac of Acre also mentions the "attachment of the thought" of the prophet Elijah. This concept of *devekut ha-maḥashavah* returns in various forms among the Gerona Kabbalists: in R. Azriel, *Perush Ha'Aggadot*, ed., I. Tishby, (Jerusalem, 1945) p. 40, and in R. Ezra of Gerona, in a section from his *Commentary to the Aggadot of the Talmud*, printed in *Likkutei Shikheḥah u-Fe'ah*, fol. 7b-8a, and in MS. Oxford 1947 fol. 204b. These places speak about the attachment of thought as a preparatory stage to more advanced mystical activities, such as "prophecy." On the ascent of thought to its source, see G. Scholem, *Les origines de la Kabbale*, pp. 320-321. Another source likely to have influenced R. Isaac's approach was *Likkutei HaRan*, which in my opinion were written by one of the teachers of R. Isaac, R. Nathan; see MS. New York JTS 1777 fol. 33b. The entire question requires detailed study. The statement by L. Kaplan, "Response to Joseph Dan," in *Studies in Jewish Mysticism*, ed. J. Dan, F. Talmage (Cambridge, Mass., 1982), p. 128, n. 13, that the intellectualist understanding of *devekut* in Maimonides influenced R. Isaac, is correct with regard to the former stage, that of "communion of thought." But R. Isaac refers to two types of *devekut*, while in Maimonides' *Guide of the Perplexed* II:51, speaks of "attainment of truth" as the first stage, while turning towards contemplation connected with God comes afterwards. For an interesting distinction among three types of *devekut*, see S. Rosenberg, "Prayer and Jewish Thought—Directions and Problems" (Heb.), in *HaTefilah HaYehudit—Hemshekh ve-ḥiddush*, ed. G. Cohen, (Ramat-Gan, 1978), p. 97.

43. See pp. 38, 41, 49, 62, 160, 213, 220, 223. In many of the quotations associated with the name "R. Abner," one can clearly see the influence of the philosophical approach. A similar approach appears in *Likkutei HaRan*, written by one of R. Isaac's teachers, cf. chapter V above.

44. MS. Moscow-Günzburg 775, fol. 138a; MS. Oxford, 1911, fol. 149b.

45. On the dangers of "sinking," see essay VI above n. 22-24. On extreme *hitbodedut* as a cause of death, see R. David Meroko Martica, *Zekhut 'Adam*, (published by Yeḥiel Brill in *Yeyn ha-Levanon*, Paris, 1866) p. 10:

> In order to maintain a compound, both parts must be used in precisely the same measure. If one is overused, then that part shall overcome, and cut off the spiritual part. So he should persist in study and concentration, to kill himself in the tent of Torah, for its combination shall remain, but the soul will be separated from the body before its perfection is finished, with the help of the organs of the body.

46. Prior to the quotation under discussion, R. Isaac writes: "Moses, the light of whose ankle dimmed the light of the sun, sought to see by the eye of his mind the light of His [the divine] countenance, and Metatron, the Prince of the Face, was prevented from showing him this light, lest his soul be detached from its dwelling, due to its great joy."

47. The belief in the ecstatic death of Ben Azzai is rooted in the thought

patterns of the Kabbalists of Gerona. I shall elaborate on this point elsewhere. Compare the understanding of Ben Azzai as a practitioner of *hitbodedut* in R. Judah Ḥallewah, *Sefer Ẓafnat Pa'neaḥ*, MS. Dublin, Trinity College 27, 5B, fol. 197b. See also below, in the quotations from *Baddei Ha'Aron* and *Sulam Ha'Aliyah*, below.

48. MS. Sasson 919 p. 215.

49. The tensions between intellect and imagination, angels of mercy and angels of destruction, etc., are doubtless connected with an approach known from the writings of Abulafia and his disciples. See chapter V above. The use of *yiḥud* here is interesting, being very similar to its use in later Lurianic Kabbalah. See the quotation from the mystical diary of R. Eleazar Azikri below, near note 147.

50. MS. Moscow-Günzburg 775 fol. 170a.

51. Ibid. fol. 170b.

52. This expression is a translation of the well-known Sufi expression: *beit al-ḥalwa*. The expression, "house of meditation," or "concentration" appears in *Sefer 'Oẓar Ḥayyim*, and is widespread in Kabbalistic and Hasidic works—again, another indication of the profound impact of Sufi terminology upon Jewish mysticism. This point will be discussed more fully in my work-in-progress on *hitbodedut*. Cf. note 11 above.

53. The passages quoted above from *Sefer Sha'arei Ẓedek* bear a certain parallel to the use of the term *hamshakhah* (drawing down) with regard to *hitbodedut*. Even though the use of the term *hamshakhah* is not identical, this parallel calls for interpretation, particularly in light of the fact that the quotation from *Sefer 'Oẓar Ḥayyim*, only a small portion of which is reproduced here, contains a clear parallel to another idea found in *Sha'arei Ẓedek;* see chapter VI above. A greater similarity in the respective usages of the term *hemshekh* exists between *Sha'arei Ẓedek* and *Likkutei HaRan;* see the passage below, in note 64. In R. Isaac of Acre, the term *hamshakhat ha-maḥshavah* (lit., "drawing down of thought") signifies pulling, generally in a downward direction. See esp. *Sefer Oẓar Ḥayyim*, MS. Moscow-Günzburg 775, fol. 39a, in several places, and compare with the passage in *Sefer Yesod 'Olam*, MS. Moscow-Günzburg 607, published in Idel, *The Mystical Experience* p. 63. In the other two kabbalists, *hamshakhah* is associated with concentration of thought.

54. MS. Sasson 919, p. 215. The context of this passage is published and discussed in my article, "History," p. 9.

55. MS. Moscow-Günzburg 775, fol. 136a, MS. Sasson 919 p. 207.

56. The expression "ruḥani" is quite common in R. Isaac: see, for example, the texts cited by Gottlieb, *Studies* pp. 233-234 and *'Oẓar Ḥayyim* MS. Moscow-Günzburg 775 fol. 93b. R. Isaac uses, apparently for the first time in Hebrew, the form *hitrawḥen* in the sense of "to spiritualize." See the quotation below, note 64, for the use of the verb *yitroḥanu*. Compare especially the use of the term *ruḥani* by Abulafia, who in his book *Sitrei Torah* (MS. Paris BN. 774 fol. 169b) refers to

Tractate *Avot* as "the spiritual (*ruḥanit*) tractate."

57. MS. Moscow-Günzburg 775 fol. 238b.

58. *Sha'ar HaAhavah*, Ch. 4. This story is very similar to the words of Diotima in Plato's *Symposium*, par. 211-212. However, he may have arrived at it via various intermediates, such as the Sufi version. Another likely possibility is that a different version of Diotima's story was received, which was then interpreted by R. Isaac in a Sufi spirit. For a case of a Sufi understanding of a Greek myth, learned by R. Isaac from a Christian, see M. Idel, "Prometheus in Hebrew Garb" (Heb.), *Eshkolot*, (N.S.) 5-6 (1980-81), pp. 119-121. Cf. Fenton, *Treatise*, pp. 63-64.

59. Note here that *devekut* of the soul follows on *devekut* of the mind. See above, note 42.

60. *Parashat Re'eh*, pp. 222-223. On R. Nathan, see chapter V above. On the ideological background of this passage see Idel, *The Mystical Experience*, pp. 133-134 and chapter I, n. 30.

61. In *Sefer 'Oẓar Ḥayyim*, the author uses only the idiom *ha-sekhel ha-Kanui* (the acquired intellect); see the sources quoted in note 62. One should note that something similar occurred in connection with another expression common in the *Likkutim* gathered by R. Isaac of Acre from his teacher, R. Nathan. I refer to the term, *'olam hademut* ("the world of imagination") which appears neither in *Me'irat 'Einayim* nor in *Sefer 'Oẓar Ḥayyim*, despite the fact that there is no doubt that R. Isaac knew the term. On this term see essay V above; likewise, a similar phenomenon occurs with regard to the term *hishtawwut;* see Gottlieb, *Studies*, p. 238.

62. This phrase is very common in the writings of R. Isaac, although its precise meaning is not always clear; here it clearly seems to refer to an entity other than the Active Intellect, but this distinction by R. Nathan was not always accepted by R. Isaac. In his book, *'Oẓar Ḥayyim*, he mentions frequently the connection between the Acquired Intellect and the Divine Intellect, without the Active Intellect between them; see MS. Moscow-Günzburg 775 fol. 1a-b; 2b; 3a; 54b; 55b; 57b; 90b; 103a; 113a.

63. See above, note 35, on the "man of God" in the quotation from Maimonides' epistle: this expression appears in connection with Moses and, possibly under the influence of R. Isaac of Acre, in R. Elnathan ben Moses Kalkish's *Sefer 'Even Sappir*, MS. Paris, BN. 728 fol. 154b. Compare the expression, "divine men," in Plotinus, *Ennead* VI: 19, in connection with those who fled worldly lives. On the attainment of the condition of "creating worlds," see Cordovero, *Pardes Rimmonim*, Sec. 27, Ch. 1. It is interesting that Cordovero portrays the highest stage of Kabbalah as involvement in the "spirituality" of the letters and their combinations, and is thus very close to the approach of Abulafia.

64. The process of casting off constitutes an ascent from the objects of sensation to the deepest levels of Godhead; see below, notes 67 and 96. Compare to one of R. Isaac's sources, *Likkutei HaRan*, chapter V, beside n. 8.

Compare the use of the verb *pashat* there and in the parable of the princess, in which the soul casts off the objects of sensation, while here the worlds cast off their own unique contents. However, in one of the discussions in *'Oẓar Ḥayyim*, one can clearly see the resemblance of the use of the term *pashat* to what we have cited from *Sefer Likkutei HaRan:*

> When an enlightened man comes to concentrate and to allow the thought of his intellect to ascend from one world to another, to the root of all the worlds (and the mind of any prophet—and even the Holy Beings—is inadequate to penetrate this secret), as long as he ascends in thought, things will be spiritualized and cast off materiality completely, until his soul will find the perfectly simple secret. And if his heart runs and it will not return to its place, then what happened to Ben Azzai will happen to him, but if he returns to his place, doing as R. Akiba, then what happened to R. Akiba will happen to him. And when this enlightened one who practices *hitbodedut* goes from world to world [returning] to the depths of the earth, below which nothing is lower, so long as he descends and thinks, things will become corporealized and embodied back down to the compounding of the four elements. (MS. Moscow-Günzburg 775 fol. 72b)

One must note that R. Isaac frequently uses the term "the world of casting-off" (*'olam ha-hitpashtut—ibid.*, fols. 73a, 86a, etc.). Compare also the connection between casting off the soul and the tendency towards communion in Plotinus, *Ennead* VI: 9, 11. As thought ascends, it apprehends the abstract and spiritual nature of things, while its concentration in the lower worlds makes it grasp the materiality and multiplicity of them. These two movements of thought are allowed by *hitbodedut*, that is, concentration.

65. Page 214. However, it seems that in *Sefer 'Oẓar Ḥayyim*, fol. 103a ff., the Divine Intellect is only a lower level of the crown (*'atarah*). Cf. *Likkutei HaRan*, in the passage quoted in my article, "The World of Imagination," p. 165: "the world of the supernal intellect, i.e., 'the *'atarah*,'" *ibid.*, p. 166, n. 6. Cf. R. Isaac of Acre's remarks concerning R. Judah ben Nissim Malka's approach, in which he says concerning the crown, i.e., *'atarah:* "And from the sensory you shall understand the intellective, for 'from your flesh shall you see God' [Job 23:16], for as it is in the created world below, so shall it be in the emanated world above. And perhaps when a sage explains this, he shall feel this secret when observing the [meaning of the] feminine [form] [of the word] 'she was.'" (published in Vajda, "Observations," p. 67). Here, the feminine form is the means of contemplating a supernal world. Cf. our discussion of Cordovero's remarks in *Sefer 'Or Yakar*, note 132 below.

66. Compare the statement in *Me'irat 'Einayim*, pp. 20-21:

> . . . The *Ẓaddik* is the seventh and the crown is his mate. Therefore, the time [of sexual union] of the sages (*talmidei ḥakhamin*), those who always commune with the Shekhinah in their good deeds and whose thoughts are connected with her, uniting all with her, is from Sabbath evening to Sabbath evening. For the Torah is called *tushiyah* (lit., advice, sagacity), for it exhausts (*mateshet*) man's strength (San. fol. 20b); but on the night of the Sabbath, when the Shekhinah is sanctified and blessed, then those who commune with her are also sanctified and strengthened.

On the special position of the righteous, between their own earthly wives and the Shekhinah, R. Isaac writes in *Sefer 'Oẓar Ḥayyim*, fol. 73b:

> I saw it said in the matter of our father Jacob, that when he was still with the physical Rachel outside of the Land [of Israel] his soul was not united with the supernal Rachel, whose domicile is in the land of holiness, but as soon as he came to the Holy Land the lower Rachel died, and his soul communed with the upper Rachel.

On the *zaddiq* who stands between two females, see also the view of the *Zohar*, as analyzed by I. Tishby, *Mishnat ha-Zohar* (Jerusalem, 1957), I: 149. We should also mention here the great similarity between this Kabbalistic approach and that of the Sufi mystic al-Arabi; see Henri Corbin, *L'Imagination creatrice dans le Soufisme d'Ibn Arabi* (Paris, 1958), p. 133; Annemarie Schimmel, *Mystical Dimensions of Islam* (Chapel Hill, N.C., 1975), p. 431; Fenton, *Treatise*, pp. 63-64. On Jacob as the husband of the Shekhinah, see the quotation from R. Moses of Burgos, alluded to in note 68 below, and the other material cited there.

67. Making do with concentration on the "intelligibles" or the Shekhinah as an end in itself would seem to have been thought improper by R. Isaac, who saw it as a religious obligation to transfer contemplation and communion to God Himself. In his book, *'Oẓar Ḥayyim*, he describes the actions of the prophets of Baal in the following words:

> And the matter of "and they prophesied," was that they did like those who practice *hitbodedut*, to negate their physical senses and to remove from the thoughts of their soul all objects of sensation, and to garb it with the spirituality of the intellect. And all depends upon thought: if his thought is attached to any created thing, even if it is the most hidden spiritual thing, which is higher than anything created in the world, namely, the created glory (*kavod nivra'*), then it is as if he literally worshipped idols. And the prophets of Baal and those who served the Asherah certainly communed in their thoughts with the queen of heaven, as the cursed women said (Jer. 44:18), "And since we have ceased to offer incense to the queen of heaven, we have lacked everything," the word *malkat* (queen) being written without the letter *aleph*, to allude to the fact that in their evil thought and corrupt intention they uprooted her, for the crown [i.e., *Shekhinah*], is the queen of heaven, upon whom is placed the rulership of this low world. But the thought of Elijah's pure soul communed with YaH the Lord God of Israel alone. (*'Oẓar Ḥayyim*, MS. Moscow-Günzburg, 775 fol. 7a)

See Gottlieb, *Studies*, p. 240; Fenton, *Treatise*, p. 63, n. 94 translates: "those that practice solitary contemplation." On the obligation to practise mystical union with God Himself, see Abulafia's remarks in *Sefer 'Oẓar 'Eden Ganuz*, MS. Oxford 1580 fol. 56a-56b, and my remark in *The Mystical Experience* p. 124 and p. 168 n. 247.

68. See R. Isaac of Acre, quoting R. Moses ben Shlomo of Burgos, in *Me'irat 'Einayim*, p. 55, and p. 245, and in *Sefer 'Oẓar Ḥayyim*, MS. Sasson 919 p. 33. Cf. Y. Tishby, *Mishnat ha-Zohar* (Jerusalem, 1961) II: 191.

69. From the Commentary of R. Joseph Ben Shem Tov to Averroes' *'Iggeret*

HaDevekut (*Epistula de Conjunctione*), MS. Berlin 216 (Or. Qu. 681) p. 325.

70. See *Kuzari* I: 13 and compare also Moses Ibn Tibbon's *Perush le-Shir ha-Shirim* (Lyck, 1874), f. 18b. It is interesting to note that there is a tradition in Moses Narboni's Commentary to *Sefer Ḥay Ben Yoqtan* which reads:

> And the latter ones blamed the pious one Socrates for bringing himself to lack of holiness because the difference between elitist study and the study of the masses was not clear to him. And I refer to the practitioner of *hitbodedut* from the polis, and the wholeness of his nature that he not take to his soul that which God and the prophets did not do, in making the fool and the wise man equal. (MS. Oxford 1351, fol. 125 a-b)

Socrates is portrayed here as one who did not understand the difference between the nature of the contemplation of the wise man and that of the masses, a misunderstanding which cost him his life.

71. In his critical comments against R. Judah ben Nissim, published by Vajda, "Observations," p. 66.

72. Vajda, "Observations," p. 47, translates this as "s'esseulant," while below (*ibid.*, p. 48), he translates the term *hamitboded* as "le solitaire." Both these terms must be understood as referring to spiritual activity, as opposed to *perishah*, which refers to abandonment of the senses.

73. The numerical equivalent (*gematria*) of *shekel* is *nefesh* (soul), i.e., 430. The reference to division of the meditator's concerns between the sensory and intellective world, i.e., "half for you, half for God," is to Pesahim 68b. Compare the anonymous *Sha'arei Ẓedek*, MS. Jerusalem 8° 148 fol. 64a: "Now, my son, if you say that you cannot attach yourself, then give half to God and half to yourself." See Scholem, "Sha'arei Ẓedek," p. 134. These statements are attributed to the spiritual guide of the anonymous author, who advises his disciple to follow an intermediary path between the desire to attain ecstasy and the difficulty in maintaining it. The usage is similar to that of R. Isaac of Acre.

74. MS. Paris BN. 840, fol. 45a.

75. Based on Jer. 8:3. Cf. Abulafia's remarks in *Sefer Ḥayyei Ha'Olam HaBa'*, MS. Oxford 1582, fol. 52b: ". . . When your soul separates itself from your body, out of its great joy in achieving and knowing what you apprehend, then it will choose death over life." It is worth mentioning that, like R. Shem Tov, Abulafia also uses the verse from Song of Songs in order to describe, albeit in a different manner, the arrival at the condition of ecstasy; see *Sefer Ḥayyei Ha'Olam HaBa'*, MS. Oxford 1592 fol. 53a; cf. Idel, *The Mystical Experience*, p. 117, n. 202.

76. Compare with the words of R. Isaac of Acre, which contain a poetic flourish:

> He who wishes to know the secret of the connection of his soul above and the communion in his thought with the Supreme God, and to acquire by that continuous, uninterrupted thought the life of the world to come, and that God be always near

him, in this life and the next—let him place before the eyes of his mind and his spirit the letters of the Unique Name, as if they are written before him in a book in scribal writing [lit., Assyrian script] . . . so that when he places the letters of the Unique Name before his eyes, your mind's eye and your heart's thought shall be in them, in the Infinite" (*Me'irat 'Einayim*, p. 217).

Compare the comments of R. Shem Tov (below, note 81) on "the light of the world to come," which appears to one who practices meditation. The expression *'olam haba* (the world to come) is already interpreted by Abulafia as referring to the ecstasy which anticipates the Afterlife, this being the significance of the title of Abulafia's major work mentioned above. On the connection between "the world to come" and the Active Intellect, see Idel, *Abraham Abulafia*, p. 94. An interesting parallel to the interpretation of "the world to come" as a prophetic state appears in a passage from MS. Sasson 290, p. 552: "I swear you by the appearance of the image of God, by the Creator, God of Abraham, God of Isaac and God of Jacob, by the Ineffable Name YH . . . that you inform me of the secret of prophecy every time that I ask you verbally, and that you teach me of the next world and teach me the law of the King . . ." This passage is based upon a *gematria* appearing frequently in Abulafia's writings, in which 999 = *be-shem ha-meforash YHWH* (by the ineffable name *YHWH*) = *we-shetelamdeni ha-'olam ha-ba* (that you teach me the world to come). On the connection between "the world to come" and the prophetic experience in Abraham Maimonides, see Gerson D. Cohen, "The Soteriology of R. Abraham Maimuni," *PAAJR*, 36 (1968), pp. 37, 40-43. See also R. Ezra of Gerona's Commentary to Song of Songs (in *Kitvei ha-RaMBaN*, ed. Chavell, II: 522: "The term *'avodah* (service) [means] to overcome pure thought in matters of the world to come and to bring about the conquest of intention [*kawannah*]." It seems probable that "the world to come" which man can thus acquire by foregoing the pleasures of this world already prior to his death is also alluded to in R. Abraham bar Ḥiya's *Hegion HaNefesh Ha'Aẓuvah* (ed. G. Wigoder, Jerusalem, 1972), p. 151.

77. Compare R. Hai Gaon's understanding of the vision of the Divine Chariot, which occurs within the heart of the perceiver and not through the soul's ascent to the world of the Chariot: see B. Levin, *'Oẓar ha-Ge'onim* (Jerusalem, 1932), *Ḥagigah, Ḥelek ha-Teshuvot*, pp. 14-15; cf. Idel, *Kabbalah: New Perspectives* ch. V.

78. MS. Paris BN 840, fols. 45b-46a. See below note 81. For the use of this verse in support of the idea of separation from society see Maimonides, *Mishneh Torah, Hilkhot De'ot* 6:1.

79. On this image, connected with the description of the Torah prior to the creation of the world, see Idel, "The Concept of Torah," pp. 43-45.

80. This refers to an inner vision of a kind of mandala; on the revelation of the circle in Abulafia and R. Isaac of Acre, see Idel, *The Mystical Experience*, pp. 109-116.

81. On the appearance of light during contemplation, see above, in the first quotation from the anonymous author of *Sha'arei Ẓedek*. Elsewhere, R. Shem Tov writes (MS. Paris BN. 840, fol. 11b): "until he chooses death over life, as he

goes out to the field to gather lights, and they become luminaries, and the light of the world appears over him, the light of the world to come and of the world of souls . . . and they reveal to him the secrets of the Torah, as is written, 'he sits alone and is silent, for it is come upon him' [Lam. 3:28], and 'The secret of the Lord is with those who fear Him' [Ps. 25:14] [etc.]." Compare the illumination coming from the lights of the holy world, "*anuar al'alam alqudusi*" in a passage from R. Abraham ibn Abu-Alrabia—the Jewish-Sufi pietist from the beginning of the thirteenth century—which was discovered and published by Naphtali Wieder, "Islamic Influences upon Jewish Cultus" (Heb.), *Melilah* 2 (1946), p. 63, who claims that this expression indicates Sufi influence. He was preceded by Rosenblatt, who also noted the Sufi background of a similar expression in Abraham Maimonides; see Rosenblatt, *Abraham Maimonides*, I: pp. 53, 65, 100. The expression already appears in R. Baḥyah Ibn Pakuda, as observed by Rosenblatt. See also the expression, "the divine lights" (*ha-'orot ha-'Elohiot*) in the Hebrew translation of Al-Ghazali's *Mishkhat Al-anwar*, MS. Vatican 209. Cf. note 149 below.

82. Based upon *Shabbat* fol. 11a. Compare *Sefer Sha'arei Ẓedek* about his literary capability during time of ecstasy: "When I entered the second week, my power of reflection was strengthened, and I was unable to write the work. Even had ten people been there, it would have been impossible for them to compose what was poured upon me." Published in Scholem, "Sha'arei Ẓedek," pp. 134-135.

83. MS. Paris BN 840, fol. 46a. See note 21 above for Abulafia's remarks about himself.

84. MS. Paris BN 840, fol. 46a. On R. Shem Tov's awareness of the problems of esoterism, see Idel, "History," pp. 9-11.

85. MS. Paris BN 840, fol. 46a. Compare the remarks of the author of *Sefer Yesod 'Olam*, who was known to R. Shem Tov:

> And when He, may He be praised, wishes that a prophet prophesy, after he has been sanctified from the womb by the perfection of his physical matter, with [even] a little learning he will gain some perception, as is written [Prov. 30:4], "And I learned not wisdom" yet even so, "I had knowledge of the holy ones"—for the holy ones, because their intellects could not receive, when prophecy was drawn down without limit upon them, their strength was weakened and they were confused, and at times even they themselves did not understand their prophecies, as the Rabbis explained [Jonah's words] "and Nineveh shall be overturned" [Jonah 3:4], that he thought this meant that it was to be destroyed. (MS. Moscow-Günzberg 607 fol. 28a).

Compare also R. Isaac b. Ḥayyim ha-Kohen, one of the exiles from Spain, to be discussed in my monograph-in-progress on *hitbodedut*.

86. MS. Paris BN 840, fol. 44a.

87. MS. Paris BN 840, fol. 47a. The expression, "the concealed letters" (*ha-'otiyyot ha-nistarot*) can be interpreted in connection with the understanding of the hidden *sefirot*, which are alluded to, according to R. David ben Judah he-Ḥasid

and his disciples, by the missing letter *yod.* See Moshe Idel, "Kabbalistic Material from the School of R. David ben Judah heḤasid" (Heb.), *Meḥkerei Yerushalayim be-Maḥ'shevet Yisra'el* 2 (1982), pp. 173-193.

Compare also the quotation from R. Shem Tov alluded to in the material in notes 91 and 92 below. One should note that it is also possible that the expression *'otiyyot mesumanot* (dotted letters) in the following passage from *Baddei Ha'Aron* may be explained as an illusion to supernal or hidden *sefirot;* as is known, the ten dots above the letters in Deut. 29:28 allude to the upper *sefirot:* see my article mentioned above (in this note), pp. 173-174.

88. MS. Paris BN 840, fol. 47b; see note 87 above.

89. See MS. Paris BN 840, fol. 45b: "and he shall know the taste of contemplation in the mountains, in a place where there are no other people, like Elisha the prophet and his friends, who killed themselves during their lifetimes . . ."

90. This work was entirely written under the influence of the Nahmanidean school of Kabbalah; on his distancing himself from the thought of that school, see the passage dealing with communion (*devekut*). In *Baddei Ha'Aron* (MS. Paris BN 840, f. 45a), we read about the experience of concentration: "for this is his life, to ascend from the lower academy to the higher academy, to enjoy the radiance of the Shekhinah, and he will have no thought of his sons or the members of his household, because of the greatness of his *devekut* (communion)." On the other hand, Nahmanides understands *devekut* as continuous thought which does not interfere with the normal life of the devotee; see Scholem, "Devekut," pp. 205-207. It should be noted that the description of the relationship to one's family during the period of *devekut* is very close to that of his Christian contemporary, Meister Eckhart, who sees the mystic relating to the world with an attitude of "Gelicheit" after he understands the equality of all things within the hidden Godhead, an understanding stemming from intimate contact with Him. See the analysis of Reiner Schürmann, *Meister Eckhart—Mystic and Philosopher* (Bloomington-London, 1978), p. 79: "Equanimity is the consequence of detachment with relation to the created as created. It is a condition of nothing." See notes 98 and 102 below. One should note the approach which understands equanimity as the result of a powerful experience of love of God; see Eleazar of Worms, *Sefer ha-Rokeaḥ, Hilkhot Ḥasidut, Shoresh ha'Ahavah.* According to Scholem, *Major Trends,* pp. 96-97, this approach is identical with the Stoic or Cynic *ataraxy.* However, among these latter inner peace is a goal in itself, and not only a side-effect of a spiritual experience of this or another kind, which it is among the Kabbalists and in Plotinus. For a criticism from another view-point of Scholem's interpretation of R. Eleazar of Worms on this subject, see Haym Soloveitchik, "Three Themes in the *Sefer Hasidim,*" *AJS review,* I (1976), pp. 328-329. Likewise, one ought to emphasize that there is no similarity between Eckhart's view of "Gelicheit" and that of R. ABNeR, as we analyzed it above, according to Scholem, *Major Trends,* p. 97, nor is there any resemblance between Eckhart's view and that of R. Baḥya Ibn Paquda, ibid., p. 372, n. 59. Baḥyah, like many of the Kabbalistic texts that we have cited here, saw in *hishtawwut* mastery over the impulses of the soul, which

are motivated by the desire or drive for honor or fear of shame; in Eckhart, "Gelicheit" is connected with an understanding of the createdness of all that exists and their equality in the eyes of God, a situation which then leads to an attitude of equanimity. Among the Kabbalists, "equanimity" (i.e., *hishtawwut*), even when it takes place after attachment of thought, is nevertheless a condition for communion of the soul, which is the main thing. See note 41 above.

91. MS. Paris BN 840 fol. 45a.

92. Ḥagigah 15a; cf. David J. Halperin, *The Merkabah in Rabbinic Literature*, (New Haven, Conn., 1980), p. 76 ff. In all versions, the interlocuter is R. Joshua rather than R. Akiba. R. Shem Tov apparently alludes to the deficient spelling of the word as *Le'an*, rather than *Le'Ayin*, as it appears in most texts of the aggadah. It may be that this Kabbalist is referring to the ten hidden or supernal *sefirot*, whose existence is represented by the absence of the letter *yod*. On the ten supernal *sefirot*, see M. Idel, "The Sefirot above the Sefirot" (Heb.), *Tarbiẓ* 51 (1982), p. 239 ff; their source is in *Sefer Baddei Ha'Aron*, MS. Paris BN 840 fol. 64a; cf. note 87 above.

93. Printed in Scholem, *MSS.*, p. 226.

94. R. Yoḥanan b. Zakkai and R. Eleazar b. Arakh, according to Ḥagigah 1:2. It is reasonable to assume that R. Judah himself might have compiled the text in Ḥagigah on the basis of the source at hand; as is known, the author was a well-known halakhic scholar.

95. Compare with *Sefer Moznei Ẓedek*, p. 49: "that their presence and absence should be equal to you." This term is the translation of the word "istiwa" in Al-Ghazali. Note the specific use of the term *shaweh* in Albotini: a man in whose eyes contradictions are nullified. This usage may be connected with the definition of the Infinite in the Kabbalah of Gerona as *hashwa'ah*, or that which is *shaweh* in the sense of being the place in which the opposites are nullified. See G. Scholem, *Les origines*, pp. 463-465. Scholem identifies R. Azriel of Gerona's comments with the scholastic concepts of "indistinctio" or "coincidentia oppositorum." There is a suggestive possible parallel between the psychological state of the human being who strives to achieve prophecy, who is defined as *shaweh*, and God, who is described in similar terms. Cf. the interesting remarks of Y. Baer, "The Sacrificial Cult in the Second Temple Period" (Heb.), *Ẓion* 40 (1975), pp. 109, 150-153. It is interesting to note that already at the beginning of the 14th century, we find the following in *Sefer Yesod 'Olam* by R. Elḥanan b. Abraham of Eskira the following: ". . . and when they reach equanimity in equal unity, as in the simile 'His left hand is under my head' [Cant. 2:6]" (MS. Moscow-Günzburg 607 fol. 104b). This indicates that the form *hishtawwut* also served in the sense of negation or the combination of contraries in God, defined as "harmonious unity" (*'aḥdut shawah*). On the resemblance of the perfect man, who is defined as *apathes* through his acquisition of apathy, to God, see the description of Philo's approach in David Winston's important article, "Was Philo a Mystic?" in *Studies in Jewish Mysticism*, ed., J. Dan-F.Talmage, (Cambridge, Mass., 1982), p. 26.

The connection between these two areas is even clearer in the quotation below from R. Joseph Karo, in which the capability of uniting God is made conditional upon reaching a state of equanimity of the soul. See also R. Ḥayyim Vital in *Sha'arei Kedushah* III:4, who includes among the conditions of prophecy: "And humility shall be deeply impressed upon his soul, until he will feel neither joy at being honored nor the contempt of those who insult him, and both shall be equal in his eyes."

96. Compare Albotini's remarks elsewhere:

> And it has already happened that one's soul was separated at the time of that casting off from everything, and he remained dead. And such a death is praiseworthy, being close to "death by the [Divine] kiss." And it was in this way that the soul of Ben Azzai, who "gazed and died," departed, for his soul rejoiced upon looking at the Source from which it was hewn, and it wished to commune with it and stay there and not return to the body, and of such a death it is said, "Precious in the eyes of the Lord is the death of his righteous ones" [Ps. 116:15]. (Scholem, *MSS.*, p. 228).

97. *Maggid Mesharim, Parashat Beshalaḥ* (Jerusalem, 1960), p. 57.

98. The meaning of *yiḥud* (union) in Karo requires clarification; it is difficult to assume that we are speaking here of *yiḥud* in the standard Kabbalistic sense: i.e., the unification of the *sefirot* of *Tiferet* and *Malkhut.* It seems very likely to me that this is based upon a reference to the Sufi concept of *tawḥid*—i.e., the unification of God by separation from everything subject to the category of time. See Benedikt Reinert, *Die Lehre vom tawakkul in der Klassischen Sufic* (Berlin, 1968), pp. 23 ff.; Reynold A. Nicholson, *The Idea of Personality in Sufism* (Cambridge, 1923), p. 13. If so, we have before us an advancing of the need for the concentration of human powers by means of transcending all contradictory arousals, so that the soul can acknowledge and experience the unity of God. This mystical level, which depends upon the achievement of equanimity, implies the separation of the soul from matters of this world. According to this analysis, in Karo one must not see *hishtawwut* as the result of communion with God, as Werblowsky states, in *Karo*, p. 162, but only a preparation for it.

99. Scholem, *MSS.*, p. 226.

100. This apparently reflects a certain influence of Maimonides' distinction between the two purposes of the Torah: the welfare of the body and that of the soul. See also R. Pinḥas b. Yair's famous saying in *Avodah Zarah* fol. 20b, as the model for this gradation. A detailed description of the meaning of *perishut* appears immediately before the above quotation, pp. 225-226. For Jewish-Sufi interpretation of this Talmudic saying, see the work described in Franz Rosenthal, "Judaeo-Arabic Work under Sufic Influence," *HUCA* vol. 15 (1940), pp. 442 ff.

101. Scholem, *MSS.*, p. 226.

102. Compare Plotinus, *Ennead* IV: 3, 32, in which the memory of one's friends,

children and wife are part of the lower levels of functioning of the soul, from which one must separate oneself. Plotinus praises their forgetting, as this enables one to flee from multiplicity to unity. Cf. note 90 above.

103. See above, note 90, and compare also the view of the Baal Shem Tov in *Ẓawa'at ha-RIBaSh;* see Schatz, *Hasidut*, p. 153. Cf. section V above, in our discussion of the precedence of communion to equanimity according to R. Isaac of Acre in his book *Me'irat 'Eynayim.*

104. Scholem, *MSS.*, pp. 228-229.

105. *Sefer Magen Dawid*, p. 49b.

106. Ibid., p. 18d-19a. On the Urim and Tummim in Abulafia, see Idel, *The Mystical Experience* pp. 105-108; compare also our discussion of *hitbodedut* in R. Ḥasdai Crescas and in R. Moses Botaril in our work-in-progress in the chapter on *hitbodedut* and the Temple.

107. Ibid., p. 19a.

108. Abraham Abulafia's *Shomer Miẓwah* was dedicated to a disciple of his from Safed: see chapter VI above.

Sefer Sha'arei Ẓedek was written in the Galilee or in Hebron, ibid., p. 120; R. Isaac of Acre was born and educated in Acre, while, R. Shem Tov Ibn Gaon concluded the writing of his book, *Baddei Ha'Aron*, in Safed.

109. See Idel, chapter VI above; *idem.*, "R. Judah Ḥalewah and his Book *Ẓafnat Pa'aneaḥ*" (Heb.), *Shalem* 4, ed., J. Hacker, (Jerusalem, 1984), pp. 133-134.

110. See Gershom Scholem, "Kabbalah" (German), *Encyclopedia Judaica*^{2} (1932), IX: 657-658; Werblowsky, *Karo*, pp. 38-39.

111. In a recently published, comprehensive monograph on the Kabbalistic doctrine of Ibn Gabbai, Abulafia's name is not mentioned even once in its own right. See: Roland Goetschel, *Meir ibn Gabbai—Le Discours de la Kabbale Espagnole* (Leuwen, 1981). Prophetic Kabbalah is also not mentioned in R. Shem Tov Ibn Shem Tov's *Sefer Ha'Emunot*, which is a reasonably representative collection of Spanish Kabbalah of the period.

112. MS. Cincinnati 586 fol. 45b. Dr. Berakha Zack has drawn my attention to several passages concerning *hitbodedut* in *Sefer Or Yakar*, for which I express my thanks.

113. This is the only source I know in which *Sefer Sha'arei Ẓedek* is ascribed to Abraham Abulafia; despite the similarity in many details of its Kabbalistic system, and even of the spiritual biography of the anonymous Kabbalist and of Abulafia, the author is not to be identified with Abulafia. Generally, Cordovero's writings contain quite a number of bibliographical confusions, one of which I mention in note 120 below; see also note 114.

114. One should not conclusively infer from this that Cordovero knew this

book by Abulafia. However, the fact that his disciple, R. Ḥayyim Vital, quotes from this work tends to confirm the assumption that Cordovero did know *Sefer Ḥayyei Ha'Olam HaBa'*, and through comparison with *Sefer Sha'arei Ẓedek* one reaches the conclusion that the two books were written by the same author. This suggests that Cordovero's copy of *Sha'arei Ẓedek* did not contain the name of its author. It follows that the circle of Kabbalists around Cordovero had all of the central Kabbalistic works describing techniques of attaining ecstasy written at the end of the 13th and the beginning of the 14th century: (1) *Sefer Ḥayyei Ha'Olam HaBa'*; (2) *Sefer 'Or HaSekhel;* (3) *Sefer HaḤeshek*, quoted in an as-yet-unpublished section of Vital's *Sefer Sha'arei Kedushah;* (4) *Sefer Sha'arei Ẓedek*, by one of Abulafia's disciples; (5) the writings of R. Isaac of Acre: *Sefer Me'irat 'Einayim* and at least portions of *Sefer 'Oẓar Ḥayyim.* See also above pp. 136-140.

115. On neo-Platonic tendencies in this work, see, e.g., Idel, *Abraham Abulafia*, p. 95. On the connection between *hitbodedut* and communion of the individual soul with the supernal soul, see our discussion of R. Ezra of Gerona in our above-mentioned work on *hitbodedut.*

116. MS. British Library 749, fol. 15b; and compare the quotation from *Sefer Shi'ur Komah*, fol. 30d, quoted below. Cf., Idel, *The Mystical Experience*, ch. II. It is difficult to determine the exact identity of the author: R. Moses Cordovero, who is mentioned on that page as the one who said certain things to R. Elijah de Vidas, who in turn conveyed them to Vital; R. Isaac of Acre, who is also mentioned there; or perhaps Vital himself. The last case seems the most probable.

117. Compare the expression, *tardemah shel hitbodedut* (slumber of concentration) in R. Ḥayyim Vital's *Sefer HaḤeziyonot* (Jerusalem, 1954), p. 55; cf. Fine, "Recitation," p. 187, 191.

118. On the parallel between music and the creation of melody, and letter-combination in Abulafia's teaching, see Idel, *The Mystical Experience*, pp. 53-55.

119. Compare with what appears in *Sefer Ha'Aẓamim*, attributed to R. Abraham Ibn Ezra (ed., M. Grossberg, London, 1901), p. 13: ". . . The Active Intellect, which they called Shekhinah, and through which he who draws it down shall apprehend the Creator, may He be blessed, and it will teach him during the time of his concentration and while he is asleep." It seems that one may conclude from the expression, "when he is asleep," the nature of this state of *hitbodedut*, namely, the breaking-off from the senses. In any event, according to *Sefer ha-'Aẓamim*, the contents revealed in those two states "shall be understood and placed in order while he is awake." See below, note 124.

120. *Pardes Rimmonim* (Jerusalem, 1962), pt. 2, p. 97a, is parallel to *Sefer 'Or HaSekhel*, MS. Vatican 233 fol. 95a. Cordovero quotes Abulafia's comments as if their source were *Sefer HaNikkud*, but it is clear that they come from *'Or HaSekhel.* This is seen, not only by textual comparison, but also because that work is mentioned by name among the compositions of Abulafia in his treatise concerning angels published in Scholem, *MSS.*, p. 232, in which he alludes to the subject referred to in the quotation from *Pardes Rimmonim.* For an explanation

of this error, see Idel, *Abraham Abulafia*, p. 25. Cordovero's words are quoted by R. Ḥayyim Vital in *Sha'arei Kedushah*, part. 4, gate 1, MS. British Library 749, fol. 10a.

121. Ibid., part. 2, fol. 69b.

122. This name is extremely significant in Abulafia's important work, *Sefer Ḥayyei Ha'Olam HaBa'*.

123. Here, the letter-combinations are understood as a means of influencing the *sefirot* and bringing about their unification.

124. Compare *Sefer ha-'Aẓamim*, attributed to Abraham ibn Ezra, p. 13: "There is a prophet to whom [prophecy] is emanated while he is awake, without him being caused to dream or his power being weakened or him falling asleep, and if he were not expert in drawing it down, along with knowing its service and its sacrifices—then he would be killed." Cf. on p. 14. See also note 119 above, and my article, "The Epistle of R. Isaac of Pisa (?) in Three Versions" (Heb.), *Koveẓ 'al Yad* 10 (20) (1982), pp. 166-167.

125. R. Moses Cordovero himself dealt with the combination of vowels of the Ineffable Name, in order to resolve a certain Kabbalistic problem; see his book *Shi'ur Komah* (Warsaw, 1885), f. 90d. Combinations of the vowels of the divine name are extremely widespread in Abulafia's system, Cordovero quoting a passage dealing with this subject in his book, *Pardes Rimonnim;* see note 120 above, and compare also R. Shem Tov Ibn Gaon, in his book *Baddei Ha'Aron*, quoted above from MS. Paris BN 840, fol. 44a.

126. *Pardes Rimmonim*, II: fol. 95d.

127. On the background to this view, see Moshe Idel, "The Magical and Neoplatonic Interpretations of the Kabbalah in the Renaissance," in *Jewish Thought in the Sixteenth Century*, ed. Bernard D. Cooperman, (Cambridge, Mass., 1983), pp. 196-201. I shall discuss elsewhere the resemblance between the conception of "spiritual force" in Cordovero, and that of R. Yoḥanan Alemanno and his sources. See also Yosef Ben-Shlomo, *Torat ha-Elohut shel R. Moshe Cordovero* (Jerusalem, 1965), pp. 41-42. *Hitbodedut* also causes the descent of souls in order to reveal secrets: see the quotation from *Sefer 'Or Yakar*, to be discussed in the chapter on concentration in the field, in my future monograph.

128. On purgation of the soul in connection with the absorption of spirituality by means of the letters, see Idel, above, p. 73.

129. Warsaw, 1885, p. 30d; on this passage, see Ben-Shlomo, *Torat he-Elohut*, p. 40. Cf. what we quoted above from MS. British Library 749, fol. 15b.

130. Here, one sees clearly the influence of Maimonides' comments in *MT, Yesode ha-Torah* 7:4, including the specific use of the term *hitbodedut* in the sense of intellectual concentration.

131. Jerusalem, 1979, vol. 10, p. 7. Compare *Sefer Shi'ur Komah* fol. 94d,

"that man should meditate on the divine wisdom, when he understands the creation of the existing things, and understand the properties of their limbs."

132. On the history of this saying, see the important article by Alexander Altmann, "The Delphic Maxim in Medieval Islam and Judaism," in *Biblical and Other Studies*, ed. A. Altmann, (Cambridge, Mass., 1963), pp. 196-231, especially p. 198 and p. 208 ff. See also Cordovero's remarks in *Shi'ur Komah* p. 34a, 94b, and Ben-Shlomo, *Torat ha-Elohut*, pp. 28-29. Altmann, p. 209, quotes *Sefer ha-Temunah* as the earliest source for the Kabbalistic understanding of Job 19:26; however, as this Kabbalistic work was written in the fourteenth century, one must see the sources for the view of *Sefer ha-Temunah* in precedents found in the Kabbalah of the circle of R. Joseph Ashkenazi: see *Perush LeSefer HaYeẓirah* of R. Joseph Ashkenazi (Jerusalem, 1954), p. 13a, and MS. Oxford 2073, fol. 170a. On the possible connection between *Sefer ha-Temunah* and the circle of Ashkenazi, see my article, "Kabbalistic Material" (op. cit., n. 87) pp. 204-205, n. 207. R. Joseph's contemporary, R. Isaac of Acre, may be one of Cordovero's sources; in a short work by R. Isaac, which appears anonymously in MS. Oxford 1638, fol. 49a, we read: "The *sefirot*, which are united with one another, and all of which are in the Infinite, in all six directions—always, when you wish to apprehend the intelligibles, look to the objects of sensation, and from the objects of sensations you shall truly apprehend the intelligibles, as is said, 'From my flesh I Shall see God.'" Compare this understanding of the transition from the sensory to the intellective, which is also associated with divinity, to the conclusion of the parable of the princess. See also the words of R. Isaac in Vajda, "Observations," p. 67 (op. cit., n. 65). A similar use of the verse in Job to that in MS. Oxford 1638 appears in *Me'irat 'Einayim*, p. 118, 237, 243.

133. Compare with *Sefer 'Or Yakar*, vol. 10, p. 8: "If you say to him, concentrate on this-worldly matters, so that you may understand, through their revealed nature, their secret nature, as several wise men did." The connection between apprehension and *hitbodedut* is seen in several passages in Cordovero: see, for example, his comments re the *sefirot:* "and the *sefirot* shall also have pleasure in their *hitbodedut* and their apprehension of their essence" (*Shi'ur Komah*, f. 43b).

134. Cordovero's treatise concerning the angels, published in Reuben Margolioth, *Malakhei 'Elyon* (Jerusalem, 1945), Appendix, p. 21. Cf. *Shi'ur Komah*, p. 94c.

135. *Tomer Devorah*, Ch. 3.

136. See *Sefer 'Or Yakar* 10: p. 8: "And when a man wishes to practice *hitbodedut* to understand some thing, he should cast off this corporeality." The relationship between *hitbodedut*, in the sense of intellectual concentration, and casting off corporeality appears in many sources: see Vital's comments, referred to in note 116 above, and Fine, "Meditation," pp. 189-190; and Cordovero in *Shi'ur Komah*, in note 129 above. Compare also R. Jacob b. Asher, *Tur, 'Oraḥ Ḥayim*, sec. 98: "who used to concentrate . . . until they reached the state of casting off of materiality and strengthening of their intellective spirit." See also Al-Ghazali's comments near

note 18 above, and Albotini, above, note 96.

137. *Sefer 'Or Yakar, Tikkunei Zohar*, Bava Batra, MS. Modena, fol. 196b.

138. Generally, Cordovero states that the spiritual Torah descends and is embodied in this lowly world. See Berakha Zack, "A Section of R. Moshe Cordovero's Interpretation of *Ra'ya Mehemna*" (Heb.), *Kovez 'al Yad* 10 (20) (1982), pp. 256-258. On the identification of the Torah with the sefirotic system, see Idel, "The Concept of Torah," pp. 49-84.

139. See *Sha'arei Kedushah* Ch. 12 (p. 176a), while chapter 2 of the same section contains the story of one of the practitioners of *hitbodedut*, which seems to have been taken from one of R. Isaac of Acre's writings. This story also seems to have served as the source for S. Y. Agnon's story, "The Tale of the Scribe" (Heb.), *Elu we-elu* (Jerusalem, Tel-Aviv, 1969), pp. 140-141 [English translation: *Midstream*, v. 13, no. 2 (Feb. 1967), pp. 16-26]. On the value of *hitbodedut*, see the quotation from R. Isaac in de Vidas', *Sha'ar Ha-'Ahavah*, Ch. 3, fol. 59a; R. Ḥayyim Vital apparently copied R. Isaac's words from here into *Sha'arei Kedushah*, MS. British Library 749, fol. 15b. One must stress that letter-combination is not mentioned in these sources, although there is no doubt that de Vidas knew of this technique: see *Sha'ar ha-Yir'ah*, Ch. 10, and Idel, *The Mystical Experience* p. 28.

140. MS. British Library 749, fol. 15b. I shall discuss the total context of this text in my monograph on *hitbodedut*, in the chapter on dream questions; cf. Cordovero's treatises on angels in Margolioth, *Malakhei 'Eliyon*, p. 83, and Albotini's discussions in several passages in *Sulam Ha'Aliyah*. The use of dream questions in connection with letter-combination already appears among Abulafia's disciples, and apparently reflects some Sufic influence here; see Trimingham, *Sufi Orders*, p. 158; Fenton, *Treatise*, pp. 16-17 and p. 61, n. 72; Idel, "Inquiries," p. 205; and note 32 above.

141. MS. New York JTS Rab. 809, fol. 210b, published in Pachter, "The Life," p. 140.

142. The active verb *shiwiti*, from the same root as *hishtawwut*, is found, at least in allusion, in *Sha'arei Kedushah* 3:4, and later in *SheLaH*, which apparently caused the spread into Hasidic literature of the understanding of equanimity in the context of this verse from Psalms. See Ze'ev Gries, "The Hasidic *Hanhagot* Literature as an Expression of Behavior and Ethos" (Heb.), Doctoral Dissertation, (Jerusalem, 1979), pp. 160-161; Schatz, *Hasidut*, p. 153; and above, note 37.

143. The use of this verse in connection with communion (*devekut*) appears in *Me'irat 'Eynayim*, p. 217 (*parashat 'ekev*), and on p. 10, and in *Sefer 'Ozar Ḥayyim;* see also the passages quoted in chapter VI, above, p. 99 n. 26. The verse also appears in an explicitly mystical context in Karo's *Sefer Maggid Mesharim, Parashat Mikez*, p. 37a, and in *Sefer Haredim*, p. 35; cf. Pachter, "Communion," p. 90, p. 117. Compare also R. Jacob Emden's comment there, in which he also mentions *hitbodedut*, apparently in the sense of intellectual concentration, in connection with this verse. Cf. Z. Gries, "The Sources and Editing of *Sefer Darkhei Ḥayyim*"

(Heb.), *Meḥkerei Yerushalayim be-Maḥashevet Yisra'el* 1:2 (1982), pp. 143-144, n. 31.

144. *Sefer Ḥaredim*, p. 256; and see Werblowsky, *Karo*, pp. 63-64, and near note 97 above.

145. See the texts cited by Meir Benayahu, *Sefer Toldot ha-AR"I* (Jerusalem, 1967), p. 154, 287. On Luria's use of *hitbodedut* in order to deeply study a Zoharic passage, see p. 166, p. 319.

146. See above, in the passage quoted from Al-Ghazali's *Moznei Ẓedek*, and the *ḥadit* brought by Abu-al-Najib al-Suhrawardi, "Contemplation for one hour is better than ritual worship for a whole year." See *A Sufi Rule for Novices. An Abridged Translation and Introduction*, by M. Milson (Cambridge, Mass.: Harvard University Press, 1975), p. 49. On the tension between meditation and Torah study, see the studies cited by Werblowsky, *Karo*, p. 64, n. 3.

147. Printed in Pachter, "Devekut," p. 88; *idem* "The Life," p. 135; compare also the description of Enoch in *Me'irat 'Einayim*, p. 47, which was known to Cordovero: see *Pardes Rimmonim* 22:4.

148. On the preceding among the Sufis of the *dhikr*, and sometimes of contemplation, by silence, see Bannerth, "Dhikr et Khalwa," p. 69, 73.

149. On the appearance of light in ecstatic states, see again Pachter, "The Life," p. 136 and 139, and especially his comments on Azikri in *Sefer Ḥaredim*, p. 256: "The early Ḥasidim . . . who refrained from study in favor of *hitbodedut* and *devekut* and described the light of the Shekhina above their heads as if it spread around them, and they sit in the midst of the light . . . And then they tremble in nature and rejoice in that trembling." For the possible source of Azikri's remarks, see Scholem, "Devekut," p. 209; the question, however, requires further study. On the appearance of the light, see also our discussion of *Sefer Sha'arei Ẓedek* and of R. Shem Tov Ibn Gaon above, section VI, and especially note 81.

150. Page 43.

151. On Abulafia, see Idel, *The Mystical Experience*, pp. 34-37; on Isaac of Acre, see *ibid.*, and note 42 above; on Albotini, see the sources mentioned in note 109 above; on de Vidas, see Pachter, "Communion," p. 104, n. 204, and p. 114; on Azikri, see Pachter, "The Life," p. 136.

152. On the shutting of one's eyes in Mussar and Kabbalistic literature, see Ze'ev Gries, "Hasidic *Hanhagot* Literature as an Expression of Behavior and Ethos" (Heb.), (Doctoral Dissertation, Jerusalem: Hebrew University, 1979), p. 168-170; Schatz, *Hasidut*, p. 108.

153. See Bannerth, "Dhikr et Khalwa," pp. 70, 73, 80. Compare also *Perakim be-Haẓlaḥah*, attributed to Maimonides (ed., S. Z. Davidowitz-D. Z. Banet, Jerusalem, 1939), p. 7. The practice of shutting one's eyes is doubtless ancient, and relates to the emergence of the term "mystic," derived from the Greek verb "muo," that is, to shut one's eyes or to close one's lips. See A. M. J. Festugiere,

La revelation d'Hermes Trismegiste (Paris, 1950) vol. I, pp. 305-306.

154. See *Sefer ha-Yashar*, attributed to (Rabbenu) Jacob Tam, sec. 13 (Jerusalem, 1967), p. 109.

155. MS. Paris, Bibliotheque Alliance Israelite Universelle, 167 VI. B.

156. Published in G. Scholem, "Chapters from *Sefer Sulam Ha'Aliyah* of R. Judah Albotini" (Heb.), *Kiryat Sefer* 22 (1945), p. 163.

157. Printed by Scholem, *MSS.*, p. 227; the description quoted here is part of the process of *hitbodedut*.

158. Sec. 3, Ch. 8 (Benai Barak, 1973), p. 115.

159. Compare *Sefer Ḥaredim*, p. 263: "The reason for closing one's eyes at the time of prayer is that it is as if he has left the world and is [standing] before the king with the closed eyes of an infant . . ." Compare also p. 277 there: "and if you close your eyes and turn to your Maker." See above, in the quotation from R. Shem Tov Ibn Gaon's *Sefer Baddei Ha'Aron.*

160. *Sha'ar Ruaḥ ha-Kodesh* (Jerusalem, 1912), 7, 52.

161. Quoted from *Sefer Mekor Ha-Shemot* by R. Moses Zacuto, MS. Laniado, fol. 68a.

162. *Sefer Sha'arei Kedushah*, MS. British Library 749, f. 16a; and compare with the above quotation from Zacuto, *Mekor Ha-Shemot*, from a MS. of Vital.

163. On the ascent of the soul during the course of meditation, see *Sefer Sha-'arei Kedushah* 3, 5 (p. 102), 3, 8 (p. 115).

164. On the use of recitation of Mishnah as a mystical technique, see Fine, "Recitation," pp. 183-199. On p. 198, he printed the passage quoted here, and on pp. 189-191 there is a translation and brief discussion of the passage.

165. MS. British Library 749, fol. 16a.

166. Compare Vital's remarks in *Sha'ar HaYiḥudim*, Ch. 7 (Jerusalem, 1963), fol. 6d: "Then concentrate and close your eyes and turn your thoughts from this world completely, and then direct your intention." Here one sees indirectly how Abulafia's teaching of letter-combination contributed to the technique of *yiḥudim* in Lurianic Kabbalah.

167. See *Sefer Ḥayyei Ha'Olam HaBa'*, MS. Oxford 1582, fol. 57b: "and close your eyes and direct your intention . . ." referring to actions during the course of letter-combination, following isolation in a room. See Idel, *The Mystical Experience*, p. 38.

168. In Yeshayahu Tishbi, *Ḥikrei Kabbalah Ushluḥoteha* (Jerusalem, 1982), pp. 131-146.

169. In Tishbi, ibid. pp. 155-156. Concerning this work, see Tishbi, ibid.,

also Yoram Jacobson *Torat HaGe'ulah shel R. Mordekhai Dato* (Ph.D. thesis, Hebrew University 1982), pp. 95-100.

170. ẒON an acronym for *Ẓ*eruf *'O*tyot *N*ekudot (combination, letter and vowel).

171. See *Targum Yonatan ben Uziel* on Exodus 3:2. This idea is cited widely in Kabbalistic literature, see especially *Ẓiyoni*, in Parshat Vezot Haberakhah, regarding this angel as Moses' teacher with the hidden numerical value of Moses' name—Me'ayin (see immediately in the text) is found earlier, in Abulafia writings.

172. Both "Zeganzagel" and "Me'ayin" have the numerical value of 101.

173. This refers to the (exegetic) numerological technique of the "hidden numerology"—in the nomenclature of the thirteenth century Ashkenazi Pietists. This amounts to figuring the numerical value of only the letters that spell out each letter (such as Alef, spelled as Alef *Lamed, Pe;* the value of the last two letters). In the case of the name Moshe the letters are Mem, *Mem*, Shin *Yod Nun*, He *Alef;* which spell the word 'Me'ayin' (meaning, from nothingness.)

174. This work was known to Cordovero and his disciples, as well as to R. Ḥayyim Vital. See Idel (citation in note 1), p. 70, note 215.

175. See Ms. Oxford 1582, f. 45b. Neither the title of this book, nor of any other by Abulafia, is mentioned in Dato's writings, though he does mention the titles of the works of many Kabbalists, all of whom are associated with the Kabbalah of the sefirot. See Y. Jacobson (note 169), pp. 120-22, also Jacobson, ibid., p. 100, note 6. There, based on the sections of *'Iggeret HaLevanon* that were brought earlier in this paper, he writes that Dato received the tradition of letter and vowel combination from Cordovero. However, he does not indicate Abulafia as a source for either Cordovero or Dato. The influence of Abulafia on Dato is noticeable in various other places in Dato's work, but this will not be elaborated upon here.

It is worth noting that mention of the "three Kabbalistic principles" is made in the works of the Italian Kabbalist R. Eliyah Menaḥem Ḥalfan, who lived one generation before Dato. See Ms. New York, JTS 1822 fol. 153b: "So too, he was a shepherd of sheep (Ro'e Ẓon), for Ẓon is an acronym for *Ẓ*eruf *'O*tiyot *N*ekudot (letter and vowel combination). These are the three fundamental principles of this wisdom." The aforementioned Kabbalist also brings this Abulafian idea without attribution.

176. See MS. Oxford 1582, fol. 23a. We note that this idea is also mentioned in the work of the Safed Kabbalist R. Shlomo Alkabetz; see *Berit Halevi*, [Jerusalem 1963 (photo-offset)] f. 14c.

177. See Idel, *Abraham Abulafia*, pp. 19, 67, note 20.

178. See *Sefer Sha'arei Kedushah* [Benei Berak 1973] pp. 105, 112, 114.

179. See Tishbi (cited in note 168 above), p. 154.

180. Exodus 3:1. Earlier, Dato indicates that Moses' shepherding of Jethro's

sheep refers allegorically to the clutivation of the "intelligence-soul."

181. See Tishbi (cited in note 168 above), p. 154, note 44.

182. 2 Samuel 23:2.

183. Quietistic expressions such as this, that occur in various of Cordovero's writings can be seen as valuable precedents for understanding the historical context of Hasidic ideology. But here is not the place for elaboration.

184. See *Sefer Ḥayyei Ha'Olam HaBa'*, MS. Oxford 1582, fol. 46b.

185. See Tishbi (cited in note 168 above) p. 155.

186. In Abulafia's Kabbalistic epistle *Vezot LiYihudah* published by A. Jellinek in *Ginzei Ḥokhmat HaKabbalah* (Leipzig 1853) p. 15.

187. Ibid. p. 19.

188. Ibid. pp. 15-16.

189. See Idel, *Abraham Abulafia*, pp. 442-43.

190. See Cordovero *Sefer Pardes Rimmonim Gate 27* (Sha'ar Ha'Otiyot—the Gate of Letters) Chapter 1.

191. Compare Cordovero *Sefer Shiur Komah* (Jerusalem 1979 photo-offset) fol. 64b: "Become learned in the writings of R. Shimeon, of blessed memory; within them you will find pleasantness for your pure intellect." So too, it is worth comparing the end of Chapter 58 (ibid.) with the words of Dato regarding the danger involved in the study of Kabbalah. What is especially noteworthy is that Cordovero seems to indicate that the study of the Zohar is merely a stage in one's Kabbalistic education. In contrast to the "pleasantness" associated with the study of the Zohar, in Cordovero's writings and by the above-mentioned quote specifically it appears that there exists a higher, more intellectual stage:

> And do not hasten to peek through the lattices of your intellectual ignorance, lest your eyes be darkened by false reasoning and you be found stricken. Rather, stand firm and contemplate until the gates of knowledge be opened for you and be like the rare one in a city, two in a family, that gather to her in peace and enter in peace. (ibid. fol. 64b.)

It is reasonable to assume that what is referred to here is not a more profound study of the Zohar, but rather, a different form of wisdom entirely. It seems to me that this form of wisdom is indicated earlier in the same chapter (fol. 63a-64a) where Cordovero mentions the "combination of letters" and the "particulars of letters" a number of times.

Regarding Cordovero's experience in combining the vowel point in his life, see ibid. fol. 90a.

192. Concerning the sources for the designation "Ruḥaniyut" (spirituality) and its influence on Kabbalah and Hassidism see M. Idel: "Perceptions of Kabbalah

in the Second Half of the 18th Century" (English), delivered at the Colloquium of Jewish Thought in the 18th Century, Harvard University, 1984.

193. As Cordovero writes in *Pardes Rimmonim* Gate 27, Chapter 1: "And in *Sefer Berit Menuḥah* this subject is dealt with briefly." This is in reference to the relation between the letters or Divine Names and the Supernal Chariot. Compare also *Pardes Rimmonim* Gate 28. (Sha'ar HaNikkud—the Gate of the Vowel Points) Chapter 1.

194. See Idel, "Inquiries" pp. 193-94.

195. See note 192.

References

Altmann, Alexander. The Delphic maxim in mediaeval Islam and Judaism. In *Biblical and Other Studies*, edited by A. Altmann, 196-231. Cambridge, MA: Harvard University Press, 1963.

———Maimonides' attitude toward Jewish mysticism. In *Studies in Jewish Thought*, edited by A. Jospe, 200-219. Detroit, MI, 1981.

———*Faces of Judaism* [Hebrew]. Tel Aviv, 1983.

Bannerth, Ernest. Dhikr et Khalwa d'apres Ibn 'Ata 'Allah. *Institut Dominicain d'Etudes Orientales du Caire. Melanges* 12 (1974): 65-90.

Fenton, Paul, ed. & trans. *The Treatise of the Pool* (*Al-Maqala al-Hawdiyya*, by Maimonides). London, 1981.

Fine, Lawrence. Recitation of Mishna as a vehicle for mystical inspiration: A contemplative technique taught by Ḥayyim Vital. *REJ* 141 (1982): 183-199.

Gottlieb, Ephraim. *Meḥqarim be-Sifrut ha-Qabbalah* (*Studies*), edited by J. Hacker. Tel Aviv, 1976.

Idel, Moshe. R. Abraham Abulafia's works and doctrine [Hebrew]. Ph.D. dissertation, Hebrew University, Jerusalem, 1976.

———On the history of the interdiction against the study of Kabbalah before the age of forty [Hebrew]. *AJS Review* 5 (1980): 1-20.

———The concept of the Torah in Heikhalot literature and Kabbalah [Hebrew]. *Meḥqerey Yerushalayim be-Maḥshevet Yisra'el* 1(1) (1981): 23-84.

———Abraham Abulafia and the Pope: An account of an abortive mission [Hebrew]. *AJS Review* 7-8 (1982-83): 1-17.

———Inquiries into the doctrine of *Sefer ha-Meshiv* [Hebrew]. *Sefunot* 17 (1983): 185-266.

———*The Mystical Experience in Abraham Abulafia.* Albany, NY: State University of New York Press, 1987.

———*Kabbalah: New Perspectives.* New Haven, CT: Yale University Press, 1988.

Pachter, Mordecai. The life and personality of R. Eleazar Azikri as reflected in his mystical diary and in *Sefer Haredim* [Hebrew]. In *Shalem*, vol. 3 (1981), edited by J. Hacker, 127-148. Jerusalem.

———The theory of Devekut in the writings of the sages of Safed in the sixteenth century [Hebrew]. *Meḥqerey Yerushalayim be-Maḥshevet Yisra'el* 1(3) (1982): 51-121.

Rosenblatt, Samuel (ed.). *The High Ways to Perfection of Abraham Maimonides*, 2 vols. New York & Baltimore, 1927-1938.

Schatz(-Uffenheimer), Rivka. *ha-Ḥasidut ke-Mistiqah* (Quietistic Elements in 18th-Century Hasidic Thought). Jerusalem, 1968.

Scholem, Gershom. *Kitvey-Yad ba-Qabbalah.* Jerusalem, 1930. (MSS).

———"*Sha'arei Zedek*, a Kabbalistic text from the school of R. Abraham Abulafia, attributed to R. Shem Tov (Ibn Gaon?)" [Hebrew]. *Kiryat Sefer* 1 (1924-1925): 127-139.

———*Major Trends in Jewish Mysticism*, New York, 1962.

———*Ha-Kabbalah shel Sefer ha Temunah shel R. Abraham Abulafia.* Jerusalem, 1966.

———Les origines de la Kabbale. Paris, 1966.

———"Devekut" or communion with God. In *The Messianic Idea in Judaism and Other Essays* by Scholem, 203-227. New York, 1971. Reprinted from *Review of Religion* 14 (1949-50): 115-139.

———*Kabbalah.* Jerusalem, 1974.

Tishby, Isaiah. *Mishnat ha-Zohar* (The Wisdom of the Zohar), 2 vols. Jerusalem, 1961.

Trimingham, J. Spencer. *The Sufi Orders in Islam.* Oxford: Oxford University Press, 1971.

Vajda, Georges. Les observations critiques d'Isaac d'Acco (?) sur les ouvrages de Juda ben Nissim Ibn Malka. *REJ* 115 [N.S. 15] (1956): 25-71.

———*Recherches sur la philosophie et la kabbale dans la pensée juive du moyen age.* Paris, 1962.

Werblowsky, Zwi. *Joseph Karo, Lawyer and Mystic.* Philadelphia, 1977.

Subject Index

Adam, 19, 33, 42, 127, 129
Armilus, 53
Aristotelianism, 2, 13, 17, 18

Cathars, 33-44
Chariot, Divine [*Merkavah*], 37, 75, 119, 120, 122, 123, 124, 155, 169
Christianity, Christians, 19, 51, 54, 141, 157
Colors, 81-82, 88, 129, 134
Combination of letters, 99, 107, 110, 111, 114, 121, 127, 133, 136, 137, 144, 161, 162, 164, 166, 167, 168
Concentration [*Hitbodedut*], 15, 103-169
Contemplation, 2, 55, 130, 132

Devekut, viii, 21, 98, 113, 117, 125, 129, 143, 148-149, 151, 157, 164. *See also* union
Diotima, 118, 151

Ecstasy, 67, 79, 94, 165
Elijah, 57, 103
Enoch, 11, 25, 26, 28, 31, 165
Equanimity [*Hishtawwut*], 107, 112-113, 122-124, 132, 146, 147, 148, 151, 157, 158, 159, 164
Eve, 37

Gabriel, 78, 96
Golem, 38, 42, 99

Ḥasidism, ix, 140, 150, 164, 168

Imagination, 37, 38, 41, 42, 43, 51, 66, 80, 107, 135, 150. *See also* sub voce *Mundus imaginalis*
Imitatio Dei, 4
Individuation, viii
Intellectus agens, 5, 6, 7, 8, 10, 13, 14, 24, 36, 52, 53, 64-65, 68, 76, 109, 151, 155, 161

Jerusalem, 46, 126
Jesus Christ, 45, 52-53, 58-60

Knesset Israel, 80

Land of Israel, 91-96, 100, 126-127, 153
Letters, 6, 58, 83, 121, 122, 128, 133, 135, 138, 140, 155, 156, 157, 158, 162, 166, 168
Light, 81-82, 111, 120-121, 129, 132, 135, 149, 155, 156, 165
Love, 7-8, 20, 24, 29, 66-67, 70, 79, 115-116

Macrocosmos-Microcosmos, 79, 82, 87
Messiah, vii, 15, 16, 28, 46, 50, 51, 55, 58, 60, 66
Metatron, 11, 16, 25, 26, 29, 36, 41, 53, 75, 78, 84, 85, 86, 87, 135, 149
Metempsychosis, 39
Mikhael, 78, 86

Author Index

Index of Works Cited